PUBLIC & PRIVATE
GARDENS
OF THE
NORTHWEST

For/Sherrie
who has a talent
for gardens and
flowers.
       Love,
     Becky
Christmas 1993.

PUBLIC & PRIVATE

GARDENS
OF THE
NORTHWEST

A personal guide to the gardens and natural areas
of the Northwest and western British Columbia.

Text & Photography by
MYRNA OAKLEY

Beautiful America Publishing Company
T.M.

Cover Photograph: Oriental Garden, Shore Acres State
Park Gardens, Charleston, Oregon.

Library of Congress Catalog Card Number 90-157
ISBN 0-89802-549-4

Published by **Beautiful America Publishing Company**©
  P.O. Box 646
  Wilsonville, Oregon 97070
  (503) 682-0173

Design: Michael Brugman
Illustrations: Elizabeth Walker
Typography: Oregon Typesetting
Printed in Hong Kong

Dedication

For garden and nature lovers everywhere and for
Doris Radebaugh Murdock, my mother, who
instilled in me a lifelong love and reverence for
flowers and for all living things.

Some Thoughts

"Reverence for nature comes from seeking to understand it. Nature is both beautiful and terrible. Human nature also is a bit that way. In working with nature, we try to bring out the best that we see in it, eagerly pursuing the beautiful and minimizing what may seem ugly. In so doing we must feel and we must think, and so we come to understand ourselves better."

—John Brainerd
Working With Nature

"Deep in the forest a gentle soul asks, for whom do the wildflowers bloom?"

—Fukoka

"But for an ever-renewing society the appropriate image is a total garden, a balanced aquarium or other ecological system. Some things are being born, other things are flourishing, still other things are dying— but the system lives on."

—John W. Gardner
Self-Renewal

Table of Contents

Foreword

ew places in the world have the diversity and beauty of the northwestern United States and western British Columbia. The geologic and climatic conditions of this region have helped to create a wide variety of both unusual as well as stunning and scenic outdoor landscapes.

These rich horticultural gifts are preserved not only in federal, state and municipal gardens and natural areas but in commercial and private gardens as well.

From redwood forests to natural preserves, from botanic and commercial gardens to the historic gardens and grounds of vintage homes and inns, from oriental and test gardens to special herb and display gardens, Myrna Oakley has compiled a valuable guide to the splendid Northwest outdoors.

For the inquisitive traveler, this guide will lead to yet another special public or unique private garden and to scenic natural areas where many bird species, wildlife species, native plants and wildflowers may also be seen.

Upon discovering the diversity of the Northwest, you will find reasons to return again and again. For new visitors as well as those well-acquainted with the region, this new guide will be a valuable companion and helpful aide for discovering many of the best horticultural and natural landscapes in the northwestern United States and western British Columbia.

Daryl Johnson, Curator
International Rose Test Garden
Washington Park
400 S.W. Kingston Avenue
Portland, Oregon 97201

Acknowledgments

A special thank you to the following garden lovers, horticulturists and friends who provided information, helpful research assistance, and inspiration. . .

Mark Carter, Carter House Inn, Eureka, CA

John Hovencotter, Portland Parks Department

Daryl Johnson, Curator, International Rose Test Gardens, Washington Park, Portland OR

Cynthia Withee, Oregon City

Nancy Bridgeford, Portland

Happy Hieronimus, Hardy Plant Society and Berry Botanic Garden, Portland

Lorna Markwart, Japanese Garden docent, Portland

Barbara Ashmun, Creative Garden Design, Portland

Jill Carlos, Vancouver Convention & Visitors Bureau, Vancouver, WA

Carla Okigwe, Friends of the Medicinal Herb Garden, University of Washington, Seattle

Madelaine Zabel, Sequim, WA

Charlene Knoop, Lake Pateros, WA

Mary Kay, Whaley Mansion, Lake Chelan, WA

Janet & Ross Woodward, Spokane, WA

Sinclair Phillip, Sooke Harbour House, Sooke, B.C.

Rod Burns, Garden & Horticultural Tours, Victoria, B.C.

The entire staff at Beautiful America for their total support.

Planning Your Itinerary

Use current state maps for California, Oregon, Washington and Idaho as well as a current Province map of British Columbia...copies are available at most local Visitors Information Centers. To order maps by mail contact:

California Office of Tourism
1121 'L' Street, Suite 103
Sacramento, CA 95814
Telephone (916) 322-2333

Washington Tourism Division
General Administration Building
Olympia, WA 98504
Telephone (206) 753-5600

Oregon Tourism Division
595 Cottage Street N.E.
Salem, OR 97310
Telephone
1-800-547-7842 outside OR
1-800-233-3306 inside OR

The Idaho Travel Council
Room 108, Statehouse
Boise, ID 83720
Telephone (208) 334-2470
1-800-635-7820 outside ID

Tourism Association of Southwestern B.C.
304-828 West 8th Avenue
Vancouver, B.C. V5Z 1E2
(604) 876-3088

Within each geographic section, local Visitors Information Center addresses and telephone numbers are included so that you may stop for local weather information, specific directions and other helpful and current advice about the immediate area.

Information is included so that you may write or telephone well in advance to make specific arrangements for visiting PRIVATE gardens, nurseries, and natural areas. Owners will appreciate your consideration of their scheduling needs.

I have yet to discover a garden or natural area which welcomes pets – garden travelers are advised to leave pets at home, or in the car.

Additional travel resource and horticultural resource information is included in the Appendixes.

Regional Map

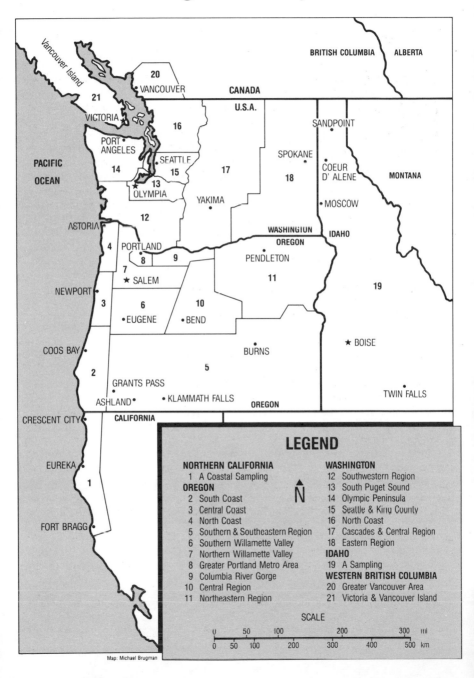

LEGEND

NORTHERN CALIFORNIA
1 A Coastal Sampling
OREGON
2 South Coast
3 Central Coast
4 North Coast
5 Southern & Southeastern Region
6 Southern Willamette Valley
7 Northern Willamette Valley
8 Greater Portland Metro Area
9 Columbia River Gorge
10 Central Region
11 Northeastern Region

WASHINGTON
12 Southwestern Region
13 South Puget Sound
14 Olympic Peninsula
15 Seattle & King County
16 North Coast
17 Cascades & Central Region
18 Eastern Region
IDAHO
19 A Sampling
WESTERN BRITISH COLUMBIA
20 Greater Vancouver Area
21 Victoria & Vancouver Island

SCALE

| 0 | 50 | 100 | 200 | 300 mi |
| 0 | 50 | 100 | 200 | 300 | 400 | 500 km |

Map: Michael Brugman

Introduction

 garden or natural area may be many things to each of us. . .a place of quiet contemplation. . .a place of wonder. . .an inspiration for one's own garden. . .and perhaps best of all, a place to celebrate life and its continued renewal.

With both gardens and natural areas as well as new garden friends discovered on each research trip, I found that seeing particular flowers and places reawakened many memories. I heard myself saying, "I remember zinnias, bachelor buttons and primroses." Or, "Those iris, dahlias and Tiger lilies look so familiar." And, "I remember traveling to this place as a youngster or years later with students, on field trips." Those dormant memories of some time ago came flooding back.

From pansies, sweet peas, nasturtiums and petunias to gladiolas, lilies, tuberous begonias and primroses I realized that my love of flowers, both annual and perennial, didn't happen by accident. From alpine wildflower meadows and snow-capped volcanic peaks to wildlife refuges, lava cast forests and ocean waysides I realized also that my love of the northwest outdoors didn't happen by accident.

Wherever we lived – first in southern Oregon (where I was born), then in the Portland-Vancouver area (during World War II), back to southern Oregon for a time, then, finally, to Portland – mother planted and nurtured both annuals and perennials. We camped and hiked at the coast and in the mountains. Later, I traveled with students on field trips into the high Oregon desert and to the coast.

As a child, I assumed that everyone had luscious tuberous begonias, stately Tiger lilies, and a half-acre of pansies (mother and dad raised them for the seed market after the war). I assumed that other 8-year-olds strung daisy necklaces and fashioned flower-princesses from petunia blossoms, just as my 5-year-old sister and I did.

I realized that during my youth I'd been surrounded by annuals and perennials and had simply absorbed both a love as well as an appreciation of them from mother and dad. This inner knowing, though dormant during busy child-rearing and career establishing years, surfaced when I began working on the garden book. Traveling, meeting plant-lovers and walking through their extraordinary gardens as well as re-visiting the region's natural areas reawakened many memories.

For example, a young mother who schools her two children at home. . .her marvelous old-fashioned garden with its wonderful clumps of perennials, scented old roses and watering cans of petunias reminded me of visiting grandmother on a hill in southern Oregon – sleeping under the stars on the old porch, surrounded by bachelor buttons, sweet William, sweet peas and wild roses. There was a well down which we dipped a wooden bucket for fresh, cold water. We picked cattails and made bouquets.

I met a husband and wife who grow peonies and daylilies and hosta high on a hill near Sherwood, Oregon. A couple who were so willing to share their knowledge and love of flowers. And I remembered the peonies and the lilies from my childhood. Mother recalled that the Tiger lily bulbs came from North Dakota, from her mother's garden.

Then, the extraordinary botanic garden of a Portland woman who loved primroses and who, I was told, communicated with and through her plants in ways that she may have been unable to communicate otherwise – she had lost her hearing as a young adult. Mother grew primroses, too, but I didn't remember until then.

Other memories, of field trips with my 7th graders to study the geology and plantlife and wildlife of the state, surfaced when I met a young man in Victoria who shared a passion for natural places and natural gardens unfettered by chemicals. We walked through a sunlit forest and along the way a cluster of yellow leaves fell softly to the ground – a nearly imperceptible greeting. And I remembered those wonderful, learning times with fellow teachers, parents and students.

I met several landscape designers who nurtured their own gardens as well as designing outdoor spaces for others. One of them said, "My garden reflects where I am emotionally, whether I'm well-centered or whether I'm fragmented. Come and visit my garden next spring." And I remembered the cycles of my own life.

Another woman designer shared her wonderful English-style perennial garden which had large garden sculptures tucked here and there, and three furry felines who scampered through the foliage and climbed on the lattice garden gazebo to peer down at us. As we ate crunchy red apples from a knarled old tree and marveled at the new hardy hibiscus she was planting that day, I remembered grandmother's garden on the hill and her crabapple and plum trees.

My intention, then, is to share both the familiar as well as lesser known of these many garden and natural area gems. And, to encourage you to also recall some of your own memories of flowers and outdoor experiences.

The book is arranged geographically, beginning with very northern California and traveling north through Oregon, Washington, Idaho and western British Columbia. While the primary emphasis is on the prolific humid transition zone between the Pacific Ocean and the Cascade Mountain Range, I've included a sampling from the colder, high desert areas east of the Cascades as well. You'll find also a bit more emphasis on Oregon and Washington in this first edition.

As we go to press all of the gardens and natural areas in this edition are accessible and open to the public either year round or during a portion of the year. Many are free of charge though some request a nominal fee.

We will appreciate hearing from you about new gardens and natural areas recommended for future editions. . .drop us a line at Beautiful America Publishing Company, P.O. Box 646, Wilsonville, OR 97070.

Happy travels and may you, too, recall your own memories of particular flowers and special places. I hope also that, in your floral forays and treks into the natural areas of the northwest, you will tread softly and walk carefully, with a reverence for all living things.

Myrna Oakley
Spring 1990

Eureka's Old Town Market, Eureka, California

NORTHERN CALIFORNIA

A Coastal Sampling

arly spring is one of the best times to visit the misty redwood forests of northern California because you may enjoy hundreds of blooming wild rhododendron which dot the lush green forest landscape much like pastel clusters daubed by a painter's brush.

Their soft pink petals contrast with the deep red bark of majestic Coastal redwoods, Sequoia sempervirens, tallest of all living things. The boundaries of THE REDWOOD EMPIRE (which also contain REDWOOD NATIONAL PARK) extend some 400 miles from the San Francisco bay area north to Mendocino, Fort Bragg, Ferndale, Eureka, Arcata and on to Crescent City and Oregon's southernmost section.

The area abounds with hiking trails, campgrounds, natural preserves, redwood groves, parks and recreation areas.

MENDOCINO ~ FORT BRAGG

One of the lovely coastal botanical gardens is found about two miles south of Fort Bragg and six miles north of Mendocino, near winding State Highway 1. MENDOCINO COAST BOTANICAL GARDENS offers 17 acres of native and ornamental plants in a lush fern-filled woodland setting by the Pacific Ocean. Stroll its surfaced paths along which are seasonal azaleas, hybrid rhododendrons, dahlias, and heathers. You may enjoy a lush 'rain forest' canyon, a lovely fuchsia walk as well as a formal garden and lily pond. The garden is wheelchair-accessible. There is a nominal fee and there is a cafe, a retail nursery and picnic areas on the grounds as well. Open year round, the garden is located at 18220 North Highway 1 (P.O. Box 1143), Fort Bragg, CA 95437. Telephone (707) 964-4352.

At TRILLIUM LANE NURSERY you may stroll among 1.5 acres of display gardens which contain some 300 species and hybrid rhododendrons in pleasing pastels as well as robust rainbow hues. Also, don't miss the native pygmy forest located just behind the display gardens. Trillium Lane Nursery is located at 18855 Trillium Lane, Fort Bragg, CA 95437. Telephone (707) 964-3282. Hours 9-5 daily. Some rhododendrons begin blooming as early as March and April with peak bloom around Mother's Day.

Rose-lovers may want to check out the HERITAGE ROSE GARDENS which are located at 16831 Mitchell Creek Drive, also near Fort Bragg. For further tourist information contact the Fort Bragg-Mendocino Visitors Information Center, 332 N. Main Street (P.O. Box 1141), Fort Bragg, CA 95437. Telephone (707) 964-3153.

North of Fort Bragg and Westport (off Branscomb Road), the Nature Conservancy has opened a 4,000-acre wilderness, including U.S. Natural Landmark Elder Creek Basin, for nature study. Those hardy nature lovers who are interested may call ahead to the COAST RANGE PRESERVE for information. Telephone (707) 984-6653.

For an impressive encounter with the giant redwoods (some have reached a height of 300 feet), detour from Highway 101 at Phillipsville onto AVENUE OF THE GIANTS, Scenic Highway 254. The two-lane asphalt ribbon winds some 33 miles into the heart of the redwood forest and allows closeup views of these towering trees. Humboldt Redwoods Interpretive Center, at Burlington Campground, is a good place to stop for park information, books, maps and nature exhibits. For further information contact Avenue of the Giants Association, P.O. Box 1000, Miranda, CA 95553. Telephone (707) 923-2555.

FERNDALE ~ EUREKA ~ ARCATA

In the Victorian village of Ferndale, just north of Avenue of the Giants, travelers can find walking and riding trails in RUSS PARK, a wilderness area within the city limits. Native plants such as elderberry, wild California lilac and huckleberry can be seen here, as well as many native birds—from the imposing great blue heron to tiny hummingbirds.

A charming private English garden can be seen at THE GINGERBREAD MANSION BED & BREAKFAST INN, located at 400 Berding Street in Ferndale. This garden is noted for its perfectly clipped topiary trees and, "visitors may view the garden from the sidewalk," says innkeeper Wendy Hatfield. The vintage inn itself is an eyeful with its elaborate Victorian scrollwork, decorative wood trim, and vibrant orange and yellow coat of paint.

It is also possible to tour nearby river channels and salt marshes where the EEL RIVER meets the sea. This invigorating encounter with nature affords views of natural vegetation and over 100 species of wildlife, including harbor seals, river otters and sea lions as well as black-tailed deer, racoon, and the elusive bobcat and fox. For information about this guided tour contact Ken Bessingpas, innkeeper, Shaw House Inn, 703 Main Street, Ferndale, CA 95536, telephone (707) 786-9958; or, local naturalist Bruce Slocum, RFD Box 248, Ferndale, CA 95536, telephone (707) 786-4187.

Further tourist information may be obtained from the Visitors Information Center, 248 Francis Street (P.O. Box 325), Ferndale, CA 95536. Telephone (707) 786-4477. Ask about annual Victorian house tours and walking tours of this charming Victorian village community. Many local gardens may be enjoyed from the sidewalk along your way.

A few miles north, visitors find binoculars handy to have along at the NATIONAL WILDLIFE REFUGE at the south end of Humboldt Bay, near Eureka. There is an egret rookery on Indian Isle which can be observed from the bridge which crosses the bay (bicycles allowed on the bridge but no foot traffic).

Much of Eureka's old town area skirts the bay; park up by the imposing Victorian painted in shades of green—Carson Mansion (now a private club)—and walk down into the restored old town area with its many shops, benches, eateries, and weekly sidewalk farmer's market. However, be sure to find a garden gem in the old town area – IMPERIALE SQUARE. The intimate space hidden just beyond the sidewalk is a delightful botanic surprise filled with colorful dahlias, hanging fuchsias, flowering fruit trees and other perennials – all carefully tended by local garden enthusiast, Bob Imperiale, whom you may encounter as you wander through this lovely oasis.

Another nearby retreat which includes 54 acres of virgin redwoods, rhododendron glen and duck pond as well as colorful annual, perennial and rose gardens, picnic area and children's playground can be found at EUREKA'S SEQUOIA PARK & ZOO, just off Harris Street at 3414 'W' Street. Those interested in guided tours may contact the park's Zoological Society. Telephone (707) 442-6552.

Additional tourist information may be obtained from the Eureka/Humboldt County Visitors Information Center, 1034 Second Street, Eureka, CA 95501. Telephone (707) 443-5097.

Another outdoor nature experience available to northern California coastal travelers is the ARCATA MARSH AND WILDLIFE SANCTUARY tour which is conducted on Saturday mornings by the Redwood Region Audubon Society. Located on the Pacific Coastal Flyway, there are trails and bird blinds on site; be prepared for a plethora of bird species as well as bay breezes. For information inquire at the Arcata Visitors Information Center near the plaza.

You might also ask here if springtime flowers are blooming along nostalgic country roads that crisscross the lush ARCATA BOTTOMS area. You'll find good photo opportunities along the way, with many wildflower-carpeted meadows, old barns and fences.

Arcata's downtown PLAZA is a unique oasis of palms, ornamental trees and colorful annuals and perennials set in lush lawn and bisected by walkways that surround a large statue of President McKinley. One of the few central city plazas left in the U.S., ask at the Visitor's Information Center about the seasonal farmer's market held here.

On a hill near the downtown area, guided tours are available of the attractive 140-acre HUMBOLDT STATE UNIVERSITY campus and arboretum. Or, simply wander the grounds yourself and enjoy sweeping vistas of Humboldt Bay as well. Telephone (707) 826-3132. In just a 5-minute walk, over the Footbridge from the campus, hungry travelers may find the Wildflower Cafe & Bakery at 16th & 'G' Streets.

The ARCATA COMMUNITY FOREST (just east of the campus) offers a 600-acre botanical paradise of towering redwoods, streams and wildlife. Its ten miles of trails can be used for walking, hiking and jogging. Telephone (707) 822-3775.

Just north of Arcata the AZALEA STATE RESERVE is a large natural plantation of azaleas which bursts into bloom during June and July and offers walking trails, educational exhibits, and lovely picnic areas among the hardy wild perennials. Turn onto North Bank Road just 2 miles north of town to find this day use reserve.

Additional tourist information may be obtained from the Arcata Visitors Information Center, 1062 'G' Street, Arcata, CA 95521. Telephone (707) 822-3619.

McKINLEYVILLE ~ ORICK ~ CRESCENT CITY ~ SMITH RIVER

At McKinleyville plan a stop at the FAIRYLAND BEGONIA & LILY GARDEN. Visitors are welcome year round and you'll see not only an all summer lily show but new lilies and begonias which are hybridized and developed here. Visitors are invited to tour the greenhouses and watch the hybridizing process. Many award-winning species can also be seen here. The gardens are open 9-5 Monday-

Saturday and 10-5 on Sundays during the summer months. Closed Saturdays during the winter. Find this unique garden and nursery at 1100 Griffith Road, McKinleyville, CA 95521. Telephone (707) 839-3034.

Heading north, hardy naturalists may want to track down the splendid array of maidenhair, five-finger and sword ferns in FERN CANYON, about 7 miles off Highway 101 on a bumpy, winding gravel road which leads to Gold Bluffs Beach Campground, north of Orick. The dainty wild Calypso orchid can be found at Bald Hills (also bumpy road), near Orick, and at Elk Prarie Campground north of Orick.

To gaze at the tallest redwood, a 368-foot giant, find TALL TREES TRAIL near Tall Trees Grove about 40 miles north of Eureka. The 1.4 mile interpretive nature trail ambles alongside Redwood Creek where you'll see fine examples of how a redwood forest grows.

For maps and specific directions to these natural areas, contact Redwood National Park Headquarters, 1111 Second Street, Crescent City, CA 95531. Telephone (707) 464-6101. Additional information, exhibits, interpretive publications, and programs are available here, as well as from the Redwood Information Center, two miles south of Orick on Highway 101. Telephone (707) 488-3461. Or, stop at the Hiouchi Redwood Information Center, just northeast of Crescent City, off Highway 199 which continues to Grants Pass, Medford, Ashland and other Oregon towns and cities along Interstate 5.

Other tourist information may be obtained from the Crescent City/Del Norte Visitors Information Center, 1001 Front Street, Crescent City, CA 95531. Telephone (707) 464-3174. And, from Orick's Visitors Information Center, P.O. Box 97, Orick, CA 95555. Telephone (707) 488-3245.

To see acres and acres of colorful lilies (90% of U.S. Easter lily bulbs are grown in this region), head north on Highway 101 from Crescent City to Smith River. An annual LILY FESTIVAL is held in July when many fields are carpeted with luscious blooms. A portion of the previous crop, lily bulbs that are a year old, are sold to greenhouses across the U.S. who carefully tend and "force" the bulbs to bloom at Easter time. More fields of lilies may also be seen as you continue north into the southern Oregon coastal area.

℘

OREGON

South Coast

BROOKINGS ~ COOS BAY ~ CHARLESTON ~ REEDSPORT

he colorful lily fields extend from northern California's Del Norte County into southern Oregon's Curry County, near Brookings. Growers have produced astonishing varieties of new lilies which vary in color, size, blooming time and perfume. July and August are good months to see the fields clothed in luscious rainbow colors.

In this temperate climate, often known as the banana belt of Oregon's coast, as many as 50 flower varieties bloom during winter months. Acacia, broom, camellias, calla lilies, fuchsias, geraniums, heather, roses, primroses, and pansies are often seen blooming here in January.

Just north of Brookings, AZALEA STATE PARK is a 26-acre natural park which abounds in colorful wild azaleas, many over a hundred years old. An annual "Azalea Festival" takes place in May, on Memorial Day weekend. For current information contact the local Visitors Information Center, P.O. Box 940, Brookings, OR 97415. Telephone (503) 469-2213.

Another natural area nearby that bears investigation is LOEB STATE PARK, located eight miles east on the Chetco River. Within its 320 acres are fine stands of virgin myrtle trees. The huge old trees spread leafy branches into wide canopies of shade, offering secluded picnic and camping areas.

On a windswept stretch of southern Oregon coastline near Coos Bay, North Bend, and Charleston awaits a botanical treasure, SHORE ACRES BOTANIC GARDEN. The garden was developed in the early 1900s by Louis J. Simpson, son of pioneer lumberman and shipbuilder, Asa Meade Simpson.

Simpson's mansion and gardens, built near the seacliff in the early 1900s, was one of the largest and finest showplaces in southern Oregon at the turn of the century. Varieties of rhododendrons and azaleas were brought here by Simpson schooner and clipper ships returning from ports around the world. Huge boulders from the rocky beach were hoisted up the steep cliffs with horse teams; they border the pond which dominates the Japanese garden section.

In 1942 some 600 acres of the estate was purchased by the State of Oregon;

Portland's Japanese Garden, Oregon

by 1948 the mansion was in such poor condition that it was razed. In its place is now a large glass-walled gazebo where you may see Simpson family photos and history as well as the ocean and spectacular wave-battered, tilted outcroppings along the windswept seacliff.

Most of the trails in the park, which wander through stands of Sitka spruce and groundcover of salal and wax myrtle, are those L.J. Simpson had built for strolling through his estate.

Now maintained by the Oregon State Parks Department, visitors will see the formal garden first, entering along a wooden walkway past the illustrated historical display developed by Oregon historian, Stephen Dow Beckham.

First views of the garden are breathtaking – the formal walkways are still there, bordered by low boxwood hedges, but wisteria-entwined pillared pergolas seen in old photographs are gone. The original garden cottage sits like a stately sentinal behind beds of prize roses and clumps of colorful annuals and perennials. Where a sense of the past permeates every nook and cranny, time seems to stand still in this botanical treasure at ocean's edge.

Flower-lined paths beckon visitors through the formal garden to stone steps which lead to the Japanese garden. Its 100-foot lily pond is encircled by a path along which are vivid azaleas, hardy rhododendron, giant rhubarb and delicate maple, bamboo, and fern. Imagine stone lanterns lighted in the evening for the Simpson's bejeweled guests – images of another time, another era. This garden is an experience to be savored, unhurried.

There are several picnic tables on the grounds and the formal garden is handicap accessible. From Coos Bay-North Bend on the southern Oregon coast, follow State Highway 14 about 15 miles through Charleston to Sunset Bay (large state campground here) and the garden. Accessible by auto or bicycle. Hours are 8 a.m. till dusk. There is a nominal fee per automobile.

Near Charleston, off Seven Devils Road, travelers may want to wander one of the three study trails open to the public at SOUTH SLOUGH ESTUARINE SANCTUARY. Most rugged is the three mile Estuary Study Trail which loops through wide-angle views of upland forest, salt marshes, tideflats and open water zones. It also passes the site of a late 1800s dike and pioneer homestead as well as an old railroad logging camp. The other two trails are both shorter and more gentle in elevation and terrain.

During summer months, the South Slough staff conducts workshops on such outdoor interests as wildflowers, edible plants, and local birds. Waterfowl migrating along the Pacific Coastal Flyway are attracted to large beds of eelgrass here and there is also a great blue heron rookery nearby.

In addition to the trails, there are canoe launch areas at the Hinch Road bridge and at Hanson's Landing in Charleston (bring your own canoe and gear). All outdoor activities within the sanctuary, including fishing, are designed to have a minimum impact on the delicate estuary environment.

The South Slough Visitor Center features displays and literature about the ecology and history of the estuary. It is open weekdays September through May and open every day June through August. Hours are 8:30-4:30. For additional information, contact South Slough Estuarine Sanctuary, P.O. Box 5417, Charleston, OR 97420. Telephone (503) 888-5558.

Other bird observation sites in the area may be found at Pony and Kentuck sloughs, Jordan Cove, North Spit, Horsfall Beach, South Jetty, Bastendorff Beach, Coos Head, and Cape Arago. Near Bandon, the Coquille River estuary (particularly Bandon Marsh), Bullard's Beach State Park, and sea stacks along the ocean's edge are good sites for viewing the some 270 species of pelagic birds, waterfowl, shorebirds, and passerines that have been seen in the south coast region.

Bird-lovers may want to use the comprehensive checklist, "Birds of Coos County Oregon," which is distributed by the Oregon Department of Fish & Wildlife. The following Visitors Centers can provide this handy brochure along with other helpful tourist information: Bandon Visitors Information Center, P.O. Box 1515, Bandon, OR 97411. Telephone (503) 347-9616. Bay Area Visitors Information Center, P.O. Box 210, Coos Bay, OR 97420. Telephone (503) 269-0215.

North Bend Visitors Information Center, P.O. Box B/1380 Sherman, North Bend, OR 97459. Telephone (503) 756-4613. Travelers are invited to use the attractive picnic area, Simpson Park, adjacent to the North Bend Visitors Center which is located at the south end of the Coos Bay bridge. Also, just next door is the Coos-Curry Historic Museum which offers a nostalgic look at the region's history through pioneer artifacts and lifelike history exhibits.

Heading north from the Coos Bay-North Bend area, travelers may want to plan a half hour or so at the informative OREGON DUNES NATIONAL RECREATION AREA Headquarters located at 855 Highway 101, Reedsport, OR 97467. Telephone (503) 271-3611. You'll see fine examples of native plants which grow in the UMPQUA DUNES SCENIC AREA as well as other educational interpretive exhibits. The area is managed by the Siuslaw National Forest (USDA Forest Service).

The nature and wildlife habitats in this dunes area of the Oregon coast range from the complex transitional forest and stabilized sand dune to the driftwood-strewn sandy beach areas. Many species of mammals and birds may be spied (or, you may find their tracks), including blacktail deer, raccoons, deer mice and mink, along with some 108 songbirds in forests and aquatic birds along the beaches and in marshy areas.

Central Coast

FLORENCE ~ YACHATS ~ NEWPORT AREAS

There are many viewpoints, numerous accessible trails, excellent places for photography, and good biking roads in the area. August is one of the best times of the year to bike on coastal byways because you may dine on a plethora of wild, juicy blackberries that often grow along the quiet county roads. The OREGON DUNES OVERLOOK, midway between Reedsport and Florence, offers wheelchair access and .4 mile Carter Dunes Trail out to the sand. Ask at the Dunes Headquarters in Reedsport for helpful information about the hundreds of trails and many campgrounds and lakes in the area.

At SOUTH JETTY DUNE access, near Florence, there is an easy road for bicyclers out to the SOUTH JETTY PIER, a popular public crabbing and fishing pier where the Siuslaw River meets the Pacific Ocean.

Just north of Florence, where an annual "Rhododendron Festival" is held each May, you'll find the DARLINGTONIA WAYSIDE. Follow the boardwalk out onto a marshy bog preserve which is home to the Darlingtonia californica. Often called the Cobra lily or pitcher plant, it has the habit of eating insects (they fall into the rounded cobra-like mouth and are broken down by bacterial action in the plant's innards). One of the few small nature preserves in the U.S. set aside for conserving a single species of native plant, you may see the unusual greenish-speckled plants here from spring through summer and into early fall.

Highway 101 winds high above the ocean a few miles north of the wayside, affording sweeping views of the salty Pacific. There are several viewpoints along the ledge and one of the most scenic, just north of Devil's Elbow State Park, offers a wide-angle view of HECETA HEAD, Heceta lighthouse, and original lighthouse-keeper's home (now used for meetings and retreats).

These viewpoints, coastal headlands that jut out into the water, may be used for aquatic bird and whale-watching (binoculars are helpful to have along) and include, heading north, CAPE PERPETUA, YAQUINA HEAD, CAPE FOULWEATHER, CASCADE HEAD, CAPE KIWANDA, CAPE LOOKOUT and CAPE MEARES.

The California gray whales migrate south from November through January from Arctic waters down the coast to warm lagoons along the central and southern coastline of the Baja. The return migration, with new offspring swimming along as well, takes place from March through May. Some 17,000 whales make this annual round-trip journey.

Warm windbreakers, jackets, hats and gloves will help to protect against the often stiff coastal breezes along these high basalt ledges between Florence and Tillamook. One of the viewpoints, north of Newport and Otter Rock, has a large grassy area and offers a closer view of the water.

The highest point on the central Oregon coast is CAPE PERPETUA, administered by the U.S. Forest Service as a natural and scenic area. The well-staffed Visitor Center offers informative maps, brochures, and displays such as "Forces of Nature" and "Flora and Fauna of the Coast."

Several nature trails are available here, including Cape Creek Trail, a 2-mile walk through a lush spruce forest and along its fern and flower lined stream. Another .4 mile trail can be taken down a salal and fern lined path and rocky steps to see ocean waves catapult and foam through a 40 million-year-old narrow fissure called DEVIL'S CHURN. Often wild carrot and huckleberry can be seen along the path. **Note:** sturdy shoes are a must on this trail.

For information about both naturalist-led hikes and a self-guided 22-mile auto tour through Douglas fir forest ridges and valleys, contact Cape Perpetua Visitor Center, Waldport Ranger District, P.O. Box 274, Yachats, OR 97498. Telephone (503) 547-3289. Additional tourist information may be obtained from the Yachats Visitors Information Center, P.O. Box 174, Yachats, OR 97498. Telephone (503) 547-3392.

Near Waldport, just east on Highway 34, you may visit WILLARD THOMPSON NURSERY to see some 19 acres of new rhododendrons surrounding an acre of large, mature rhododendrons — one of the largest commercial collections on the coast. The hardy plants, which are well-labeled, bloom during spring months with peak bloom around Mother's Day. The nursery is located at 2874 Alsea Highway. Telephone (503) 563-3676. Hours are 9-5 daily.

At the HATFIELD MARINE SCIENCE CENTER in Newport, north of Yachats and Waldport, you may see a comprehensive interpretive exhibit of coastal birds and wildlife as well as marine plants and aquaria filled with unusual saltwater fish. A friendly octopus greets visitors from a saltwater tank located in the foyer and there is a small tidepool filled with sea urchin and other live sea creatures that children may investigate.

During summer months wildlife, botany and marine education specialists conduct workshops on such topics as Coastal Birding, Coastal Plants, and Bay Crabbing & Clamming. Those interested may also inquire about trips and treks, Yaquina Head bird walks, tidepool excursions, and estuary walks. Contact the Center, which is open every day, at Marine Science Drive, Newport, OR 97365. Telephone (503) 867-3011. Additional tourist information may be obtained from the Greater Newport Visitors Information Center, 555 S.W. Coast Highway, Newport, OR 97365. Telephone (503) 265-8801. U.S. toll free, 1-800-COAST-44.

DEPOE BAY ~ GLENEDEN BEACH ~ LINCOLN CITY

A traditional "Fleet of Flowers Ceremony" takes place on Memorial Day each year in the small coastal community of Depoe Bay located north of Cape Foulweather. Floral wreaths and flowers are cast out on the ocean from a parade of boats from Depoe Bay's fishing fleet, in memory of those who have lost their lives at sea. For current information contact the local Visitors Information Center, P.O. Box 21, Depoe Bay, OR 97341. Telephone (503) 765-2889.

Along the south shore of SILETZ BAY, near Gleneden Beach and south of the Lincoln City area, a wide nature path along much of the estuary can be found at the north end of the MARKETPLACE shops. At low tide, you'll see cranes, herons, egrets, and bitterns standing guard in the mud flats. Overhead may be redtail hawks, marsh hawks, harriers, numerous noisy gulls and many species of migrating shore birds. An easy and invigorating trek either rain or shine, the nature path may also be followed a short distance out onto the sandy beach. Many native plants can be identified along the path, including salal and fireweed.

Additional tourist information may be obtained from the Lincoln City Visitors Information Center, 3939 N.W. Highway 101 (P.O. Box 787), Lincoln City, OR 97367. Telephone (503) 994-8378.

North Coast

SANDLAKE ~ NETARTS ~ OCEANSIDE ~ TILLAMOOK AREAS

Continuing north on Highway 101 from Lincoln City, travelers may find nature trails at both CASCADE HEAD and CAPE KIWANDA. Trails may wind through green forests, over small streams and through open meadows which abound with wildflowers in the early spring; or, high atop sand dunes for lofty views of the ocean and wave action.

In this section of the Oregon coast, hundreds of skunk cabbage with their spiky yellow blossoms carpet low marshy-meadow areas during early spring, beginning in April. Pale pink blossoms also burst from gnarled limbs of old apple trees, the slender alder are beginning to leaf and the bushy Oregon grape, low-lying salal, and prickly salmonberry will be in bloom as well. Here and there you may spy the pale lavender blooms of wild lilac.

As if this weren't enough, the next wave of spring color in May, includes pink wild rhododendron, purple camass, vivid yellow Scotch broom, blue lupine, bright yellow buttercups, and the delicate pink wild roses which grow along most state and county roadsides throughout the northwest. Many travelers feel that spring blossoms here are the best show of the season, and they're free for everyone to enjoy.

Many of these early spring blooms can be seen along THREE CAPES SCENIC DRIVE which begins just north of Lincoln City at a junction from Highway 101. The scenic drive ambles along to Pacific City, Sandlake, Netarts, Oceanside and Tillamook and offers nature stops along the way at Cape Kiwanda, Cape Lookout, and Cape Meares.

Just north of Sandlake, nature trails at CAPE LOOKOUT offer a close-up view of a typical coastal rain forest, including Sitka spruce, western hemlock, western red cedar and red alder. A thick tangle of salal, box blueberry, salmonberry, sword fern and pacific waxmyrtle covers the forest floor. Skunk cabbage, lily-of-the-valley, and trillium flower in the early spring. For maps and camping information contact the Oregon State Parks Office, 13000 Whiskey Creek Road West, Tillamook, OR 97141. Telephone (503) 842-4981.

Another nature stop is the 5-mile-long NETARTS SPIT, protected under the Oregon State Park designation of Research Natural Preserve. Dunes with knee-high beach grass cover much of the spit which extends like a narrow finger just north of Cape Lookout and west of Netarts Bay. You may see Sitka spruce, shore pine, and huckleberry which thrive here. You may spy the tracks of deer and racoons as well. Park rangers suggest checking current tide tables before walking out too far on the spit.

At the tiny community of Oceanside, offshore island formations called THREE ARCH ROCKS were set aside as the first wildlife preserve on the Pacific Coast by President Theodore Roosevelt in 1907. Covered with a carpet of sea grass and yellow flowering sulphur weed, it is home to thousands of black petrels, colorful tufted puffins and penguin-like murres as well as several varieties of gulls and cormorants. The bellow of resident sea lions and sea pups may also be heard at times. Binoculars and telephoto lenses will be helpful to have along on this nature stop.

There are also within the state some 40 natural preserves which are protected and maintained by non-profit conservation groups such as The Nature Conservancy. This national organization is dedicated to preserving natural diversity and since 1951 has preserved nearly 3 million acres of land in 50 states. Because of the delicate ecosystems which are involved, interested travelers are asked to contact the Oregon Field Office for current regulations and conditions for visiting these fragile areas. The address is 1205 N.W. 25th Avenue, Portland, OR 97210. Telephone (503) 228-9561.

At CAPE MEARES, located at the northernmost section of Three Capes Scenic Drive, an unusual Sitka spruce can be seen. It's named Octopus Tree because it has not just one but six trunks reaching skyward. Along the nearby walk down to the Cape Meares lighthouse are many native shrubs and plants, including wild roses and huckleberry. There are nature trails and several picnic tables as well as restrooms here.

Additional tourist information may be obtained from the Tillamook County Visitors Information Center, 2105 First Street, Tillamook, OR 97141. Telephone (503) 842-7525.

Just east of Tillamook, travelers can take a 25-mile interpretive auto tour through the reforested TILLAMOOK STATE FOREST. It is the site of a massive fire which burned more than 300,000 acres during the period between 1933 and 1951. Several nature trails within the forest offer rewarding excursions.

The King Mountain to Elk Creek Park trail section introduces visitors to a rare and fragile ecosystem, a COAST RANGE ROCK GARDEN. In addition to wildflowers, rare plants here include the smooth douglasia and the fringed synthyris. **Note:** this trail is categorized as difficult.

Maps of both the auto tour and nature trails can be obtained from the Oregon State Department of Forestry, 4907 Third Street, Tillamook, OR 97141. Telephone (503) 842-2545. There is also an office in Forest Grove, near Portland. Telephone (503) 357-2191.

GARIBALDI ~ CANNON BEACH ~ SEASIDE ~ ASTORIA

Near Highway 101, north of Tillamook, Garibaldi and Rockaway Beach, NEHALEM BAY estuary is another stop on the coastal birdwatcher's itinerary. Both spring and autumn are good times to see a plethora of Canada geese as well as a myriad of migratory waterfowl who rest and feed here. The Nehalem Bay Canoe Races take place each spring when wildflowers bloom along the North and South forks of the Nehalem River.

Located at Cannon Beach, HAYSTACK ROCK has been designated part of the Oregon Islands National Refuge Wildlife Range. At its base are numerous tidepools filled with sea anenomes, tiny crab and other sea creatures easily seen at low tide. Tufted puffins, known as sea parrots, can be seen on its high grassy ledges.

Just north of Cannon Beach, ECOLA STATE PARK offers some of the most spectacular panoramic views of the northern coastline from eight nature trail outlooks high above the salty Pacific. The 1,100 acre park abounds with native plants, bird species and wildlife. Less than a mile off shore a rookery of sea lions can be seen. Deer and elk often browse nearby. Picnic tables are tucked here and there, many in places sheltered from coastal breezes.

Additional tourist information may be obtained from the Cannon Beach Visitors Information Center, 2nd & Spruce Streets, Cannon Beach, OR 97110. Telephone (503) 436-2623 or 1-800-452-6740.

For those who want to plan hikes along the OREGON COAST TRAIL, some of which passes through scenic Ecola State Park, maps and current information can be obtained from the Recreation Trails Coordinator, State Parks and Recreation Division, 525 Trade Street S.E., Salem, OR 97310.

Along the NECANICUM RIVER, a tidal river that flows through the historic coastal community of Seaside, belted kingfishers are often seen diving like pelicans to catch small fish. Tourist information may be obtained from the Seaside Visitors Information Center, 7 North Roosevelt Street (P.O. Box 7), Seaside, OR 97138. Telephone (503) 738-6391.

At the FLAVEL MANSION, which houses Clatsop County's Historic Museum in Astoria, a garden of rhododendrons and ornamental trees fills the entire city block near 8th and Duane Streets. Nominal fee for the museum. Nearby, see a splendid array of flowering fruit trees which surround the ASTOR COLUMN high atop COXCOMB HILL. Peak blooming time happens in April. Inquire at the museum about walking tours of Astoria's many vintage Victorian homes, many of whom have lovely gardens which can be viewed along the way.

Additional tourist information may be obtained from the Astoria Visitors Information Center, Port of Astoria Building (P.O. Box 176), Astoria, OR 97103. Telephone (503) 325-6311.

Southern & Southeastern Region

BURNS ~ MALHEUR NATIONAL WILDLIFE REFUGE ~ FORT ROCK

Although southern and southeastern Oregon haven't the array of public gardens found in other parts of the region, there are several specialty gardens and outstanding natural areas worth noting on the travel itinerary – particularly if you enjoy spying and identifying a wide variety of native plants and wildflowers as well as waterfowl and birdlife. Most viewing areas are accessible by car or by easily accessed nature trails.

In the High Desert area near Burns you may enjoy an outdoor nature walk on the SAGEHEN HILL NATURE TRAIL. Stopping at eleven stations along the half mile trail you'll get acquainted with the native plants, birds and animals who live in this enormous region of wide open spaces where the desert landscape stretches unbroken for hundreds of miles in all four directions.

You'll identify both Big Sagebrush, which dominates some 20 million acres in eastern and southeastern Oregon, and Low Sagebrush which provides food for resident antelope and nesting areas for sage grouse. Deer like the big sage brush because it provides places to hide while browsing.

You'll notice Bitterbrush with its dark green leaves which are loved by the elk as well as the deer and antelope. The Big Sagebrush has large silvery leaves with soft white hairs and fills the desert with lush carpets of yellow when it blooms in the spring and summer. The Bitterbrush has smaller flowers which are creamy white and the Low Sagebrush also blooms bright yellow.

At another station you'll learn about the Western Juniper which thrives on the high desert and on dry rocky hillsides and ridgetops. Growing in many sizes and shapes and often living more than 500 years, juniper provides shade for wildlife and its pungent blue-green "berries" are plucked and eaten by many birds.

At Station 4 you may see Harney Valley to the east where two large lakes, Harney and Malheur, are part of the MALHEUR NATIONAL WILDLIFE REFUGE. Thousands of noisy migrating and nesting geese, ducks, shorebirds and wading birds use the refuge waters each year. This area was first explored in 1826 by trappers led by Peter Skene Ogden and the first ranches and farms appeared in the later 1800s.

On a clear day you'll see 9,733-foot Steens Mountain to the southeast from Station 5. A huge fault block of hundreds of basalt lava layers, the mountain was shoved and thrust more than a mile above the desert floor some 15 million years ago. The distant U-shaped valley is Kiger Gap, carved by enormous valley glaciers during the ice ages. It's an impressive sight, to say the least.

You'll spot a variety of native plants along the trail including Wax currant, Diffuse phlox, Idaho fescue, Bottlebrush squirreltail and Dwarf monkey flower as well as Western yarrow, Blue-eyed Mary, Taper-tip hawkbeard, Owl clover and Wild parsley. Several Penstemons have also been identified. Among the raptors and songbirds you'll see among the juniper and sagebrush are the Red-tailed hawk, Prairie falcon, Golden eagle and Turkey vulture as well as Mourning doves, Mountain bluebirds, Western kingbird, Common flickers and Brewer's sparrows. The self-guided leaflet and map provide a longer list of the native plants and birds.

Access the area via Highway 140 about 96 miles from Klamath Falls to Lakeview, then Highway 395 north about 140 miles to Burns. Pick up hearty snacks and beverages in Klamath Falls and be sure to fill the gas tank before heading north from Lakeview. There are cafes, restaurants and overnight lodging in Lakeview, Hines, Burns and Frenchglen. The area may also be accessed from Bend via Highway 20 some 130 miles southeast to Burns.

Additional information and a copy of the Sagehen Hill Nature Trail leaflet and map may be obtained from the Harney County Visitors Information Center, 18 West 'D' Street, Burns, OR 97720. Telephone (503) 573-2636. Ask also about weather and road conditions into the high desert area – summer days are generally hot, with cool nights.

Information about guided treks and the best current spots to view some 300 species of migrating birds and 58 species of wildlife on the refuge may be obtained from the Malheur National Wildlife Refuge, P.O. Box 245, Princeton, OR 97721. Telephone (503) 493-2323. Ask for a copy of the excellent auto-tour map.

The Refuge Visitor Center, located about 40 miles south of Burns, offers helpful orientation and interpretive exhibits and the George M. Benson Memorial Museum with some 200 mounted specimens of local birds. The Visitor Center is open 8-4 weekdays and the Museum 6 a.m.-9 p.m. daily.

Information may also be obtained from the Malheur Field Station, Box 260-E, Princeton, OR 97721. Telephone (503) 493-2629. There are numerous camp-grounds and a vintage hotel at Frenchglen where the birdwatchers like to gather. The address is Frenchglen Hotel, Frenchglen, OR 97736. Telephone (503) 493-2825.

For those heading toward Klamath Falls and Crater Lake, consider a side-trip from Highway 395 about 54 miles south of Burns. Head west on the all-weather gravel road about 45 miles to Christmas Valley, then onto a paved road some 12 miles west and 16 miles north to FORT ROCK STATE MONUMENT. Fort Rock is actually the enormous remnant of an ancient volcano, now surrounded by sagebrush and bitterbrush rather than the seas of eons ago.

It's an easy hike up into the center of the volcano where you can have a close-up look at native plants, wildflowers and towering basalt ledges showing wave action by those ancient waters. Raptors glide on air currents high above and songbirds twitter and chatter among the sagebrush and bitterbrush. Sometimes baby eagles can be seen in nests on the high rocky ledges. You'll enjoy the same wide-angle panoramic views of the High Desert as are seen from the Burns and Malheur area. **Note:** there are a couple of picnic tables and outdoor restrooms but no water here. Sturdy shoes are a must.

From Fort Rock, you may contine seven miles to the west, head south on Highway 31 to Silver Lake, then west again 46 miles to Highway 97 to access southern Oregon.

CRATER LAKE ~ KLAMATH FALLS ~ KLAMATH BASIN

Half the fun of seeing CRATER LAKE NATIONAL PARK is first navigating the winding asphalt ribbon high to the rim and, second, that first breathtaking panoramic view of the mammoth crystal-blue 1,932-foot deep lake, nestled in the remains of an ancient volcano. Mount Mazama, once 12,000 feet high, collapsed in a fiery shower of lava and ash some 6,000 years ago and formed the caldera that houses the lake.

Wildflowers bloom late and disappear early here, but you may see phlox, pearly everlasting, and knotweed from July to early August. The leisurely trail through CASTLE CREST WILDFLOWER GARDEN, about half a mile from the Park Headquarters, offers a host of summer wildflowers including Indian paint brush, bleeding heart, Lyall lupine, Western pasque flower and Lewis monkey flower. Some 750 species of native plants are found in the park. You'll also see chattering golden-mantled ground squirrels, often looking for crumbs at viewpoints and parking turnouts. You may see bald eagles, golden eagles and California gulls soaring over the lake. Jays and nutcrackers often accompany visitors on trails and pathways.

The spectacular 33-mile Rim Drive around the lake is a must and you may also enjoy the new William Steel Center near Park Headquarters which features interpretive displays, a film about the lake's geologic history, and a library of resource materials for the naturalists and rangers who plan interpretive hikes and programs for visitors. The park's two entrance stations are open from mid-May until after Labor Day; there is a small fee for each automobile entering the park. For additional tourist information contact Crater Lake National Park, P.O. Box 7, Crater Lake, OR 97604. Telephone (503) 594-2811. You may want to ask about the campfire programs held on summer evenings at Mazama Campground, and, about cabins and lodge accommodations near the Rim Village.

Heading southeast from Crater Lake along State highway 62 toward Klamath Falls, groves of aspen contrast with open cattle range and pines. The aspen are especially vibrant clothed in yellow and orange, announcing the fall season in southern Oregon.

Near Klamath Falls, just a few miles north of the California border, travelers may visit one or more of the six National Wildlife Refuges which make up the KLAMATH BASIN. Each season of the year offers unlimited opportunities to see more than 250 species of birds plus many varieties of ducks and geese.

Red-necked grebes, white pelicans, blue herons, cormorants, sandhill cranes, osprey, terns, and avocets as well as the long-necked white tundra swan can be seen on the hundreds of lakes, streams and rivers in Klamath County.

Located on the Pacific Flyway, the six wildlife refuges in the Klamath Basin provide resting as well as nesting and feeding grounds for the birds who migrate along the flyway trail twice each year—some two million ducks and one million geese make pit stops here in the spring and again in the fall.

Scores of White pelicans, one of the largest North American water birds, arrive in March to nest and remain until November. Among the best places to view these striking birds are Upper Klamath Lake, the Link River, Lake Ewauna and Tingley Lake.

As if on cue, when the white pelican families depart in striking formation in November, the bald eagles arrive for the winter. The eagles can be seen until late March from self-guided auto tour routes on the Tulelake and Lower Klamath refuges.

Near downtown Klamath Falls many birds and waterfowl may be spied along a graveled nature trail which skirts the Link River. It begins near the Favell Museum of Western and Indian Art and Artifacts, on West Main Street. Often the white pelicans can be seen early in the morning on Lake Ewauna, also visible from the museum and nature trail.

For helpful maps, travel tips and informational exhibits plan a stop at the Klamath Basin Refuge Headquarters, U.S. Fish and Wildlife Service, Route 1, Box 74, Tulelake, CA 96134. Telephone (916) 667-2231. There is also an office in Klamath Falls at 4343 Miller Island Road. Telephone (503) 883-5732. Additional tourist information can be obtained from the Klamath County Visitors Information Center, 125 N. 8th Street, Klamath Falls OR 97601. Telephone (503) 884-5193.

ASHLAND – MEDFORD – JACKSONVILLE

Visitors to the southern Oregon theater community of Ashland will find two lovely public gardens and a self-guided nature trail within walking distance of the picturesque downtown area. The largest, LITHIA PARK, was designed in the early 1900s by landscape architect John McLaren, who also designed San Francisco's Golden Gate Park.

McLaren took advantage of large granite boulders and native vegetation when he laid out the park in a series of sweeping curves rather than angles. Stroll along paths which encircle the spacious grounds; you'll be shaded by cool sycamores, towering Douglas fir, and large rhododendrons. "Woodland Trails" and "Lithia Park–the History" help visitors identify the unusual variety of trees and flowering shrubs found here; the two booklets are available from the Visitors Information Center for a small fee.

You may feed the ducks and geese which paddle about in several ponds; there is a play area for children as well. The chilly waters of Ashland Creek bisect the park and there are several footbridges to cross along your stroll. During the summer months, weekly concerts are held at the band shell near the Butler-Perozzi Fountain.

At one of several drinking fountains in the park, you may want to taste the mineral water for which Lithia Park was named. Lithium is one of the ingredients of the salty tasting liquid which bubbles from a mineral springs just up the canyon.

On a gentle slope across from the Bulter-Perozzi Fountain, you'll find an intimate well-tended JAPANESE GARDEN. Stroll its graveled paths and giant stepping-stones, perhaps pausing to sit at one of several benches placed to catch the best views of native shrubs and plants. It is a lovely, quiet and contemplative space which offers a pleasant contrast to the more active happenings in nearby Lithia Park.

OREDSON-TODD WOODS TRAIL begins near Green Meadows Way at the south edge of town—it's a gentle .5 mile self-guided nature walk which winds through 8 acres of woodland. It is particularly colorful when clothed in autumn colors, during late September and October. You might ask at the Visitors Information Center about another .5 mile self-guided walk, ASHLAND NATURE TRAIL, from which Reeder Reservoir and Wagner Butte may be seen.

The Ashland community lends itself to walking and strolling quiet streets and boulevards where many turn of the century homes and gardens have been restored. Notice the spacious grounds and native plants surrounding the historic and stately CHAPELL-SWEDENBURG HOUSE MUSEUM, located on the Southern Oregon State College campus at the corner of Siskiyou Boulevard and Mountain Avenue. The museum is open 1-5, Tuesday-Saturday.

At the north end of Main Street are a number of imposing restored Victorians which can be enjoyed on a walking tour. An especially well-tended English style garden can be seen at THE HERSEY HOUSE, which is now a bed & breakfast inn. The colorful garden may be enjoyed from the sidewalk; the inn is open just to guests.

Many of Ashland's bed & breakfast inns have notable gardens which are available to inn guests and not visible from the street. Among the lovliest of these private gardens are those at ROMEO INN and at THE MORICAL HOUSE. A map of historic homes along a walking tour is available from the Visitors Information Center, 110 E. Main Street (P.O. Box 606), Ashland, OR 97520. Telephone (503) 482-3486.

Just south of Ashland, herb growers Richard and Elizabeth Fujas invite visitors to their RISING SUN ORGANIC HERB FARM. You may learn about the large variety of herbs grown here as well as sample a plethora of some 36 organically grown specialty herb products. The farm is nestled in the Siskiyou Mountains at 2300 Colestin Road, Ashland, OR 97520. Telephone (503) 482-5392. Hours are 9-5 Monday-Saturday.

On old Highway 99, between Ashland and Medford, there is a lovely ROSE DISPLAY GARDEN on the grounds of Jackson and Perkins, one of the world's largest rose growers. Open every day, you'll see an excellent display of new and old rose varieties with a kalidescope of blooms showing from June until well into September. The address is 2836 S. Pacific Highway, Medford, OR 97501. Telephone (503) 776-2277.

Nearby is the CLAIRE HANLEY ARBORETUM at Oregon State University's southern Oregon Experiment Station. Located at 569 Hanley Road, Medford, this arboretum was established to display and test plants which are suited for landscaping in southern Oregon. A miniature JAPANESE DISPLAY GARDEN, an HERB GARDEN and a lawn test area can be seen here. Open weekdays and some weekend hours. Telephone (503) 772-5165.

The Siskiyou Mountains are known throughout the world as one of the world's best sources of alpine species and the plantsmen at SISKIYOU RARE PLANT NURSERY have developed a premier collection of hardy alpine and rock-garden perennials on four acres near Medford. For appointment-only visits to the nursery, contact plantsman Baldissare Mineo, Siskiyou Rare Plant Nursery, 2825 Cummings Road, Medford, OR 97501. Telephone (503) 772-6846.

Additional tourist information may be obtained from the Medford Visitors Information Center, located at 304 South Central, Medford, OR 97501. Telephone (503) 772-5194.

Also near Medford garden lovers may want to search out the historic BIRDSEYE HOUSE during mid-summer when tall phlox, pink and white hollyhocks, golden yarrow and rudbeckias create an old-fashioned tapestry of color about the lawns. For information about arranging a visit, contact the Birdseye House, 3791 Rogue River Highway, Gold Hill, OR 97525.

Mid-April is another special time to visit southern Oregon, when acres of blooming pear trees fill the Rogue Valley with a canopy of creamy white blossoms. Find them along the Old Stage Road from Medford to Jacksonville as well as dotting gentle hills and valleys to the east of Ashland. Snowcapped Mt. McLoughlin provides a striking background for this annual spring spectacle. Between Medford and Jacksonville, a private garden and broad sweeps of lawn surround UNDER THE GREENWOOD TREE, a historic farm home which is now a bed & breakfast inn. Shading the large home (it was an early weigh station for hay and grain) are 300-year-old vintage oaks.

The summer harvest also finds local markets brimming with pears, apples, peaches, nuts and fresh vegetables of all kinds. Pinnacle's Orchard Store, on Highway 238 entering Jacksonville, offers farm-fresh fruits, unique cheeses and delectable desserts.

In historic Jacksonville, visitors may park along California Street and walk up First Street to the PETER BRITT GARDENS, site of the former Peter Britt home. Britt came to the area in the 1850's and became one of the northwest's first professional photographers.

You may enjoy a picnic here, sitting near the historic garden which is being restored. Old roses are blooming again and waxmyrtle trails purple blossoms on tendrils which cling to moss-covered rocks. This lovely spot is best viewed mid-week and early in the day. It is the site of the well-attended Peter Britt Music and Dance Festival during late June, July and August.

Strolling along the side streets of Jacksonville is a nostalgic trek back into the 1800s, for there are some 80 restored Victorian houses and other vintage structures to see. Many have their own private gardens which can be enjoyed from the sidewalk.

Not far from the center of town, the historic Pioneer Cemetery offers quiet paths through a stand of old oak trees. Waxmyrtle trails around vintage headstones (many date back to the mid-1800s) and spring wildflowers appear here and there in shady nooks and crannies.

For additional information about Britt Gardens, other historic homes, and walking tours contact the Southern Oregon Historical Society, 106 N. Central Street, Medford, OR 97501. Telephone (503) 773-6536.

Additional tourist information may be obtained from the Jacksonville Visitors Information Center, 185 N. Oregon Street (P.O. Box 33), Jacksonville, OR 97530. Telephone (503) 899-8118.

For a spectacular wildflower show, usually peaking in April, don sturdy walking shoes and walk the 1.5 mile trail to the top of LOWER TABLE ROCK (a climb of about 780 feet), a 1,650-acre preserve of The Nature Conservancy. You may see displays of goldfields, fawn lilies, scarlet fritillaries, buttercups, camas, cat's ears, lupine, monkey flower, saxifrange, and violets. Some 140 different species, both native and cultivated, have been identified here. The trail can be accessed from Central Point which is about four miles north of Medford.

For another nostalgic trek through the past continue to Grants Pass on old Highway 99 instead of the I-5 freeway. The old macadam ribbon winds through vintage oak and madrone and skirts the scenic Rogue River. Should you pass through on a Saturday between March to November, stop at the splendid outdoor GROWER'S MARKET located between 6th and 7th Streets at 'L' Street in Grants Pass. You'll find an abundance of fresh seasonal produce, colorful annuals and perennials for sale as well as herbs, houseplants and homebaked goodies of all kinds. It's billed as the longest-running open air market in the state. Open from 9-1. Telephone (503) 476-5375 for other summer market locations in southern Oregon.

Just off Highway 199, west of Grants Pass and Cave Junction toward Crescent City, the ROUGH AND READY BOTANICAL WAYSIDE is easily found. This area has been set aside by the State Parks Division to preserve the hardy native plant life found here.

Late summer and early fall is wild blackberry time and those traveling through the area during this luscious annual happening may want to check out what is reported to be the world's largest blackberry patch near the tiny community of Holland. It's located on the winding asphalt ribbon which detours from Cave Junction up to the Oregon Caves National Monument. **Note:** to avoid the throngs heading up to visit the caves, try mid-week and quite early in the day for this edible side trip.

Hardier travelers may want to check out a number of other nature trails and natural botanic areas in the nearby Kalmiopsis Wilderness. The area was named for the rare rhododendron-like plant, Kalmiopsis leachiana, which grows only in the remote wilderness area. For information about Big Craggies Botanical Area (near Cave Junction and the Oregon Caves), Rough and Ready Botanical Wayside, and the remote nature trails, contact the Siskiyou National Forest, 200 N.E. Greenfield Rd., Grants Pass, OR 97526. Telephone (503) 479-5301. The office is easily reached from 7th Street at the north edge of town as you're heading toward the Interstate-5 freeway.

Southern Willamette Valley

EUGENE ~ SPRINGFIELD ~ JUNCTION CITY

For one of the best and most accessible urban spring wildflower displays, detour from the I-5 freeway macadam at Eugene and find ALTON BAKER PARK near the University of Oregon. You can take a trail from Franklin Boulevard near Agate Street to a footbridge across the Willamette River and into the park.

It's worth a stop to just walk, or jog, or paddle your way through the flower displays along the park's 9.2 miles of trails, 3 miles of canoe run, and 9 acre pond. Large stands of fringecups, Oregon grape, California poppy, larkspur and bleeding heart can be seen along with patches of bluebells and redmaids. Bigleaf maples and black cottonwoods create dappled sunlight through leafy canopies overhead.

To obtain a species list, "Spring Flowers of Alton Baker Park," and for information about guided spring and fall walks, contact the University of Oregon Herbarium, Eugene, OR 97403. Telephone (503) 686-3033. The director of the herbarium is David Wagner.

If you like your wildflowers farther away from civilization, stop just south of Eugene at MT. PISGAH ARBORETUM, a 118-acre natural area nestled within the HOWARD BUFORD RECREATION AREA. A place of solitude far from the joggers and bicyclers, the arboretum offers shady trails and sunny paths along the flank and up the sides of 1,520-foot Mt. Pisgah. Stop by early in the spring to see fawn lilies, baby blue eyes, blue camas and a host of other delicate wildflowers along with more than 22 native species of trees on the hillside and river bank areas—this is the curved east bank of the Willamette River's Coast Fork. **Note:** there is also poison oak in the areas away from the established trails.

Arboretum volunteers plan to add to the fine native selection trees from all over the world, gathering enough variety to create many of the world's growth zones. A Tasmanian grove, a European woodland, and a small Chilean forest from the Andes Mountains all are part of this future plan.

Autumn is a colorful season at Mt. Pisgah as well, where you may see Western grey squirrels busily collecting acorns fallen from white oaks, pocket gophers which inhabit a marsh on the upper slopes, and animated frogs from a bridge which spans the lily pond near the river. Bird-lovers will want to keep an eye out for ospreys, pileated woodpeckers, and red-tailed hawks.

To access the arboretum, take the 30th Avenue exit from I-5 at the south edge of Eugene and head east on Seavey Loop Road; cross the wooden bridge over the Willamette Coast Fork and turn right at the arboretum sign onto the upper gravel entrance road, just past the field of u-cut flowers. There are picnic tables (and restrooms) in a quiet grove of trees near the headquarters cottage.

Information about the Arboretum, its annual Spring Wildflower Show & Plant Sale, its Fall Festival & Mushroom Show, and a map can be obtained from Friends of Mount Pisgah Arboretum, Box 5621, Eugene, OR 97405. Telephone (503) 345-6241.

Since it was established in 1951, the GEORGE OWEN MEMORIAL ROSE GARDEN at the foot of Jefferson Street in Eugene has offered visitors a kaleidoscope of colors from over 3,000 rose plants. The 4.89-acre garden was donated to the city by lumberman-philanthropist Owen who was a city councilman in the 1950's. The Eugene Rose Society as well as numerous other

Eugeneans have donated roses throughout the years. In addition to this display of roses, especially notable is the large resident cherry tree — it's nearly 140 years old. There are paths to stroll, jog, or bicycle and there are also picnic tables and restrooms nearby.

Equally as popular as the rose garden, HENDRICKS PARK RHODODENDRON GARDEN is a shady 20 acre garden glen situated within Hendricks Park on the east end of Eugene's forested south ridgeline.

The land for the park was donated by Thomas and Martha Hendricks in 1906 and the development of the rhododendron garden was initiated by the Eugene Men's Camellia and Rhododendron Society in 1950. In early spring of 1954 the garden was dedicated by the newly formed Eugene Chapter of the American Rhododendron Society. Members donated the earliest plantings from their own collections and propagations.

The spring rhododendron display in this lovely garden is a colorful and stunning spectacle not to be missed. The main entrance, just off Fairmount Blvd. and Summit Ave. (access from Franklin Blvd. onto Walnut Street), is flanked with massed plantings of colorful azaleas which flower in middle to late May. Pick up the helpful self-guided interpretive brochure from the box near the tall pillars of columnar basalt — these are ancient volcanic lava formations characteristis of the area. A guided tour of the garden may be arranged by contacting the Eugene Parks & Recreation Department maintenance office at (503) 687-5334.

Rhododendron and azalea lovers may want to search out the display garden at GREER GARDENS NURSERY as well, just north of town. Plantsman Harold Greer has received both Bronze and Gold medals from the American Rhododendron Society for outstanding achievement in the world of rhododendrons. More than 4,000 hybrids have been developed here under his expert guidance. Greer Gardens is located at the north edge of town, at 1280 Goodpasture Island Road, Eugene, OR 97401. Telephone (503) 686-8266 for hours in April and May.

To visit another fine rhododendron and azalea collection in a display area which is organized in a residential garden design, find BOWHAN'S NURSERY located at 27194 Huey Lane. Telephone (503) 688-1431. Hours are generally 9-6 daily except Wednesdays.

For a lovely collection of elegant ornamental perennials, including some of the choicest magnolias in the entire region, plan to visit GOSSLER FARMS NURSERY which is run by plantsman Roger Gossler and his mother. They also have many winter blooming shrubs as well. Find the nursery and well-landscaped grounds at 1200 Weaver Road, Springfield, OR 97478. Telephone (503) 746-3922 for directions and for current hours.

One of the loveliest Autumn leaf extravaganzas in the state is found on the McKENZIE LOOP DRIVE, east of Springfield via Highway 126 to McKenzie Bridge and on a few miles to Highway 242. The old asphalt ribbon curves and twists up through flaming vine maple, yellow bigleaf maple, and russet dogwood against a backdrop of Douglas fir to the top of the 5,324-foot pass. The ancient lava fields at the summit, along with several distant snowcapped Cascade peaks, are an impressive sight best seen from the lava rock observation gazebo. For maps and weather information stop at the McKenzie Bridge Ranger Station, 2.5 miles east of McKenzie Bridge. Telephone (503) 822-3381.

If your schedule won't allow this autumn side trip, at the very least plan an hour or so to stroll the lovely grounds of the UNIVERSITY OF OREGON where you'll see a grand display of native and non-native deciduous trees shouting colors of russet, deep golden yellows, vivid oranges and burnished tans. Find parking near Franklin Boulevard at Agate or Onyx Streets.

Additional tourist information may be obtained from the Eugene-Springfield Visitors Information Center, 1401 Willamette Street (P.O. Box 10286), Eugene, OR 97401. Telephone (503) 484-5307.

A pleasant spring drive northwest of Eugene, near Junction City, takes visitors along the eight mile FERGUSON ROAD DAFFODIL DRIVE. From a plethora of bulbs planted by rural residents beginning in the late 1960's, you'll find the bright yellow flowers along pasture boundaries and against wooden fences along Ferguson Road. Peak bloom time is usually mid-March. If you happen by on a Sunday in March, around the 20th, you might ask whether or not homemade cinnamon rolls and coffee are available at the Long Tom Grange Hall. Be prepared for long lines though — everyone else has heard about the cinnamon rolls, too.

Additional tourist information may be obtained from the Junction City Visitors Information Center, 516 Greenwood St., Junction City, OR 97448. Telephone (503) 998-6154.

If the notion of strolling through two acres of colorful annual and perennials sounds appealing, find PIMM FARM FLOWERS at 29415 Blueberry Road, Halsey, OR 97348. The best surprise is that at Pimm's, you may cut your own bouquet. Halsey is located a few miles north of Junction City on Highway 99E. Telephone (503) 491-3703.

CORVALLIS ~ ALBANY

For the scenic route to Corvallis, try old Highway 99W, from Junction City, which meanders through lush green farmland and skirts one of the Willamette Valley Wildlife Refuges near Monroe.

For a pleasant stroll amid a bevy of geese, ducks, hooded mergansers, grouse, pheasants, quail, mourning doves and Blacktail deer, plan a stop at the WILLIAM L. FINLEY NATIONAL WILDLIFE REFUGE just 11 miles south of Corvallis off Highway 99W. Here you'll find a self-guided trail. The refuge was named for the naturalist who persuaded President Theodore Roosevelt to create the first national wildlife refuge in the U.S. Also nearby are the 2,796-acre ANKENY NATIONAL WILDLIFE REFUGE (just south of Salem) and the BASKETT SLOUGH NATIONAL WILDLIFE REFUGE, 25 miles north of Corvallis. For further information and a map contact the Refuge Manager, Western Oregon Refuges, 26208 Finley Refuge Road, Corvallis, OR 97339. Telephone (503) 757-7236.

In Covallis, home of Oregon State University, there are several notable places to visit.

In AVERY PARK, located at 15th Street and Avery Lane, there is a ROSE GARDEN guarded by a dozen or so magnificent towering redwoods. A wide expanse of luscious green grass invites picnics and frisbee throwing contests. For further information contact the Corvallis Parks & Recreation Office, 760 S.W. Madison Street, Corvallis, OR 97333. Telephone (503) 757-6918. The rose garden may be accessed from Highway 99W, turning west onto Western Avenue then south onto 15th Street and directly into the park.

PEAVY ARBORETUM, located 8 miles north of the campus, offers 40 acres of many species of native and non-native trees and shrubs. For information and to arrange a tour, telephone The College of Forestry, (503) 737-2650. You'll find two interpretive trails here along with pleasant spots to picnic.

Just southwest of Corvallis, from the summit of MARY'S PEAK (the highest mountain in the Coast Range), you'll have a wide-angle view of not only the Cascade Mountains to the east but also the broad Willamette Valley and, on a clear day, the Pacific Ocean to the west. There are trails for walking and wonderful spots to picnic among the wildflowers and trees. Drive southwest on State Highway 34 and turn on Mary's Peak Road. A self-guided auto tour map (about 2 hours in length) is available from the Siuslaw National Forest regional office, U.S. Forest Service, 4077 Research Way, Corvallis, OR 97333. Telephone (503) 757-4480.

Additional tourist information may be obtained from the Corvallis Visitors Information Center, 420 N.W. Second Street, Corvallis, OR 97330. Telephone (503) 757-1544.

About halfway between Corvallis and Albany on Highway 20, the GARLAND NURSERY offers some five acres of annuals and perennials at one of the region's largest retail nurseries. Browse through Don and Sandra Powell's garden store and lovely gift shop as well. You'll want to plan at least and hour at this lovely oasis. Open 9-5:30 Monday-Saturday, near the 5-mile marker, 5470 N.E. Highway 20, Corvallis, OR 97333. Telephone (503) 753-6601.

Albany, a 19th century river town, boasts some 350 historic homes, most of which have been restored and awarded a place on the National Historic Register. From Federal, Classic and Stick styles to Georgian Revival, Italianate, Gothic and Colonial Revival styles, visitors may have an eyeful of one of Oregon's best collection of vintage homes along with many of their lovely gardens (you may find another impressive collection of turn-of-the-century homes and their gardens in Astoria, on the north coast).

During Albany's late July Victorian Heritage Week, you may pick up a map for free VICTORIAN GARDEN TOURS, Monday-Friday, at the Visitor's Gazebo on S.W. 8th & Ellsworth Streets. You'll see the gazebo as you come into town on Highway 20.

Park in the public area just next to it and enjoy the collection of wonderful old flowers — a lush fragrant stand of lavender, deep purple Heliotrope, pink and white and yellow snapdragons and phlox, pale lavender clematis and a hollyhock with double blossoms surround the picture-filled gazebo and an old-fashioned bench. The Visitors Information Center is located at 435 W. First Street (P.O. Box 548), Albany, OR 97321. Telephone: (503) 926-1517.

Unless you're looking for NICHOLS GARDEN NURSERY, you could easily pass by the barn red vintage buildings along the Old Salem Road near Albany. However, don't be put off by its unspectacular appearance because the well-tended gardens are behind the weathered buildings. Look for the weathered sandwich board announcing this world-reknowned grower of herbs and mail-order herb seeds.

Nicholas P. and Edith Rose Nichols moved to Oregon and began growing and selling seeds some 40 years ago. Their daughter, Rose Marie Nichols McGee, now runs the nursery with her husband, Keane.

Visitors enjoy a variety of gardens which have been planted here over the past several years, including a colonial garden, a shade garden, a "teas, bees and potpourris" garden, a culinary garden, and an intriguing knot garden.

Included is a display of All-America flowers and vegetables which are the special focus of the nursery's annual plant day, usually the third Saturday in May. You can also see and sniff some ten varieties of sweet basil as well as chocolate mint, lavender mint, applemint, pineapple mint, and the familiar peppermint and spearmint.

Open 9-5:30 Monday-Saturday, Nichols Garden Nursery is located at 1190 N. Pacific Highway, Albany, OR 97320. Telephone (503) 928-9280. Take the first Albany Exit (heading south on I-5) or Exit 234 (heading north on I-5) and bear to the west and north at the first light (Albany Street) to Old Salem Road, turning right. The nursery is less than a mile from the freeway interchanges.

Northern Willamette Valley

SALEM ~ AURORA ~ CANBY

The landscaped grounds surrounding the Capitol building in Salem offer both a lovely fountain and a stroll through native dogwood, rhododendron, azaleas, and colorful annual beds. The ancient Calapooya Indians who once lived in the broad Willamette Valley called this area Chemeketa, meaning "place of peace." Trek to the top of the capitol rotunda for a 360-degree view of the surrounding countryside where these peaceful Indians once roamed.

A few blocks south of the Capitol building and the adjacent Willamette University grounds, two Victorian mansions rest among 89 wooded acres. HISTORIC DEEPWOOD ESTATE, an elegant Queen Anne style Victorian, was built by a druggist and land speculator, Dr. Luke A. Port around 1893. In 1895 the house was sold to Judge and Mrs. George Bingham and in 1925 the mansion was purchased by a hop and wool broker, Clifford Brown for his wife Alice.

By 1929 Alice Brown began developing the formal gardens which were designed by landscape architect friends Elizabeth Lord and Edith Schryver. With a champagne toast on New Year's Eve, 1935, Alice (now widowed) christened her home "Deepwood."

She incorporated into her formal gardens a delicate and ornate wrought iron gazebo from the 1905 Portland Lewis & Clark Exposition, an ivy arch walk, and an English tea house garden with perennials as well as a boxwood garden with ornamental fencing, an old spring water well, and a spring house gazebo (which has been relocated to the north end of the tennis court).

Included now in the 5.5 acre estate is the wooded RITA STEINER FRY NATURE TRAIL which winds through native trees, plants and wildflowers along Pringle Creek. In late March-early April the ground carpet of Lamb's Tongue is especially grand. At the south end of the estate, near the parking area, you may browse in the greenhouse which features tropical plants, cacti and succulents.

Notice also the mansion's stunning stained glass windows, collections of apothecary bottles and costumes, original 1894 electric light fixtures and solarium over the old carriage port. For further information contact The Friends of Deepwood, 1116 Mission Street S.E., Salem, OR 97302. Telephone (503) 363-1825. The estate and gardens are open every day except Tuesday and Saturday, May-September. Modified hours during the winter months. Nominal fee.

Located just next door to Deepwood Estate is the historic BUSH'S PASTURE PARK and BUSH HOUSE which was built in 1877 by Asahel Bush II, editor of the Oregon Statesman newspaper. The stately Victorian's grounds feature a collection of old and new roses, espaliered shrubs and native trees. The adjacent BUSH BARN is home to the 63-year-old Salem Art Association where a large Art Fair is held in mid-July each year.

Additional tourist information may be obtained from the Salem Visitors Information Center which is located in historic Mission Mill Village and shops, 1313 Mill Street S.E., Salem, OR 97230. Telephone (503) 581-4325. Tourist information is also available in the Capitol rotunda. You may also want to search out the small HERB & DYE GARDEN located at Mission Mill Village.

To feast your senses on acres and acres of stately bearded iris, from stylish yellows and classic blues to exotic purples and seductive pinks, plan to visit the display gardens at two world renowned Willamette Valley iris growers. The iris Germanicus was brought to Oregon from southern France in the early 1800s and active hybridizing began in the late 19th century.

A Swiss-American named Francis X. Schreiner turned his iris hobby into a business, compiling his first "Iris Lover's Catalogue" in 1928. Still in the family two generations later, SCHREINER'S GARDENS may be found at 3625 Quinaby Road N.E., just north of Salem. The field irises are rotated yearly on Schreiner's 200 acres, some of which are located alongside Interstate 5 so motorists can enjoy the kaleidoscope of spring colors as well. The display gardens are open daily, 8 a.m. till dusk and best blooming times are mid-May to early June.

Just 15 minutes east of Salem, near Silverton, at 11553 Silverton Road N.E., you may discover more world renowned iris growers at COOLEY'S GARDENS. Rholin Cooley became interested in growing irises in the 1920s through the family physician, Dr. Richard Kleinsorge, whose hobby was the hybridization of the iris. In honor of Cooley's 60th anniversary a deep caramel-pink iris with a red beard was named for grandmother Pauline Cooley. At 89, she still works in the gardens with the younger generation of Cooleys who now manage the business.

Each year around May 20 Cooley's Gardens celebrates its anniversary with ten days of special events, including a cut-flower show featuring some 300 varieties of the bearded blooms and an evening of tasting wines from local wineries.

The display garden is open each day and camera buffs are encouraged to catch the colorful blooms early in the morning while still coated with dew.

Tourist information may be obtained from the Silverton Visitors Information Center located at 216 Oak Street (P.O. Box 257), Silverton, OR 97381. Telephone (503) 873-5615.

In the small community of Aurora, between Salem and Canby, on State Highway 99E, you may see many of the German colony's original buildings including the Ox Barn Museum, the Kraus House, and the Steinbach Cabin. The log cabin dates to 1876.

Walk through the museum to the backyard to find the cabin and an excellent display of early farm equipment as well as the charming EMMA WAKEFIELD HERB GARDEN. The garden, which contains both medicinal and culinary herbs, is tended by members of the Willamette Valley Herb Society. For information about the community's annual Aurora Colony Day held in August contact the Old Aurora Colony Museum, Aurora Colony Historical Society, P.O. Box 202, Aurora, OR 97002. Telephone (503) 678-5754.

In Canby, just next door to Aurora, flower lovers may enjoy strolling through some 50 acres of late summer blooming dahlias at SWAN ISLAND DAHLIAS. The peak blooming time is August through frost (usually the end of October). During the first two weekends of September you may catch the indoor dahlia show and watch professional designers arrange the voluptuous blooms.

With names like "Cuddles," "Cameo," and "First Love," to "Matchmaker," "Playboy," and "Tahiti Sunrise," dahlia blooms may range in size from miniature, dwarf and pompon to ball, collarette and formal decorative. The smallest may be one or two inches in diameter while the giants are seven to twelve inches across. Located just off Holly and N.W. 22nd Avenue, Box 800E, Canby, OR 97013, the office is open Monday through Friday, 9-4:30 p.m. Telephone (503) 266-7711.

Located west of Canby, off I-5 at Exit 278, the CECIL & MOLLY SMITH GARDEN can be found at 5065 Ray Bell Road in St. Paul. Plantsman Cecil Smith has had a love affair with rhododendrons for much of his life and the garden is filled with superior examples of his hybrids. They are known throughout the world because of his generous sharing of seeds and pollen.

In the spring of 1983, the Portland chapter of the American Rhododendron Society purchased the garden and a volunteer group of Portland, Tualatin Valley and Willamette Chapter members now manage it. Their work parties maintain the lovely garden, selected plant varieties are propagated, pollen is collected, and hybridization continues under Cecil Smith's direction.

Along with the rhododendron collection are choice trees, shrubs, wildflowers and bulbs. Each garden pathway leads to another botanic treasure — licorice fern tucked into crevices of moss-covered logs, carpets of delicate bleeding heart, native huckleberry thriving in its favorite spot atop old tree stumps.

The garden is open during selected Saturdays in mid-March, April and May or by appointment. Nominal fee. Further information about visiting the Cecil & Molly Smith Garden may be obtained from the Portland Chapter, The American Rhododendron Society, Paula Cash, Executive Secretary, 14885 S.W. Sunrise Lane, Tigard, OR 97224. Telephone (503) 620-4038.

Other luscious perennials such as peonies, iris and daylilies may be seen at the CAPRICE FARMS NURSERY located between Wilsonville and Sherwood. Al and Dorothy Rogers came to Oregon from the east coast some 40 years ago, and when they first settled high atop Parrot Mountain, there were only one or two other neighbors. To find their picturesque spot with its view of Mount Hood to the east, exit from I-5 north of Canby at Wilsonville (exit 283), head west on Wilsonville-Newberg Road, right on Brown to 110th, then onto Tooze Road for about 4.5 miles. Angle onto McConnell then left on Pleasant Hill Road to the Caprice Nursery sign. April, May and June are peak blooming times. For further information contact Caprice Farm Nursery, 15425 S.W. Pleasant Hill Road, Sherwood, OR 97140. Telephone (503) 625-7241.

NEWBERG ~ FOREST GROVE ~ CORNELIUS

In the small rural community of Newberg, travelers may find the HOOVER-MINTHORN HOUSE, the childhood home of Herbert Hoover, our 31st president. In Hoover's boyhood days the yard was devoted to vegetables, herbs, lilac trees and a small orchard. Later, when the house became a museum, the landscaping team of Elizabeth Lord and Edith Schryver performed the same magic which they achieved at Deepwood Estate in Salem.

As a model for the gardens at Hoover-Minthorn House, Elizabeth Lord used her mother's rose-filled gardens of the 1890s. A new addition, in 1987, was a seedling from a tulip tree planted by George Washington at Mount Vernon. The museum is located at 115 S. River Street (off Highway 99W), Newberg, OR. Telephone (503) 538-6629. Hours Wednesday through Sunday, 1-4. You may also enjoy a picnic at Hoover Park, just across the street.

North of Newberg, toward Forest Grove and Hillsboro via Highway 219, flower lovers may enjoy stopping at BLOOMING NURSERY to meet plantswoman Grace Dinsdale and her genial staff. From scented geraniums and roses to hardy succulents and herbs; from hydrangeas, vines and groundcovers to trees and shrubs you'll see one of the largest selection of regional plant material in the area.

Stroll through the attractive lath display area which is attached to the huge country barn just next to the general retail area. The nursery is located two miles south of Cornelius, off Highway 8 between Forest Grove and Beaverton, at Rt. 4 Box 90, Cornelius, OR 97113. Telephone (503) 359-0317. Hours 9-6 Monday-Friday, 9-5 on Saturday and 10-4 on Sunday.

WILSONVILLE

Located near Wilsonville, off I-5 at exit 286, the BARN OWL NURSERY offers a lovely display herb garden which includes Potpourri, Colonial, and Culinary herbs, a Drying and Dye section, Silver and Grey area, Blue and White Flowering area and the Barn Owl motif. Owners Chris and Ed Mulder specialize in annual, biennial and perennial herb plants for both culinary and medicinal as well as ornamental and fragrant use. Among the best are the scented-leaf geraniums — rose, lemon, mint, fruit and spice.

Numerous classes and workshops are held in the large, well-stocked gift shop and Chris usually has a tasty herbal dip and crackers for everyone to sample, along with steaming herbal teas. On coolish mornings, a wood stove offers warmth and the resident cat can often be found snoozing close by.

A 10-day Herb Festival is held at the nursery the first two weeks in May and a Holiday Open House in early November. Open to the public April through July, Wednesday through Saturday, 10-5. The address is 22999 S.W. Newland Road, Wilsonville, OR 97070. Telephone (503) 638-0387. From exit 286, head east and bear to the right onto Stafford Road. Continue north on Stafford Road to Barn Owl Nursery signs.

For those rose lovers there are two well-known Portland & Tri-County Area nurseries in the Wilsonville area — FRED EDMONDS ROSE NURSERY at 6235 S.W. Kahle Road, Wilsonville, OR. Telephone (503) 638-4671. And, JUSTICE MINIATURE ROSES, 5147 S.W. Kahle Road, Wilsonville, OR 97070. Telephone (503) 682-2370. Both are off Stafford Road between Wilsonville and the Barn Owl Nursery.

Additional tourist information may be obtained from the Wilsonville Visitors Information Center, 8880 S.W. Wilsonville Rd. (P.O. Box 111), Wilsonville, OR 97070. Telephone (503) 682-0411.

Head north on Stafford Road to rejoin the I-205 freeway, either toward Portland or east to Oregon City, Milwaukie, West Linn and Lake Oswego.

Greater Portland Metropolitan Area

OREGON CITY ~ MILWAUKIE

In this area, at the terminus of the Oregon Trail where Oregon's roots run perhaps the deepest, are a number of notable historic homes with lovely grounds and gardens worth adding to the travel itinerary.

The ROSE FARM, which boasts the distinction of being the oldest pioneer house in Oregon City, was built in 1848 by the William Holmes family. It was the site of the swearing in ceremony of the first Territorial Governor, Joseph Lane, and served as the legislative hall for the fledgling Oregon Territory.

On the grounds are lovely vintage roses and many old-fashioned flowers, shrubs and fruit trees. Located at 534 Holmes Lane, Oregon City, OR 97045, visitors may telephone (503) 656-5146 for hours and to arrange a tour.

The GLENNON HOUSE, a rural gothic built by stonecutter Francis Glennon in 1884, boasts a lovely cottage garden reclaimed by the current owners. The inviting trellised entry garden combines foxglove, lavender, iris, columbine, campanula, veronica, and old scented roses. Tall spikes of blue delphinium march along the picket fence into a mixture of daylily, poppy, daisy, sweet william, geum and globeflower. For information about visiting this private garden, contact OLD HOME FORUM member, Claire Met, at the JAGGER HOUSE Bed & Breakfast, 512 Sixth Street, Oregon City, OR 97045. Telephone (503) 657-7820.

The Old Home Forum sponsors an annual self-guided summer tour of vintage homes in the Oregon City area, many of whom have lovely gardens. Many local historic homes are dressed in holiday finery and open during the Christmas season as well. For information contact the historic McLOUGHLIN HOUSE, 713 Center Street, Oregon City, OR 97045. Telephone (503) 656-5146.

The BROETJE HOUSE, at 3010 S.E. Courtney Road in Milwaukie, is an 1889 Queen Anne style home which was built for John F. Broetje, a noted pioneer horticulturist and floriculturist. The impressive house, its 50-foot water tower and lovely grounds have been restored for use as a bed & breakfast inn. For information about an annual open house, usually held during Historic Preservation Week in May, contact the Milwaukie Historical Society Museum, 3737 S.E. Adams, Milwaukie, OR 97232. Telephone (503) 659-2998.

Volunteers from the Oak Grove Garden Club are maintaining RISLEY LANDING GARDENS, a recently reclaimed private natural area along the Willamette River between Milwaukie and Oregon City. The property was originally included in a mile-long riverfront land grant deeded in 1866 to Jacob Risley. In the late 1800s, riverboats plied between Oregon City and Portland, stopping at numerous river landings like Risley's to pick up passengers as well as produce and goods for the Portland market. It wasn't until 1903 that the electric car line reached out to Milwaukie and replaced the riverboats for transportation in the growing region.

The riverfront property, first settled by Jacob's father, Orville Risley, was deeded to the garden club by Jacob's grandson in memory of his mother and sisters. It has now been transformed from overgrown blackberry brambles and a plethora of poison oak into a natural park which is open to the public on a limited schedule.

Risley Landing Gardens is a happy blend of cultivated and natural landscaping. In addition to stately old oaks visitors find Douglas fir, holly, cedars, honey locusts, European birch, sequioa, pine, filberts and magnolia. Additional native plants will be incorporated so that the gardens may be used as a nature study area as well.

Near the center of the garden is a lovely cedar gazebo which was designed by J.S. Risley IV, a descendent of Jacob Risley. Meander the main path through colorful flower beds and up a gentle slope to the old boat landing site which overlooks the Willamette River. The old stone foundation has been preserved. For information about visiting this private garden, contact Oak Grove Garden Club members Irma Knapp, (503) 654-2337 or Marian Morton, (503) 654-6836. The garden is located off McLoughlin Boulevard, turning west onto Concord, north on River Road, west on Risley, and north on Oak Shore Lane to the park's locked gate.

For another quiet stroll along shady paths which encircle a large wildlife pond, plan to spend an hour or so at the JOHN INSKEEP ENVIRNOMENTAL LEARNING CENTER located on the campus of Clackamas Community College.

Also on the campus, near the softball field, is a lovely PERENNIAL & ANNUAL GARDEN and small rose garden. Curator Richard Marx tends more than 100 plant and tree species native to Oregon.

Although the garden is hidden behind an expanse of boxwood hedge and may be easily passed by, it is worth a stop. When visited, beds were carefully laid out in geometric shapes and the annuals and perennials were well tended and arranged in color-coordinated groupings. Bees hummed happily over purple salvia, pale pink silver cup, colorful daisies of all kinds, numerous daylilies and a large bed of statis as well. To access the campus from I-205, take exit 10 and follow State Highway 213 to Beavercreek Road. Turn left .5 mile, right into the campus and left to the Perennial Garden. Telephone (503) 657-6958.

Additional tourist information may be obtained from the Oregon Tri-City Visitors Information Center, 500 Abernethy Road, Oregon City, OR 97045. Telephone (503) 656-1619.

WEST LINN ~ LAKE OSWEGO ~ LAKE GROVE

Across the Willamette River from Oregon City take the West Linn exit from I-205, turn right onto State Highway 14 and just past the service station turn right to the McLEAN HOUSE and PARK at 5350 River Street in West Linn. Stroll the grounds shaded by towering Douglas fir and find the path through old rhododendrons, azaleas, fern, and ivy. The only discordant note in this lovely setting is the incessant roar of traffic from the I-205 bridge which spans the nearby Willamette River. One imagines the loudest noises heard by the McLean family, when the house was built, were the chattering of squirrels and melodious early morning bird songs. Although there is a shady space to picnic here, I suggest continuing north on Highway 14 to nearby HAMMERLE PARK. Its colorful entry greets visitors with a colorful bed of well-tended bulbs and annuals. Plenty of space for a picnic here, even on misty days beneath a large shelter. For further information contact the West Linn Parks Department, (503) 656-6081.

On the rocky bluffs above the West Linn High School, a rare white larkspur with a blue center is now being preserved at the Nature Conservancy's 27-acre CAMASSIA NATURAL AREA PRESERVE. A member of the ranunculus family, the pale white larkspur usually blooms late May to early June. The flower may have been observed first by botanists in the late 1800s in the Columbia Gorge. The Nature Conservancy is also protecting the delicate plant on nearby Little Rock Island in the upper Willamette River above Oregon City. Clackamas Community College botany instructor Bob Misley and his students are mapping out and counting the delphinium leucophaeum in both areas, the only two places in the northwest where the delicate native plant now grows.

SOUTHWEST PORTLAND

Heading north on Highway 14 through Lake Oswego, find THE BISHOP'S CLOSE at Elk Rock which offers an imposing specialty garden on a bluff high above the Willamette River. Serene graveled paths beckon the visitor around a wide expanse of lawn, trees, shrubs and plantings which open to graceful vistas around every turn. For some 60 years, Scotsman Peter Kerr worked in his beloved garden which was designed in tandem with John Olmsted. For some 10 years Kerr and Olmsted corresponded, drew plans and changed them, dug into the hillside, spread out the expanse of lawns, and both pulled and pruned as well as planted trees and shrubs.

When he died in 1957, at the age of 95, the Scotsman's estate was deeded to the Episcopal Diocese of Oregon. The manor house serves as the Diocese headquarters and the lovely grounds are maintained by an endowment from the Kerr family.

A single gardner, Mike Black, now tends this 13-acre paradise (in Kerr's day there were six gardners). If possible, plan to visit the garden in April and early May when pink dogwood, elegant magnolias (Kerr's favorites), dozens of rhododendron species and Japanese cherry burst into bloom. Hopefully, you'll also encounter the enchanting cascade of white blossoms on the tangle of wisteria which climbs a weathered wall near the garden's entry path.

A lily pond with an island on which bloom rhododendron, deep blue wood hyacinth and pale blue-violet iris can also be seen along your gentle stroll around The Bishop's Close. Open daily from 8-5 in winter and 8-7 in summer. There is parking but no public facilities here; there is no admission fee. From Macadam Avenue (Highway 14) turn east (toward the river) on S.W. Military Road and take an immediate right onto Military Lane to the entry.

In this high bluff scenic river area between Lake Oswego and Portland are many elegant homes with well-manicured private gardens. In earlier times, before the turn of the century, wealthy cityfolks built summer cottages on the rocky Douglas fir-coated bluff and traveled out a dirt road via horsedrawn means.

When all-weather roads were constructed in the early 1900s, some families moved out to the area permanently, building large homes with gatehouses and stables and developing those rocky bluffs and cascading streams into beautifully landscaped estates. While many of the gardens are over 70 years old, some have been updated. New gardens have also been created by local landscape architects well known for their innovative designs and use of native plants.

Visitors may visit several of these elegant private gardens on the biennial DUNTHORPE HOUSE AND GARDEN TOUR. For information about dates in 1990 and 1992, and cost, contact the Riverdale School Parent Committee, Riverdale School, 11733 S.W. Breyman Avenue, Portland, OR 97219. Telephone (503) 636-4511.

For additional information about other spring garden tours in the Portland area, contact the Association of Oregon Gardens, P.O. Box 15013, Portland, OR 97215.

Just off Macadam and S.W. Riverdale garden lovers may find one of the choicest gems in the northwest, THE BERRY BOTANIC GARDEN. This unique species garden had its beginnings in 1938 when Rae Selling Berry moved her extensive plant collection from northeast Portland to her new home in this shady wooded bower in the southwest hills.

A world renowned plantswoman, she pursued new plants from all corners of the globe and since 1932 had subscribed to major plant hunting expeditions to western China, Tibet and the Himalayas. From these exotic seeds she grew those first seedlings that ripened into a love for rhododendron, magnolia, Meconopsis, alpines, and her lifelong passion, Primula or primroses.

In 1932 she wrote, in the National Horticultural Magazine: "I wonder how many of us who garden, start with the definite idea of growing or specializing in any particular plant? . . . but to me has come the joy of almost having a plant choose me, of happening on the particular plant that fitted my garden, my purse, my surroundings, bringing with it the opportunity of growing up with the species, expanding with it as my horizon expanded, and my love for it and my interest in it grew."

After her death in 1976, her gardening and botanist friends at home and abroad united to provide a way to save her irreplaceable collections. The garden is now a non-profit corporation supported by membership dues, special gifts and income from an endowment fund.

Some 30 endangered native Pacific Northwest and northern California plants are being collected and preserved here as The Berry Garden has been named one of some 20 regional gardens across the U.S. representing the national Center for Plant Conservation. In addition to the native plants, alpines, and over 145 rhododendron species, the garden is dedicated to expanding its major collection of species primula and is also developing an extensive collection of species lilies from the western United States.

A quiet stroll through Rae Selling Berry's 6-acre garden is a walk through five distinct micro-environments. The elegant magnolias may capture your interest first, particularly the Chinese magnolias whose dramatic blooms emit a poignant melon scent in the early spring. Next, the moist area between upper lawn and woodland where colonies of primroses thrive, and up a gentle slope to a meadowy bog and small stream where marsh marigolds, forget-me-nots, ferns, irises, Indian rhubarb and horsetail live.

Behind the main house you'll stroll across an open sunny alpine rock garden and continue past the raised growing platform and greenhouse to the garden's northerly sections. Here are the groves of tall rhododendron, now half a century old, and a self-guided Native Plant Trail through the forest canopy. Wild ginger, wild bleeding heart and salal are here along with bunchberry, snowberry, salmonberry and Oregon grape. Near the bubbling stream are found skunk cabbage, Indian rhubarb and the rare Darlingtonia Californica or cobra lily.

For information about membership in The Berry Botanic Garden and to make an arrangements to visit the garden, contact the horticulture or conservation directors, or garden volunteers, at 11505 S.W. Summerville Avenue, Portland, OR 97219. Telephone (503) 636-4112. The hours are 10-4, Monday-Saturday, by appointment only.

Nearby, on Palatine Hill Road, you may stroll the lovely campus of Lewis & Clark College. The best panoramic view can be seen from the far side of the original manor which houses the administrative offices. Rhododendron, azaleas and tall Douglas fir are mirrored in a lovely reflecting pool just down stone steps from the spacious lawn. Mount Hood is also seen on clear days rising above the Cascade Mountains to the east. This lovely reverie may be disturbed only by the happy chuckles and laughter of students playing frisbee on the lower lawns.

Located just a mile from the college, at 11321 S.W. Terwilliger Boulevard, find wooded and shady TRYON CREEK STATE PARK. One of the special features of this natural park is barrier-free, paved Trillium Trail, for those with limited mobility. This trail, the first of its kind in the state parks system, was constructed in two years with hundreds of hours of volunteer help, including design help from wheelchair nature-lover Robert Pike, founder of Environmental Access. Landings and benches provide rest spots and water fountains are reachable from a wheelchair.

A 640-acre mini-wilderness within the city, the park is laced with some 14 miles of trails which are enjoyed by hikers, strollers, and bikers. There are sections for riding horses as well.

The forest is primarily second-growth but the native flowers and plants continue to thrive under the loving care of the Oregon State Parks rangers and dedicated Friends of Tryon Creek who helped to ensure that the park remains a wilderness area between Lake Oswego and Portland.

Numerous nature study classes, wildflower workshops, and slide-talks are offered at the spacious Nature House, located near the public parking area. An annual Trillium Festival is held in early April, honoring the arrival of the northwest's first spring wildflower. When the trilliums bloom, we know that spring has truly arrived!

For further information contact the park rangers and Friends of Tryon Creek State Park volunteers at Nature House. Telephone (503) 636-4398. The park is open daily from dawn to dusk and 10-6 on Sundays.

Visitors are welcome to visit nearby KLINE NURSERY where plantsman Phil Parker specializes in native wildflowers as well as cyclamen, lilies, begonias, ferns and a variety of spring bulbs. From delicate Fawn and Avalanche lilies to lively Shooting Star and Red Columbine, many propagated native plants are available at the nursery.

Native plant lovers are urged to grow the delicate plants from seeds or cuttings rather than to try and transplant them from the wild. The chances of successfully transplanting full grown plants from the wild are slim because of their large root systems and close interrelationships with soil fungi.

Propagated plants are more readily adapted to city gardens and they are available from not only Kline's but several other plant nurseries in the Northwest who, like Phil Parker, are carrying on the fine tradition of propagated natives begun by dedicated northwest plantsmen like Edgar Kline. Edgar passed away in 1988. The Kline Nursery is located at 17401 S.W. Bryant Road, Lake Grove, OR 97035. Telephone (503) 636-3923. Hours 10-3 Monday-Friday year round and 12-4 on Saturdays during March, April and May. Find the nursery by driving south on Boones Ferry Road (just west of Tryon Creek State Park) about 3 miles, through Lake Grove to Bryant Rd. Left on Bryant for about a mile to the nursery's white fence. The address numbers are on a post to the left of the driveway.

Those lovers of birds as well as flowers may want to plan a stop at GERBER GARDENS, located at 15780 S.W. Boones Ferry Road, in Lake Oswego. Richard Clarke handcrafts, to Audubon specifications, a wide variety of birdhouses for those feathered species that frequent the northwest, particularly Oregon. He also offers bird baths, seeds, and helpful bird books as well as a selection of locally grown flowers and plants. Telephone (503) 227-3232. Open 10-5 daily.

Another nursery nearby which specializes in species rhododendron, azaleas and other hardy plants is THE BOVEES NURSERY. Driving north on Boones Ferry Road find the small sign just beyond the light at Kerr Parkway. Turning left (west) onto Stephenson Street, follow the nursery's direction signs to 1737 S.W. Coronado Street. The telephone is (503) 244-9341 and the friendly plantswoman is owner Lucy Sorenson.

Additional tourist information may be obtained from the Lake Oswego Visitors Information Center, 47 North State Street (P.O. Box 368), Lake Oswego, OR 97034. Telephone (503) 636-3634.

You may continue north on Boones Ferry Road to Terwilliger Boulevard, bearing left on Terwilliger to the Interstate 5 freeway which accesses the downtown Portland area.

PORTLAND'S DOWNTOWN AREA

Known as the City of Roses, Portland is aptly named for the climate here is especially friendly for growing the thorny-stemmed perennials with the exquisite blooms. A visit to the gardens of Portland's downtown area naturally begins with the INTERNATIONAL ROSE TEST GARDENS in WASHINGTON PARK.

Situated high above the city, and with one of the best views of Mount Hood to the east, these public gardens welcome thousands of visitors each year. Stroll among row upon row of carefully tended hybrid teas, floribundas, grandifloras, and climbers. Dedicated volunteers from The Portland Rose Society donate countless hours to help tend the beds and remove the spent blooms from June through September.

The society had its beginnings in 1888 when Georgiana Burton Pittock, wife of pioneer publisher Henry Pittock, invited her friends and neighbors to exhibit their roses in a tent set up in her garden.

In 1915 a former society president, Jesse A. Currey, convinced city fathers to inaugurate a rose test garden and in 1918 the world was invited to send its roses to Portland's new municipal rose garden.

In spite of a war raging in Europe, roses from England and Ireland arrived to compete with American roses in The Portland Test, as the gardens were first known. In 1966 the half acre Gold Medal Garden was established, separate from the test area and general garden area, for the purpose of displaying in chronological order those roses that have received the coveted medal since 1919.

Expert volunteers serve on the panel of judges who evaluate the hybrid roses in the test garden area. Catalogued and numbered rather than named, roses still arrive from all over the world to have their growth tested in this mild humid transition climate between the Cascade Mountain Range and the Pacific Ocean.

Tucked over in the southeast corner is the high-walled Shakespeare Garden with its colorful assortment of poppies, lavender, rosemary and other flowers and herbs mentioned in the bard's plays.

Above the Rose Gardens, on the former site of the city's old municipal zoo, is another botanical treasure, THE JAPANESE GARDEN.

Stroll through five traditional gardens here, including "Shukeiyen" (the Natural Garden), "Rijiniwa" (the Tea Garden), "Chisen-Kaiyui-Shiki" (the Strolling Pond Garden), "Seki-Tei" (the Sand and Stone Garden), and "Hiraniwa" (the Flat Garden). This garden masterpiece was designed by Professor P. Takuma Tono, a noted authority on Japanese landscaping.

The Japanese Garden is impeccably beautiful in spring and summer, fall or winter. Each season brings visitors again and again to this tranquil, serene, traditional oriental garden high above the city.

In early May, colorful "koi Nobori" (carp kites) fly in the breeze high atop a flagpole to signal the opening of the annual Children's Festival. One of the features of the day-long festival is the Tea Ceremony which dates back to the 15th century in ancient Japan.

Find the entrance just across from the tennis courts, above the Rose Test Gardens. There's plenty of free parking but a nominal fee is charged for this garden which is nurtured and cared for by the Japanese Garden Society, a nonprofit organization. Information about the membership may be obtained from the Japanese Garden Society of Oregon, P.O. Box 3847, Portland, OR 97208. Telephone (503) 223-1321 or (503) 223-4070. Hours are 10-4 daily.

Nearby, at the WASHINGTON PARK ZOO, you may enjoy a butterfly garden, a selection of exotic bamboos and ornamental grasses, a small herb garden (next to the planetarium) and an impressive display of colorful annuals at the zoo's entrance. Find the collections of bamboo at the southwest end of the Primate Building and next to the Elephant Museum.

The zoo's BUTTERFLY GARDEN was developed by a local affiliate of the

Oregon State Federation of Garden Clubs. This organization has actively promoted gardens and gardening since 1924. Further information about the organization and about local garden tours open to the public may be obtained from membership chairwoman Larcel Abendroth, 7535 S.E. 21st Avenue, Portland, OR 97202.

Next door to Washington Park on a forested hump, Tualatin Mountain, are five thousand acres of Portland's own urban forest, FOREST PARK and HOYT ARBORETUM. Amble along sections of the 25-mile Wildwood Trail which begin near the Zoo and World Forestry Center for a close encounter with peaceful vistas and wide-angle views as well as shady nooks. Just likeminded souls and a jogger or two may occasionally interrupt your pleasant trek. More than 30 species of wildflowers, including trilliums, wild violets and buttercups show off for visitors in March, April and May. The park is also home to some 100 bird species and 50 mammals.

In the Hoyt Arboretum section of the park, hundreds of identified deciduous trees and conifers from all corners of the globe await spring and summer visitors. Autumn, of course, may bring you back again to enjoy the vibrant fall colors here. You'll find oaks, maples and magnolias as well as splendid examples of Himalayan spruce, Dawn redwood, Chinese Lacebark pine and Brewer's Weeping spruce. Stop at TREE HOUSE, the visitors information center on upper Fairview Boulevard, for maps and other information about the 175-acre arboretum and its network of trails. Telephone (503) 248-4492. The arboriculturist is Fred Nilsen.

Access all of these botanic treasures in Portland's southwest hills from West Burnside, downtown. Above 23rd Avenue, turn onto Tichenor at the yellow blinking light, then onto Kingston and across Fairview Boulevard to Washington Park, the tennis courts, and Japanese Garden. Wind from there over to the Zoo, World Forestry Center, and Wildwood Trailhead. You'll find plenty of places to picnic as well as restrooms nearby.

Also close by, at 5151 N.W. Cornell Road, just north of Forest Park and West Burnside, you may want to stop by the Portland Audubon Society's AUDUBON HOUSE for maps and information about the two nature trails within walking distance of the center. Guided nature hikes and workshops are offered throughout the year and each fall an Annual Art, Craft and Book Fair features the work of wildlife artists and crafters, authors, and nature photographers. Audubon House is open 10-4, Tuesday-Sunday. Telephone (503) 292-6855. An annual Birdathon fund-raiser is held each spring around the first weekend in May.

Often the bird lovers will be found out on SAUVIE ISLAND near the historic BYBEE-HOWELL HOUSE and AGRICULTURAL MUSEUM. An 1850s territorial homestead, much like the ROSE FARM in Oregon City, the house and barn have been restored, furnished and maintained by the Oregon Historical Society. A lovely spot to picnic, you'll sit among dozens of old-fashioned scented roses and beneath the shade of vintage fruit trees over a hundred years old.

Located at 18901 N.W. Howell Park Road, access the island from northwest Portland by heading west on Highway 30 for about 10 miles to the Sauvie Island bridge. Open noon-5, Wednesday through Sunday, June through Labor Day. Admission is free and guided tours are available. Information about special events at the farm may be obtained from the Oregon Historical Society, 1230 S.W. Park Avenue, Portland, OR 97201. Telephone (503) 222-1741.

There are also many places to bird watch on Sauvie Island and with or without binoculars you may spot marsh and red-tailed hawks, Canada geese, tundra swans, sandhill cranes and great blue herons as well as the smaller shore birds, ducks and Passeriformes (perching birds).

PORTLAND'S WEST SIDE HISTORIC MANSIONS

The PITTOCK MANSION, located at 3229 N.W. Pittock Drive in northwest Portland, was the elegant turn-of-the-century French Renaissance chateau-style home of Henry and Georgianna Pittock. Henry founded Portland's Daily Oregonian newspaper in the late 1800s. On the landscaped grounds are stately rhododendrons, azaleas and flowering trees. A couple of picnic tables offer a pleasant spot to lunch overlooking the city and mountains beyond. Also on the grounds, the quaint restored Gatehouse offers tea and crumpets on selected days. Telephone: (503) 248-4469. Access the Pittock Mansion off West Burnside, just above Washington Park.

Another lovely old estate can be found further west, up West Burnside to Highway 217 (just past the hospital) and out through Beaverton on Highway 10 to Aloha. The JENKINS ESTATE sprawls on 68 acres atop Cooper Mountain. Lush pink and purple rhododendrons, planted in the 1920s, arch over a gravel path to the rear of the main house which looks like a wealthy sportsman's hunting-lodge. A fish pond and rock garden emit rich scents from exotic imported flowers. Don't miss the herb garden, down a side road from the front of the house.

Formerly the home of garden and horse-lovers Belle Ainsworth and Ralph Jenkins, the estate was purchased in 1976 by the Tualatin Hills Park and Recreation District. Assisted by local garden clubs, the grounds have been restored to their turn of the century granduer. Find the Jenkins Estate at 209th Avenue & Grabhorn Road, just off Farmington Road (Hwy. 10). The gardens are open weekdays, 9-4. The house, by appointment only. Telephone (503) 642- 3855.

In nearby Aloha you may enjoy a strolling pond garden at CLEARWATER AQUATIC GARDENS. Gene and Barbara Bunch specialize in pond, tropical and salt water fish, including the colorful koi, a hybrid of carp which comes from Japan and Hawaii. Luscious pink and yellow water lilies dot the pond and there are plans for several more ponds and a picnic area. Find the pond garden at the rear of their storefront, Clearwater Pond Filters, located at 19800 S.W. Farmington Road, Aloha, OR 97007. Telephone (503) 649-7211.

PORTLAND'S EAST SIDE

The Rose City's oldest public rose garden is the lovely SUNKEN ROSE GARDEN at PENINSULA PARK, located at 6400 N. Albina Street, just off Interstate 5 north at the Portland Boulevard exit. Developed from 1908 to 1912, its long grassy walkways, dwarf boxwood hedges and symetrically pruned trees are reminiscent of the Elizabethan style of landscape architecture.

Among nearly 10,000 roses here is Mme. Caroline Testout, a pink rose which was popular at the turn of the century in many Portland neighborhoods. You'll find Mme. Caroline planted around the octagonal 1913 bandstand which overlooks the far side of the garden. Its pillars now marred through years of amateur whittling, the bandstand is the last of its kind in the city.

A cascading waterfall in the Jane Martin Entrance Garden welcomes visitors to the 7-acre CRYSTAL SPRINGS RHODODENDRON GARDEN which is located at S.E. 28th Avenue and Woodstock Boulevard, and near the lovely REED COLLEGE campus. In May the garden bursts into cascades of blooming azaleas and rhododendrons, so well known for thriving in the northwest climate. Meander around the spring-fed waters of Crystal Springs Lake and enjoy the waterfowl who nest here as well. The duck families especially love the day-old bread crumbs you might bring along to this popular garden cared for by the City of Portland.

Open daily, more information may be obtained from the Portland Park Bureau, 1120 S.W. 5th Avenue, Portland, OR 97204. Telephone (503) 771-8386 or 796-5193.

The Reed College campus is particularly colorful in the fall when many varieties of maple, oak, pine, ginkgo, elm, alder and birch are clothed in autumn shades of red, yellow and russet. A walking trail winds through a canyon wildlife sanctuary and around Reed Lake. The campus is located at 3203 S.E. Woodstock Boulevard. Telephone (503) 771-1112. From downtown Portland, take the Ross Island Bridge onto Powell Boulevard to S.E. 39th, turning south to Woodstock, then west (right).

If you prefer your flowers blazing with vibrant color and a hearty lusciousness, plan a visit to Lucy Bateman's DAHLIA SHOW GARDEN located at 6911 S.E. Drew Street. Telephone (503) 774-4817. Her garden is open to the public beginning around the 5th of September. A licensed nurseryperson and national dahlia authority, Lucy Bateman and her family have grown the luscious perennials and operated a mail order business for nearly 40 years. A lifetime member of the Portland Dahlia Society, Lucy also travels about the northwest judging at accredited flower shows. Call for directions and current hours.

A few miles farther to the east, out Foster Road, visitors may find the LEACH BOTANICAL GARDEN and manor house which was formerly the "Sleepy Hollow" home of John and Lilla Leach. For some 30 years, the couple explored the mountains of Oregon and Washington in search of botanical specimens. John said that Lilla finally consented to marry him because he convinced her that he could "handle a pack mule, talk mule talk, throw the diamond hitch, and could pack her back where the flowers were different and cake-eating botanists could never get . . ."

In the Siskiyou Mountains of southern Oregon, Lilla discovered a rare rhododendron-like plant and this small wilderness shrub with deep rose blossoms was named for her—Kalmiopsis leachiana.

She also discovered a rare saxifrage in 1928 and more than a dozen other new species. One, a wild iris called Iris innominata ("iris the unknown") was introduced into domestic gardens and won various horticultural awards. Lilla Leach was the first to receive the Eloise Payne Luquer medal for distinguished achievement in botany from the Garden Club of America. At "Sleepy Hollow," the couple developed their 9-acre woodland and Johnson Creek setting into a splendid natural and native garden.

John Leach died in 1972 at the age of 90; Lilla passed away in 1980 at age 94. Their botanical treasures, a lifetime collection of over 1,000 native species, hybrids and cultivars, can be enjoyed on a self-guided tour, your own map of the garden in hand.

The garden is cooperatively sponsored by Leach Garden Friends and the City of Portland Bureau of Parks and Recreation. Future plans for the complete restoration of John and Lilla's paradise include work on the Display Collections, Native Woodland gardens, Bog Garden, Riparian Zone, Shaded Rock Garden, Sunny Rock Garden and Leach Discoveries section. Open 10-4, Tuesday through Sunday. Access from the Foster Road exit off I-205, continue east to 122nd Avenue and turn south (right) to the parking area. The garden is located at 6704 S.E. 122nd Avenue, Portland, OR 97236. Telephone (503) 761-9503.

A fitting conclusion to one's departure from the Portland area to the east must be the lovely GROTTO GARDENS. A spiritual place of solitude, a quiet stroll through its shady woodland trails offers a sense of peace and timelessness. Enjoy an old variety rose garden and a selection of magnolias, spring bulbs and native plants surrounded by towering redwoods, spruce and Douglas fir.

A 10-story elevator connects the two levels of this wooded sanctuary. From the ponds at the top of cliff you'll have wide-angle views of the Columbia River Gorge and Cascade Mountains to the east as well as the city to the west. The Grotto Gardens are located at 8840 N.E. Skidmore Street, Portland, OR 97220. Telephone (503) 254-7371. Grounds open daily, daylight hours. Gift shop open 9:30-5. Access from I-205 at the Sandy Boulevard exit, to 85th Avenue. Mass is celebrated outdoors from May through September on Sundays and daily in The Chapel of Mary throughout the year.

Columbia River Gorge

HOOD RIVER ~ MOUNT HOOD LOOP ~ MOUNT ADAMS AREAS

Heading east from the Portland metropolitan area on Interstate 84, travelers encounter the western section of the scenic Columbia River Gorge – a broad chasm of ancient volcanic lava layers fringed with Douglas fir and broadleaf species, laced with old Indian trails, and home to many waterfalls as well as numerous wildlife, bird species and thousands of wildflowers. The ancient river serves also as the boundary between Oregon and Washington.

If your schedule allows you may want to motor the more leisurely scenic Lewis & Clark Highway 14 which heads into the Gorge from Vancouver, Washington. Bridges connect the two sides of the river at Cascade Locks, Hood River, The Dalles, and Umatilla – offering travelers a choice of pace as well as access to backroad excursions into the wildflower meadow areas.

In the shadows of both Mount Adams (to the north of Hood River, in Washington) and Mount Hood (south and west of Hood River, on the Oregon side) are numerous alpine meadows which bloom in mid to late summer. Carpets of avalanche lilies at higher elevations, mountain buttercups and purple lupine at lower elevations, desert parsleys and wild primroses at the drier eastern end of the Gorge, reddish Indian paintbrush and blue gentian tucked here and there – all are part of the natural legacy which many local and regional groups are endeavoring to protect.

From the Native Plant Societies of Oregon and Washington to local chapters of the Audubon Society and the Nature Conservancy, from the Friends of the Columbia Gorge to the U.S. Forest Service, and from Oregonians and Washingtonians as well as out-of-state visitors who enjoy and explore the year round treasures of the Columbia River Gorge – literally thousands of folks are dedicated to preserving this unique, fragile and irreplaceable habitat. For information concerning membership in local and national wildflower and native plant preservation groups, see the expanded resource list following the final chapter.

For those who want to get acquainted with the botanical treasures of the Gorge, one of the best resources is Russ Jolley's "A Comprehensive Field Guide: Wildflowers of the Columbia Gorge" published by the Oregon Historical Society Press. A handy 348-page pocket-size guide, it includes some 750 color photographs and a list of field trips to take from early March through September along with charts that show blooming times. A color-coded fold-out map shows various vegetation zones, roads, rivers, trails and mountains within the gorge boundaries. The guide may be ordered from the Oregon Historical Society bookstore, 1230

S.W. Park Avenue, Portland, OR 97205. Telephone (503) 222-1741.

If you're interested in learning more about the preservation of native plants and wildflowers across the country, information may be obtained from the National Wildflower Research Center, 2600 FM 973 North, Austin, TX 78725. The Director is David Northington. The center was created in 1982 under the leadership of Lady Bird Johnson who has nurtured a lifetime interest in nature and in wildflowers. Oregon has some 34 native plants in danger of becoming extinct within the next 10 years, including the Golden paintbrush, once native to the Willamette Valley.

Another resource is Don Eastman's new book, RARE AND ENDANGERED PLANTS OF OREGON, published by Beautiful America© and available in local bookstores.

Additional information about trails and hikes in the gorge may be obtained from the U.S. Forest Service, Mount Hood National Forest, c/o Information Desk, 2955 N.W. Division Street, Gresham, OR 97030. Telephone (503) 666-0700.

Information about finding wildflower meadows in the Mount Adams area can be obtained from the Gifford Pinchot National Forest, 400 West 12th Street, Vancouver, WA 98660. Telephone (206) 696-7500 or (503) 285-9823. Or, if you're heading up toward Mount Adams from Hood River, a distance of about 20 miles, stop at the Ranger Station in Trout Lake for local information. Autumn drives and hikes are especially lovely in this area as well.

For one of the easiest ways to experience a close-up encounter with the area's unique habitat, access a section of the old Columbia Gorge Scenic Highway from I-84 at the Bridal Veil exit. You'll meander about 20 miles along the historic highway ribbon before returning to the freeway and along the way you may see many roadside flowers, bird species, and lacy waterfalls such as Horsetail, Waukeena, and Multnomah. To see Latourell Falls and the panoramic view from the historic Vista House, some 750 feet above the river at Crown Point, first loop back to the west for a few miles before continuing east on the Scenic Highway.

There are many places to stop and hike short distances to get closer views of not only the waterfalls but of the ancient layers of volcanic basalt as well. Many delicate ferns and wildflowers grow in the nooks, crannies and crevices as well as along the hiking trails. You can easily find salmonberry, huckleberry, Oregon grape, salal, licorice fern, maidenhair fern, sword fern, and wild strawberry at the lower elevations. The vast huckleberry fields long-used by ancient Indian families may be seen near Trout Lake and the luscious berries are free for the picking from mid-August to mid-September.

To enjoy another spring spectacle, that of pink and white blooming apple and pear trees which cover the Hood River Valley like a giant patchwork quilt, take the Mount Hood/Government Camp exit from I-84 at Hood River. Follow State Highway 35 as it ambles up into the blossoming fruit trees and around the southeastern flank of Mount Hood. This lovely drive loops around past the Cooper Spur and Mt. Hood Meadows ski areas to State Highway 26.

For information about the annual Hood River Valley Blossom Festival which takes place late April, contact the Hood River Valley Visitors Information Center, Port Marina Park, Hood River, OR 97301. Telephone (503) 386-2000.

GOVERNMENT CAMP ~ RHODODENDRON ~ WELCHES AREA

Late spring to early summer, you'll also find pale pink wild rhododendron and creamy white bear grass blooming on the loop drive from Hood River around Mount Hood to Government Camp at the 3,000-ft. level and up to Timberline

Lodge at the 6,000-ft. level.

Other native perennials such as red Indian paintbrush and blue lupine may also be seen at lower elevations. The wild rhododendrons, among the loveliest springtime sights on the mountain, can easily be spotted from the car along your drive around the venerable mountain, especially below Government Camp toward Rhododendron and Zigzag.

To determine peak blooming times, which may vary according to spring and summer weather, contact the Zigzag Ranger Station, 70220 East Highway 26, Zigzag, OR 97049. Telephone (503) 622-3191. The ranger station is located right on Highway 26, about 15 miles down the mountain from Government Camp between the communities of Rhododendron and Welches.

If you're interested in waterfalls and ferns ask at the Ranger Station about the easy three-mile hike into RAMONA FALLS which is accessed from Lolo Pass Road. The trail loops to the impressive falls with its many frothy cascades, then back along shady moss and fern-lined paths to the trailhead.

Information about tourist facilities may be obtained from the Mt. Hood Area Visitors Information Center, P.O. Box 819, Welches, OR 97067. Telephone (503) 622-3017. And, from the Mt. Hood Recreation Association, P.O. Box 342, Welches, OR 97067 (same telephone number).

THE DALLES ~ MARYHILL ~ KLICKITAT AREAS

Heading east from Hood River toward The Dalles on the I-84 freeway or on the scenic Lewis & Clark Highway 14 on the Washington side of the Columbia River, travelers are swept along to higher elevations and afforded countless wide-angle views of the ancient gorge. Douglas fir thins out just beyond Hood River as the drier and higher elevations of the gorge's eastern sections are approached. Low hills hunched along the gorge on both sides of the Columbia River show brownish-tan shoulders no longer clothed in verdant Douglas fir but now sparsely clad with the flowering sagebrush and bitterbrush characteristic of the high desert.

In this high desert region where one is more likely to see cowboy hats and cowboy boots than formal gardens, there are several botanic locations and natural areas worth adding to the travel itinerary.

One such possibility is to take the final preserved section of the Scenic Columbia Gorge Highway which is accessed from I-84 at Mosier, a few miles east of Hood River. This picturesque 9-mile loop ambles above the freeway and offers marvelous views of the river, gorge and mountains along the way to The Dalles. The best wide-angle view is found at ROWENA CREST VIEWPOINT which is just next to the TOM McCALL PRESERVE, a refuge for a host of native plant species, many of which are rare and endangered.

As you come into this historic city via the Rowena Loop, angle onto West 6th, then 3rd Place to West 2nd Street for a stop at the Visitors Information Center. Here you'll find maps and directions for historic walking tours and to a local scenic drive off Lincoln Street which winds up to SOROSIS PARK and the Pioneer Cemetery. The park was developed by a local pioneer women's club on 15 scenic acres above the city. A number of vintage homes with lovely grounds and gardens, like the historic WILLIAMS HOUSE (now a bed & breakfast inn), can be enjoyed on a walking tour.

Ask also about nearby auto tours into the blossoming cherry orchards – some 5,000 acres of them bloom in the early spring and there is an annual Cherry Festival in early April. The Dalles Area Visitors Information Center address is 404 West 2nd Street (P.O. Box 460), The Dalles, OR 97058. Telephone (503) 296-2231.

Crossing the Columbia River at The Dalles, turn west on Lewis & Clark Highway 14 and north on Highway 142 at Lyle to visit ICE HOUSE BIRD SANCTUARY. This old abandonded gas ice plant near Klickitat provides a nesting area for a large population of bird species.

Heading east again on Highway 14, you may want to stop at HORSETHIEF LAKE STATE PARK where there are many native wildflowers as well as a fine sampling of ancient Indian petroglyphs on huge basaltic rock outcroppings. Dating back to the Stone Age, the irreplaceable petroglyphs, as well as pictographs, painted and scratched on the ancient rocks by prehistoric travelers are also being protected and preserved in other sections of the Gorge as well.

This also is a fine place to stop for a picnic. Those vivid colors bobbing about on the river aren't water lilies, they're the perennial wind surfers who habitually flock to the Gorge every spring, much like those bird species who biennially fly the Pacific Flyway.

At MARYHILL MUSEUM, located just east of Horsethief Lake State Park, you may enjoy the lovely grounds of this lavish Flemish-style chateau which was built by roadbuilder-lawyer Sam Hill. Dedicated in 1926 by Queen Marie of Rumania, the imposing castle is perched high on the gorge wall and is known for its art collection, rare chess sets and extensive assortment of mid-Columbia Indian artifacts.

Just north, on Highway 97 to Goldendale, Columbia Gorge explorers may find the PRESBY MANSION, a turn of the century 20-room Victorian which now houses the Klickitat County Historical Museum. The museum houses a large collection of vintage coffee grinders. On the grounds are a selection of old roses and hardy perennials.

PENDLETON ~ MILTON FREEWATER ~ WALLA WALLA AREAS

Located in Milton-Freewater, just north and east of Pendleton on Highway 11, the historic FRAZIER FARMSTEAD MUSEUM offers travelers an authentic slice of pioneer life as it was during the late 1800s. Situated at the base of the Blue Mountains in the fertile Walla Walla Valley, the area's long growing season was possible because of the mild micro-climate created in the protected valley. The region is still known for its fine orchards of cherry, plum and apple trees which flower in mid to late April.

The vintage farmhouse, barns and well preserved farm equipment, furnishings, photographs, farm records and memorabilia are now cared for by the Milton-Freewater Area Historical Society. Opened as a museum in 1984, an annual Frazier Farmstead Festival is held on the first Saturday of October.

To see the wide variety of herbs and flowers which are offered for sale at the festival, stop by the farmstead during the summer months when you'll find scores of statis and other everlastings blooming about the six-acre site. Curator Diane Biggs manages the gardens as well as the museum.

Should you stop by in October, you'll get to see demonstrations of old pioneer crafts and skills, munch an authentic farm-country lunch, and buy homemade preserves, herbal vinegars and voluminous bouquets of the harvested everlasting flowers.

The homestead may be visited from 11-4 on Thursday-Saturday and 1-4 on Sundays, April through December. For further information contact the Frazier Farmstead Museum, 1403 Chestnut Street, Milton-Freewater, OR 97862. Telephone (503) 938-4636 or (503) 938-3480.

Tourist information be obtained from the Milton-Freewater Area Visitors

Information Center, 505 Ward Street, Milton-Freewater, OR 97862. Telephone (503) 938-5563. The center is open 8-3, Monday-Friday.

About 10 miles north of Milton-Freewater, just across the Washington state line on Highway 11, you may want to visit the WALLA WALLA CITY PARK GARDENS. Located at Division and Alder Streets, the gardens are open every day during daylight hours. For information about annual events and festivals contact the Walla Walla Area Visitors Information Center, P.O. Box 644, Walla Walla, WA 99362. Telephone (509) 525-0850.

Central Region

LAPINE ~ BEND ~ REDMOND ~ TERREBONNE AREAS

Situated on the high desert and with a short growing season, this region isn't as amenable to the nurturing of year round formal gardens, perennial or otherwise, as are the milder areas west of the Cascades. There are, however, several outstanding natural areas worth noting on the travel itinerary.

During late spring and into summer, many high desert native plants bloom in shades of pink, yellow, and white. For a closeup look at blooming wild currant, bitterbrush (often called rabbitbrush) and sagebrush walk the easy self-guided nature trail at LAVA CAST FOREST, between LaPine and Bend. This 0.9 mile loop is an especially intriguing trek and offers a chance to learn about one of the chapters in the story of the High Desert's volcanic origins.

You'll peer down inside the innards of ancient trees, just their round lava cast remains indicating that a tall pine once thrived here. Bright red-orange Indian paintbrush blooms here and there in lava crevices as well as pink wild currant along the trail. Contorted and distorted pine and juniper struggle to grow again in the encrusted black lava fields. Rock pentstemon pokes up here and there around tree casts.

Access the self-guided trail at Lava Cast Forest on a well-maintained cinder gravel road which winds about 9 miles east from Highway 97. The self-guided brochures are located at the beginning of the trail. **Note:** there are a couple of picnic tables and outdoor restroom facilities here but no water. The paved trail is handicap accessible.

After visiting Lava Cast Forest you may want to stop at the LAVA LANDS VISITORS CENTER located just a couple of miles north, on Highway 97. Here you'll see realistic diorama exhibits of ancient volcanic eruptions and learn more about this unusual high desert region, its native plants and wildlife. For a wide-angle view of the Cascade Mountains volcanic area, drive up the short but steep circular road to the top of 500-foot LAVA BUTTE, a reddish-brown cinder cone.

On the interpretive trail which encircles the rim are many places to see wide panoramic views of the ancient lava fields (about 6,000 acres spread below in all directions) and several of the snow-capped peaks and icy lakes in the volcanic chain.

For a close encounter with native plants, wildlife and birdlife of the area plan a stop at the OREGON HIGH DESERT MUSEUM located about six miles south of Bend. On the 110 acre site you can see and experience several high desert environments on your own self-guided stroll – a rimrock canyon, marshy areas, meadows, a flowing stream, a prehistoric cave and other habitats for desert plants and wildlife. You'll see native plants in bloom during spring and summer months along with river otters, porcupines, lizards and birds of prey. Offering numerous natural history and educational programs throughout the year, the museum is located at 59800 South Highway 97, Bend, OR 97702. Telephone (503) 382-4754.

In the high desert area between Crater Lake, Crescent, LaPine and Bend you may often see deer, hawks, pinyon jays and magpies along the way. For a scenic side excursion, turn west onto Cascade Lakes Highway just north of LaPine. This historic loop, once called Century Drive, winds past Pringle Falls, Crane Prairie Reservoir, Cultus Lake, and at least five other mountain lakes on the way to Bend. The everpresent wild currant, bitterbrush, and red and green manzanita can be seen along the way.

Information about other side excursions, ice caves, lava caves, obsidian flows and high desert wildflowers and birdlife may be obtained from the Deschutes National Forest Regional Office, 1645 Highway 20E, Bend, OR 97701. Telephone (503) 382-6922.

For a handy 80-page resource, "Wildlife Viewing Guide," which contains regional maps and information about 123 sites (accessible by car, foot, boat or a combination of the three) for viewing native wildlife and birds in natural settings throughout the state, contact DEFENDERS OF WILDLIFE, 333 South State Street, Suite 173, Lake Oswego, OR 97034. Telephone (503) 293-1433. The guide is available for a nominal fee and may also be found at Forest Service offices and ranger stations as well as at some visitors information centers.

Tourist information may be obtained from the Bend Area Visitors Information Center, 164 N.W. Hawthorne Street, Bend, OR 97701. Telephone (503) 382-3221.

Just north of Bend and Redmond, turning east at Terrebonne, you may follow signs to SMITH ROCK STATE PARK. At the far end of the deadend access road is the best and most scenic view of the gigantic reddish-orange pinnacles, native flowers and grasses, stands of pungent juniper and the winding Crooked River which meanders at the base of the narrow canyon. It's a most impressive sight and well worth the short excursion from Highway 97.

When last visited, the charming Huckleberry Junction gift shop was open as well and still offering its delicious huckleberry ice cream. It's located near the entrance of this day use state park. There are picnic tables, water, restrooms and an easy trail down to the river where you'll have closeup views of native plants, the junipers and chattering birds. The friendly calls and echoes of those ever-present rock climbers who scale Smith Rocks every weekend can also be heard along your walk.

Highway 97 joins Highway 26 at Madras where you may continue down into the picturesque Warm Springs canyon and Indian Reservation, looping toward Mount Hood and Portland. Or, you may elect to head north on Highway 97 from Madras, driving through cattle and wheat country toward Shaniko, Grass Valley, Moro, and Wasco, accessing Interstate 84 at Biggs or Rufus which continues east and west through the Columbia Gorge.

Tourist information may be obtained from the Central Oregon Recreation Association, P.O. Box 230, Bend, OR 97709. Telephone (503) 389-8799. And, from The Dalles Visitors Information Center, 404 West 2nd Street, The Dalles, OR 97058. Telephone (503) 296-2231.

Northeastern Region

JOSEPH ~ HALFWAY ~ NYSSA ~VALE AREAS

In this high alpine area reminiscent of the Swiss Alps, travelers who take the time to visit the Wallowa Mountains – including the Wallowa-Whitman National Forest and Eagle Cap Wilderness – will be rewarded with discovering an enormous region of natural scenic panoramas, high mountain lakes, alpine meadows carpeted with late summer wildflowers, and high altitude wildlife and birdlife as well as a number of areas rich in Oregon pioneer history.

At THE OLD CHURCH on Main Street in Halfway, 53 miles east of Baker, travelers may meet Sandy Kennedy and take in a pleaseant visual and fragrant overdose of over 150 varieties of lovely handmade wildflower wreaths, sumptuous dried flower bouquets and sensual scented sachets and potpourris as well as hand-woven baskets.

Visitors may take a tour of the whole operation as well as browse through the retail area. A second shop has also been opened in the community of Joseph which is accessed from I-84 at LaGrande onto State Highway 82 for some 70 miles into the heart of the Wallowa Mountains. Find WILDFLOWERS OF OREGON next to Bronze Gallery on Main Street, Joseph, OR 97846. Telephone (503) 742-6474 for both locations.

Information about alpine wildflower meadows and nature trails may be obtained from Wallowa County Visitors Information Center, P.O. Box 427, Enterprise, OR 97828. Telephone (503) 426-4622. And, the Wallowa-Whitman National Forest office, P.O. Box 907, Baker, OR 97814. Telephone (503) 523-6391.

Information about annual events and festivals may be obtained from the Northeast Oregon Vacationlands Information Center, 490 Campbell Street, Baker, OR 97814. Telephone (503) 523-5855.

To see fields of wildflowers grown for the seed market, continue traveling on I-84 to the Oregon-Idaho border, and find the community of Nyssa just south of Ontario on Highway 201. Waves of corn poppies, bachelor buttons, baby blue eyes and a plethora of other wildlflowers produce the tiniest of seeds which are sold through northwest retail markets. Other areas where similar wildflower fields may be seen are found near Medford, in Central Oregon, and near Albany in the Willamette Valley.

Tourist information may be obtained from the Nyssa Visitors Information Center, 212 Main Street (P.O. Box 2515), Nyssa, OR 97913. Telephone (503) 372-3091.

You may also see a section of the historic Oregon Trail where wagon ruts are still visible just south of Vale. Wagon trains paused to rest at the hot springs on the Malheur River, a welcome stop for the weary mid-1840s and early-1850s travelers. Sagebrush and bitterbrush bloom here in the spring, brightening the high desert landscape with blotches of yellow and white.

Tourist information may be obtained from the Western Treasure Valley Tourism Association, 173 S.W. First Street, Ontario, OR 97914. Telephone (503) 889-8012.

❦

WASHINGTON

Southwestern Region

VANCOUVER ~ CAMAS - RIDGEFIELD ~ BATTLE GROUND

 ocated just north of the Columbia River, which bisects Oregon and Washington, historic VANCOUVER is home to several fine gardens, natural areas and specialty nurseries.

Founded during the winter of 1824-1825 as a fur trading post and supply depot for the British Hudson's Bay Company, historic Fort Vancouver has now been reconstructed much as it was during those early days of the territory. Located in Vancouver's CENTRAL PARK, you'll also find here a British pioneer garden and a lovely rhododendron garden as well as places to picnic, walk, jog, and bicycle.

Volunteers, along with National Park Service staff members, are bringing to life once again the HUDSON'S BAY GARDENS planted in 1825. In those days, grapevines trailed over greenhouses for shade and a large vegetable garden yielded Thomas Laxton peas, English broad beans, blue potatoes, yellow pear tomatoes and white carrots. In the reconstructed gardens visitors may also find 19th century purple Peruvian potatoes, white Belgian carrots, cardoons, lemon cucumbers and West Indian gherkins.

The British also grew herbs, dahlias and planted marigolds to ward off insects. You may find a sampling of heirloom flower and vegetable seeds from the reconstructed pioneer garden for sale in the Fort's gift shop.

The RHODODENDRON GARDEN is located in the Waterworks Park section near the natural outdoor amphitheater. To see a vintage apple tree which was planted in 1826 by Hudson's Bay Company's chief factor Dr. John McLoughlin, find the OLD APPLE TREE PARK section on Columbia Way just east of the I-5 bridge (take the Camas exit).

In another section of Central Park, on East Evergreen Boulevard just north of the fort, is a collection of stately Victorian homes built between 1849 and 1906 when the area was a U.S. Army post. The restored OFFICER'S ROW, with well-tended grounds and stately old trees, is listed on the National Register of Historic Places.

Native Rhododendrons on Hood Canal, Washington

The FORT VANCOUVER NATIONAL HISTORIC SITE and CENTRAL PARK are located at 1501 East Evergreen Boulevard, Vancouver, WA 98660. Telephone (206) 696-7655. Hours 9-4 winter, 9-5 summer. There are handicap facilities. The Fort is operated by the National Park Service and the gardens are open until dusk. From I-5 take the E. Mill Plain Boulevard exit, head east to Fort Vancouver Way, right to the traffic circle where Officer's Row begins, and to the east end of the row for the entrance to the fort.

Nearby, at 400 East Evergreen Boulevard, you may want to stop and view the lovely grounds of the PROVIDENCE ACADEMY which was built by French-Canadian nun Mother Joseph in 1873. Notice the thick tangle of wisteria vines which climb the weathered columns at the entrance. They bloom around the first of May. A portion of Mother Joseph's garden is located at the east side of the academy. Now privately owned, the building is not open to the public but visitors may walk around the grounds.

At 8th and Esther Streets, also in downtown Vancouver, a lovely VICTORIAN ROSE GARDEN may be found at ESTHER SHORT PARK. Dedicated in 1853, this five-acre site is the oldest public square in Washington State.

In the park you'll find pleasant places to sit, vintage drinking fountains and Victorian lamp posts along with a turn of the century railroad engine, children's play area, wooden outdoor sculpture and a bronze statue dedicated to pioneer women.

Also on the grounds is the SLOCUM HOUSE, an 1867-era home, moved to the park in 1960, which now houses the local Slocum House Theatre Company. A Victorian festival of plays from the 1880s is offered during August when the roses are still blooming in a profusion of rainbow colors.

Additional tourist information and a calendar of annual events and festivals may be obtained from the Vancouver/Clark County Visitors Information Center, 303 East Evergreen Boulevard, Vancouver, WA 98660. Telephone (206) 693-1313. Ask also for a copy of the helpful Washington state map.

Those avid bird-watchers and wildlife lovers can find the RIDGEFIELD NATIONAL WILDLIFE REFUGE north of Vancouver by taking the Fairgrounds exit from I-5. Follow N.W. 269th Street to the west for a couple of miles to find this 3000 acres of protected woodland, marsh, and pasture which scores of deer, beaver, otter and many bird species call home.

Nearby is SINCLAIR ARBORETUM, a 15-acre private collection of native trees and hardy plants. Group tours can be arranged with one day's advance notice. Located at 18816 N.W. 41st Avenue, Ridgefield WA, take the Fairgrounds exit from I-5, head west on 179th two miles, then right on N.W. 41st Avenue.

For a country drive and a special treat, add POMEROY HOUSE near Battle Ground to your garden travels itinerary. A delightful herb and old-fashioned flower garden are located beside the log house near the vegetable garden. The log house was built by Englishman E.C. Pomeroy in 1915 and remains, both inside and out, as it was in those early pioneer days.

The oldest house in the Lucia Falls area, the logs were felled on the property and other lumber came from old mill buildings. In the living room is the original brick fireplace from the first house built in 1910 which was destroyed by a forest fire.

Owners Lil and Len Freese, Pomeroy's grand-daughter, vacationed in England in the early 1970s, re-discovered British roots and decided to open a British Isles style gift shop at the farm. You'll sniff herbs, spices, potpourri, seeds, pomanders and oils as well as try samples of strained and combed honey from the area. A bubbling teapot fills the air with pleasant aromas and guests are invited to enjoy a very British cup of tea.

Nearly all the family's flowers, herbs, fruits and vegetables are grown on the farm and visitors are encouraged to wander about the gardens and grounds as well as explore the 1930s barn, granary, chicken coop and original blacksmith shop. Displayed in the horse barn is the old Pomeroy buggy and an example of a vintage northwest corduroy road (narrow logs laid side by side to form a solid roadbed above muddy areas for early automobiles before macadam highways were constructed).

The gift shop, which offers delectable goodies and interesting gift items from England, Ireland, Scotland and Wales, is located in the old carriage house which, years ago, served as the wash house and cream separating building.

About 35 minutes from Vancouver, find this bucolic country farmstead nestled in an old apple orchard along the Lewis River at Rt. 1, 20902 N.E. Lucia Falls Road, Yacolt, WA 98675. Telephone (206) 686-3537 or (206) 694-5294. The gift shop and gardens are open to the public 10-5 Monday-Saturday and 1-5 Sundays. The Tea Room is open 11:30-3:00 Friday-Saturday. The farmstead is open on six selected weekends May through October, Saturday 11-4 and Sunday 1-4. There is a nominal admission charge.

Call ahead for directions or venture out on your own by taking the Battle Ground exit from I-5, turn east (right) on N.E. 219th (State 502) to State highway 503, north on Highway 503 about 5.5 miles to N.E. Rock Creek Road, east about 4.5 miles on Rock Creek Road across Heisson Bridge and onto Lucia Falls Road to the farm.

In the greater Vancouver environs are several specialty nurseries worth noting on your floral itinerary. Horace and Gloria Jackson invite those interested in grafted Japanese maples, newer rhododendrons, rock garden and trough plants, sculptured pines and junipers, flowering trees and dwarf conifers to visit their large display garden of mature plants and shrubs at JACKSON NURSERY.

They're located at 31805 N.E. George Road, Camas, WA 98607. Telephone (206) 834-2555. Hours are 9 a.m. till dusk, Saturday-Monday and other times by appointment. From Vancouver head east on Lewis & Clark Highway 14 which parallels the Columbia River and winds into the Columbia Gorge on the Washington side of the river. From Camas (about 15 miles east of Vancouver) head north and east on Highway 500 (E. Fourth Plain Road), turn east (right) at Fern Prairie store and follow signs.

If you're heading east into the Columbia Gorge on Highway 14 consider stopping in Carson to visit WIND RIVER NURSERY, maintained by the Gifford Pinchot National Forest. The nursery grows some 30 million seedlings, of 16 species of conifers, for the national forests of Washington and Oregon. Pick up a self-guided booklet and tour the nearby arboretum which was established in 1912. Hours are 8-4:30 Monday-Friday. Telephone (206) 427-5679. Carson is about 30 miles east of Camas and Washougal.

Collectors and propagaters of unusual plants, Bill Janssen and Diana Reeck welcome visitors by appointment only, year round, to COLLECTOR'S NURSERY. In their display garden and nursery are a varied collection of more than 1800 species and varieties of unusual perennials, daylilies, iris, Hosta, hardy perennials and shade plants. They may be contacted at Collector's Nursery, 1602 N.E. 162nd Avenue, Vancouver, WA 98684. Telephone (206) 256-8533.

In her home nursery, ROBYN'S NEST NURSERY, plantswoman Robyn Duback specializes in hostas (some 150 varieties) along with companion shade and bog perennials. She also grows other unusual perennials and rockery plants and invites interested gardeners and garden-lovers to browse through her display garden where established specimens can be seen.

Robyn's Nest Nursery is located at 7802 N.E. 63rd Street, Vancouver, WA 98662. Telephone (206) 256-7399. Her hours are 10:30-5:30 Thursday & Friday and 10:30-2 most Saturdays, March-June and September-October; other times by appointment. A catalog is available for $1. From Vancouver take the Camas exit onto Lewis & Clark Highway 14 to Andresen, turn north on Andresen to 63rd and east to sixth house on the left.

At ALICE'S PERENNIAL WONDERLAND, Alice Engels offers a variety of hardy field grown perennials and rock plants for all four seasons of the year. From carefully cultivating and tending dwarf iris, daylilies, asters and astilbes to campanula, dianthus, phlox, and hosta; from grasses and herbs to some 200 sedums and sempervivums, plantswoman Alice is busy year round. She is located at 13012 N.W. 117th Avenue, Vancouver, WA 98662. Telephone (206) 254-3420. Hours are 10:30-6, Thursday-Saturday, May-October. From Andresen, north to 78th, turn east to 117th Avenue (Highway 503), then .6 mile north of the Par 3 Golf, on west side of the road.

For a gander at a viewing garden filled with exotic lilies – from Asiatic hybrids which bloom in June (the least fragrant but easiest to grow) to the Aurelians (also called trumpets) which burst into bloom in July, and the fragrant Oriental varieties which bloom in late July through August, stop at LILIES AND MORE to meet plantswoman Billie Mathieu and husband Robert.

You can even depart with a luscious bouquet of the gorgeous blooms which are for sale from June through August. An interesting selection of perennials, ornamental trees and shurbs is also available and bulbs can be ordered for fall planting. Find the viewing garden, and Billie, at 12400 N.E. 42nd Avenue, Vancouver, WA 98686. Telephone (206) 573-4696. Hours 10-5, on Mondays and Fridays, May through September. Other times by appointment except Sundays. A catalog is available for $1. From Vancouver take the Hazel Dell exit onto Highway 99 to 119th Street, turn east to 42nd Avenue and north to the nursery (it's a deadend road).

To learn more about growing lilies, contact the Pacific Northwest Lily Society, which has monthly programs at Mt. Hood Community College (in Gresham, near Portland), bulb sales in spring and fall, a bulletin, tours, and an annual lily show. An annual membership is $5. Write to PNLS, c/o 19766 S. Impala Lane, Oregon City, OR 97045.

At AITKEN'S SALMON CREEK GARDEN visitors may encounter some 500 varieties of quality iris hybrids and the best time for gazing at this kaliedoscopic two-acre spectacle is from late April to early June when the stately bearded Dwarfs, Medians, Tall Beardeds, Siberians, Japanese and Pacific Coast (to name just a few) irises are in full bloom at Terry and Barbara Aitken's place. Old garden favorites, our grandmothers often called the vintage (and much smaller) purplish clumps "flags." Find this sea of colorful rhizomes at 608 N.W. 119th Street, Vancouver, WA 98685. Telephone (206) 573-4472. Hours are daily during daylight hours during bloom season, April-June. A catalog may be ordered for $1. From the Hazel Dell exit turn west (left) on 114th Street and north (right) on 7th Avenue to N.W. 119th Street. The Aikens can also provide information about membership in the Greater Portland Iris Society.

Note: information about two large, nationally known Oregon iris growers can be found in the Willamette Valley section beginning on page 19.

Friends Susan Henke and Rosanna Long invite perennial-lovers to stroll through the lovely woodland walk which connects their two nurseries, FRIENDS & NEIGHBORS PERENNIAL GARDENS. Specializing in unusual and hard-to-find perennials and native plants, the two plantswomen offer over 500 varieties in their two next-door locations.

They may be found at 24708 N.E. 152nd Avenue and 14825 N.E. 249th Street, Battle Ground, WA 98604. Telephone (206) 687-2962 and (206) 687-4475. Hours 8-6, Monday-Wednesday and most Saturdays from April to frost (usually mid to late October). From Main Street in Battle Ground (about 15 miles northeast of Vancouver), turn north (left) on Parkway, east (right) on 249th and about .6 mile to the two nurseries.

For a copy of a four-page guide which includes an additional seven Vancouver area nurseries write to: Specialty Nursery Association of Clark County, 4806 N.W. 122nd Street, Vancouver, WA 98685.

WOODLAND ~ LONGVIEW ~ LONG BEACH AREA

It may seem old-fashioned to like lilacs but for many flower-lovers they conjure up memories of childhood, playing at a special grandmother's, hiding beneath leafy branches, draping pale lavender or snowy white blossoms about one's queenlike shoulders.

Thanks to the work of Hulda Klager, during most of the 96 years of her life as "The Lilac Lady," gardeners and garden-lovers enjoy some 250 different hybrid varieties and colors of the frothy blooms. Early spring is the time to see many of them in bloom at the HULDA KLAGER LILAC GARDENS located about 20 miles north of Vancouver in Woodland.

Hulda's family settled in this area in 1877, immigrating from Germany first to Wisconsin in 1865. It is said that she often spoke of her love for flowers and wandered through the woods near her home looking for wildflowers. After reading a book on Luther Burbank, in 1903, she began experimenting first with apples then lilacs and also grew roses and dahlias.

By 1910 Hulda had 14 new lilac varieties and 10 years later even more. Her annual spring open house, when the lilacs were in full bloom, was held every year until her death in 1960. Through the years she was honored by many organizations, including an arboretum in Cambridge, Massachusetts, for her work as a leading hybridizer of lilacs.

Dedicated volunteers from the Hulda Klager Lilac Garden Society, a non-profit organization formed by the Woodland Federated Garden Club, now devote countless hours to maintaining the gardens and grounds as well as the original farmhouse, carriage barn, windmill and water tower.

The annual open house happens again, around the last week of April and first week of May, when the lavender, purple and white hued lilacs are in full, gorgeous bloom. Lilac starts, often some 75 varieties, are offered for sale during the open house. The gardens are open year round; a nominal donation is welcomed. An appointment needs to be made to tour the house other than during lilac week when garden club members don old-fashioned dresses and greet visitors who come to see "The Lilac Lady's" garden.

From I-5 take the Woodland exit, turn west under the freeway and angle south on Goerig Street, turn west on Davidson Street and south on Perkin Road to the garden (about one mile from the freeway). For additional information about the non-profit Hulda Klager Lilac Garden Society, write to P.O. Box 828, Woodland, WA 98674. Telephone (206) 225-8996.

For a jaunt of about 70 miles west into the sunset and onto the narrow Long

Beach peninsula which juts into the Pacific Ocean north of Astoria (a toll bridge can also be taken from Astoria across the mouth of the Columbia River to Megler and the peninsula on the Washington side), head west from I-5 at Longview on State Highway 4, turning onto Highway 101 to Seaview, Long Beach, Ocean Park, Oysterville and Nahcotta.

On the sandy peninsula travelers may visit a wildlife refuge, a world-renowned rhododendron nursery, and a private nursery and garden. The WILLAPA NATIONAL WILDLIFE REFUGE is located on Long Island which lies between the east side of the peninsula and the Washington mainland. Another section of the refuge can be seen by driving to Leadbetter Point at the northern end of the peninsula. More than 100 bird species have been recorded feeding and nesting on the waters of Willapa Bay and the salt marshes.

Although the tip of the point is reserved for snowy plover nesting from April-August, visitors may enjoy the short loop walk, ELLIOT TRAIL, in nearby Leadbetter Park. The area is also known for its delicious oysters, Dungeness crab and shrimp.

Between Ocean Park and Nahcotta travelers may find THE HALL GARDENS. Don and Marva Hall nurture a wide variety of perennials and, to the rear of their home nursery, tend display gardens surrounding a large pond filled with exotic water lilies. The gardens are brimming with species Primulas, Eucryphia, species Rhododendrons, Crinodendron and Meconopsis—nearly two thousand different plants are featured in this lovely oasis.

The Halls also welcome inquiries about hard to find perennials, herbs, shrubs and trees. Their address is Rt.1, Box 231/F, Ocean Park, WA 98640. Telephone (206) 665-4753. Hours are 9-4:30 daily. Find The Hall Gardens by following the signs to The Ark Restaurant; they're .5 mile north on Sandridge Road.

Nearby, also on Sandridge Road, you may want to stop and visit CLARKE NURSERY, one of the largest rhododendron venues on the west coast. Offering a plethora of species rhododendrons and azaleas, peak blooming time is about mid-May. Telephone (206) 642-2241. Hours are 8-6 daily, April-July; 8-4:30 daily August-October and February-March.

Information about annual events and festivals may be obtained from the Peninsula Visitor's Bureau, P.O. Box 562, Long Beach, WA 98631. Telephone (206) 642-2400. The Visitor's Center is located at the junction of Highways 101 and 103.

For an optional loop farther north (via Highway 105 from Raymond) into coastal cranberry country and opportunities to visit another wildlife-filled estuary, see the Olympic Peninsula section which begins on page 58.

For a second option, another scenic loop back to Interstate-5, leave Highway 4 (from the Long Beach area through Nemah and South Bend) and continue east on Highway 6 from Raymond along the Willapa River through Pe Ell and Doty, past Rainbow Falls (near Doty), rejoining I-5 at Chehalis.

On this route herb lovers, especially those interested in medicinal and culinary herbs, may want to call ahead for an appointment to visit BEARS, HERBS, HEARTS & FLOWERS HERB FARM located just east of Raymond. Plantswoman and master gardner Verona Latta has logged in over 30 years growing herbs and offers at the farm a display garden of some 500 varieties, including scented geraniums and culinary mints. The Lattas have two open houses each year, in June and September. A tour of the gardens may be arranged through Verona or husband, Bear. The farm's address is 81 E. Raymond-Willapa Road, Raymond, WA 98577. Telephone (206) 942-2122. Hours 9-4 during open house; by appointment only during remainder of year.

NORTH COVE ~ GRAYLAND ~ WESTPORT ~ HOQUIAM ~ ABERDEEN

Another option for coastal travelers is continuing north from the Long Beach Peninsula to the northernmost section of Willapa Bay, via Highway 105 from Raymond to the North Cove-Grayland area. In this region you'll find one of the major cranberry producing areas on the west coast (Bandon, on Oregon's south coast is another large cranberry growing area). The bogs are in bloom in mid-June and harvesting of the tangy red berries can be seen in mid-October.

You can find numerous cranberry bogs by turning east, away from the ocean, off Highway 105 anywhere between the Shoalwater Indian Reservation near Tokeland and the north end of Grayland. Rather than big bushes or orderly rows of plants, look for a solid mass of small-leaved vines covering wide bogs, pinkish-white blossoms in June, loaded with small red berries in October, and a russet-tinged ring most of the rest of the year.

Cranberries like growing in the misty climate near the sea and in those ancient peat bogs with ground water near the surface. Years ago the bright red berries were picked by hand with a wooden toothed scoop. Before that wild cranberries were picked and used by the Indians who lived in the area. Now machine-picked rather than scooped by hand, if you tour the cranberry bogs during October's harvest, watch carefully on narrow roads for large trucks picking up full boxes and barrels for transport to the Ocean Spray processing plant in Aberdeen, about 20 miles northwest. The bright red and white Cranberry Coast flag, designed by a local artist, can be seen flying at many businesses in the area.

Information about the annual CRANBERRY FESTIVAL and other annual events may be obtained from the Westport/Grayland Visitors Information Center, 1200 N. Montesano Street (P.O. Box 306), Westport, WA 98595. Telephone (206) 268-9422.

The GRAYS HARBOR ESTUARY, just north of Grayland and Westport, offers the unique environment which is created when fresh water and salt water combine at ocean's edge. Bird-watchers can obtain information about the most accessible current harbor viewing areas from the Westport/Grayland Visitors Information Center. Or, grab the binoculars and board the summer passenger ferry from Westport (access at the float dock area on the harbor) across the harbor to Hoquiam and Aberdeen. The passenger ferry operates from about June 30 to Labor Day with several scenic trips each day. A 49-passenger ferry also runs to and from nearby Ocean Shores.

In Hoquiam, on the east side of the harbor, you'll find the BURTON ROSS MEMORIAL ROSE GARDENS on the grounds of Polson Park and Museum. Also surrounding the park is a collection of exotic tree species. Hours are 9-5 daily from June-August. The museum, which was the 26-room mansion of the Arnold Polson timber family, houses antiques and historical memorabilia of Grays Harbor and early logging days.

Now on the National Historic Register the museum is open noon-4 Wednesday-Sunday during summer months and noon-4 Saturday-Sunday during the rest of the year. The address is 1611 Riverside Avenue (P.O. Box 432), Hoquiam, WA 98550. Telephone (206) 533-5862. The gardens are accessed from Highway 101 turning right just before the Riverside Bridge on the way into town.

Information about both the annual Spring Festival and Rhododendron Show may be obtained from the Grays Harbor Visitors Information Center, 2704 Sumner (P.O. Box 450), Aberdeen, WA 98520. Telephone (206) 532-1924. Hours are 9-5 Monday-Friday.

Nature lovers may want to ask about the STEWART PARK NATURE WALK, a self-guided walk into a nearby deep forest area. BOWERMAN BASIN, next to the Hoquiam-Aberdeen airport is the last area in Grays Harbor to be flooded at high tide and the first to be exposed, offering extra feeding time for western sandpipers, dunlins, short-billed and long-billed dowitchers as well as numerous wading birds, gulls and terns. Peregrine falcons, northern harriers, and red-tailed hawks can often be sighted along with black-tailed deer, coyotes, voles and songbirds who use the uplands area.

Soon to become a National Wildlife Refuge, the 500-acre Bowerman Basin also has a variety of typical coastal wetland vegetation including red alder, black willow, Scouler's willow, western crabapple, wild blackberry, salmonberry, Scot's broom, cattail, American bullrush, a variety of sedges and pickleweed along the tideflats.

Bird watchers with rubber boots can trek a marshy trail along the northernmost edge of the peninsula, next to the Bowerman Field Airstrip. Come prepared with rain gear, rubber boots, tide tables and binoculars to enjoy watching the array of birds who feed and nest here. The best viewing times are the hour before and the hour after high tide and the heaviest concentration of shorebirds occurs around the last two weeks of April.

To find the trail, head west on Highway 109 from Hoquiam .5 mile to Paulson Road, left to Airport Way and look for Bowerman Basin signs. Park only in the gravel strip parking areas and do not wander onto the airstrip. There is a public restroom near the parking area.

Bird-lovers may also elect to continue on to Ocean Shores to visit the OYEHUT GAME PRESERVE, a salt-marsh area which offers more bird-watching and interesting native plant material. The preserve is located about 18 miles west of Hoquiam and information may be obtained from the Ocean Shores Visitors Information Center located in Catala Mall, N. Point Brown & Ocean Shores Blvd. (P.O. Box 382), Ocean Shores, WA 98569. Telephone (206) 289-2451. Hours are 9-5 Monday-Saturday during summer months, 10-4 Monday-Friday during the rest of the year.

MONTESANO ~ SATSOP ~ ELMA

For those who elect to head back to Olympia and I-5 via Highway 12 from Aberdeen, be on the lookout during early spring months for acres of colorful tulips, daffodils and iris grown by the SATSOP BULB FARM folks. You'll spy the kaliedoscope of colorful fields between Montesano and Elma. Telephone (206) 482-4223 for current hours and directions if you wish to visit the farm.

You may also want to plan a stop at HAUS EDELWEISS NURSERY in Elma. This nursery offers hardy plants and shrubs, including the European lingonberry. Luscious lingonberry sauces, preserves and baked goods are also available in the retail shop. The address is P.O. Box 1132, Elma, WA 98541. Telephone (206) 482-3691. Call ahead for current hours and directions.

The Olympia-Tumwater section begins on page 53.

South Puget Sound

CHEHALIS ~ CENTRALIA ~ MOSSYROCK ~ MOUNT RAINIER AREAS

Located in FORT BORST PARK, just off I-5 at Centralia, travelers may find the twin cities' prize RHODODENDRON GARDEN and ROSE GARDEN. The park, which is adjacent to the historic BORST HOME, has shady places to picnic and play areas for children as well. Hours are dawn to dusk daily. To find the gardens take exit 82 from I-5 onto Borst Avenue.

Information about the Borst Home may be obtained from the Lewis County Historical Society, 599 N.W. Front Street, Chehalis, WA 98532. Telephone (206) 748-0831. Information about annual events and festivals may be obtained from the Twin Cities Visitors Information Center, National Avenue at I-5, P.O. Box 1263, Chehalis, WA 98532. Telephone (206) 748-8885.

Located between Silver Creek and Morton on Highway 12, the DEGOEDE BULB FARMS can be found about 20 miles east of Interstate 5. In the early spring you'll see acres of tulips and iris which carpet surrounding fields with eye-catching colors. The Mossyrock community also celebrates the peak blooming time with a lively Street Festival, usually in mid-April.

You may select your own bouquet of cut flowers to take along and there are also dormant bulbs, perennials, potted plants and baskets for sale in the large retail shop. In the spring, for tulips and iris, and again in early December, for poinsettias, a gala Open House welcomes visitors to the large greenhouses at Degoede Bulb Farms.

The farm, greenhouses and retail shop are located at 409 Mossyrock Road West, Mossyrock, WA 98584. Telephone (206) 983-3773. Hours are 8-6 Monday-Friday and 10-6 Saturday-Sunday during spring and summer months.

Just east of Mossyrock RAINTREE NURSERY specializes in dwarf shrubs and plants, including the delicious European lingonberry which ranges in the wild across Europe and Asia. The nursery is located at 391 Butts Road, Morton, WA 98356. Telephone (206) 496-6400. Call ahead from Degoede's for current hours and directions.

For a scenic loop into mountain meadows and alpine wildflowers, during mid-July and August, continue east on Highway 12 through Randle and Packwood to venerable 14,410-foot Mount Rainier, the highest peak in the Cascade Mountains' volcanic chain. Take the scenic drive up to PARADISE or continue north on Highway 123 to the scenic drive up to SUNRISE. Both drives are spectacular and afford panoramic views of mountains, hills, streams, glaciers and valleys of Mount Rainier National Park and the Gifford Pinchot National Forest.

If you prefer your wildflower treks at lower elevations try the TRAIL OF SHADOWS, an easy self-guided .5 mile stroll through meadows and forest near Longmire. Find the trail just across from the Longmire Hiker's Center.

At Paradise, 12 miles farther up the mountain, there are several wildflower meadows laced with accessible trails, at the 5,400-foot level. You'll find also a cafeteria, snack bar, log lodge-inn and gift shop at Paradise.

At Sunrise, on the eastern slope, you may travel the highest paved highway in the state to an elevation of 6,400 feet. There are a variety of short trails through nearby wildflower meadows which offer marvelous photographic vistas. There are many places to stop and picnic as well as a picnic area at Sunrise (along with a snack bar, gift shop and lodge).

For current road information and wildflower meadow locations as well as information about fishing, mountain climbing and camping, contact Mount Rainier National Park, Ashford, WA 98304. Telephone (206) 569-2211. You may also contact the Region #6 tourism office, Mount Rainier Guest Services, 55106 Kernahan Road East, Ashford, WA 98304. Telephone (206) 569-2400. And, the Mount Rainier Visitors Center, P.O. Box 63, Elbe, WA 98330. Telephone (206) 569-2285. The park is open year round, with the eastern entrance road from Highway 123 closed during the winter. There is a nominal fee per car for entrance into the park.

OLYMPIA ~TUMWATER ~ PUYALLUP

On the 160-acre landscaped grounds of Washington's State Capitol in Olympia are several notable botanic areas worth investigating. If you're in the area during early spring begin your tour at CHERRY BLOSSOM LANE where some 33 cherry trees bloom in pink profusion in April. The lane is located just south of the Capitol Greenhouse and stretches in a colorful canopy toward the Public Lands Building.

In the WASHINGTON STATE CAPITOL GREENHOUSE you may see displays of tropical and sub-tropical plants as well as cacti and succulents. The Greenhouse is located off 11th and Water Streets. Hours 8-4:30 daily during June-September, Monday-Friday other months. Telephone (206) 753-1752. Group tours may be arranged by calling ahead a couple of days.

Just north of the World War II monument find the lovely SUNKEN GARDEN which contains a collection of roses and perennials. The FORMAL ROSE GARDENS are located west of the Temple of Justice. Peak bloom times are from June through September and the gardens are open daily from dawn to dusk. Information about an annual June rose show may be obtained from the Olympia Rose Society, c/o P.O. Box 2231, Olympia, WA 98507.

The State Capitol Campus Information Center is located at Capitol Way and 14th Street. Telephone (206) 586-3460.

At the WASHINGTON STATE CAPITOL MUSEUM located in the historic C.J. Lord Home at 211 W. 21st Avenue (a few blocks south of the Capitol grounds), visitors enjoy browsing through the PIONEER HERB GARDEN and PERENNIAL PLANT GARDEN. Both gardens are maintained by the Associates of the Museum. Telephone (206) 753-2580. Hours are 10-4 Tuesday-Friday and 12-4 Saturday & Sunday.

For an early spring spectacle plan a stroll through ZABEL'S RHODODEN-DRON & AZALEA PARK which is located at 2432 N. Bethel Street, Olympia, WA 98506. Telephone (206) 357-6977. Hours are noon-8 May 1 through May 31. With advance notice groups may visit the park during morning hours.

In nearby Tumwater, the FAIRIE HERBE GARDENS invite travelers to a summer open house and plant sale at the gardens located at 6236 Elm Street. Telephone (206) 754-9249. Hours are 10-6 on weekends and sometimes the herbal teapot is on as well. Call ahead for an appointment and directions.

The 60-acre TUMWATER HISTORICAL PARK along Capitol Lake offers canoeing, bird-watching, walking and picnicking in a quiet area away from the freeway. Walk the mile-long riverbank trail where you'll pass marsh areas noisy with melodious bird songs. Early Indian families used to camp here and catch salmon at the base of Tumwater Falls. In 1845 the first white settlers arrived, making Tumwater the first permanent settlement north of the Columbia River. To find this shady oasis take exit 103 from I-5 and follow signs to the park.

For another accessible though more peopled walk along the water, plan to take in the Olympia Area FARMER'S MARKET which sets up shop near the one-mile boardwalk along the waterfront just a few blocks from the Capitol grounds and adjacent to the downtown area. Plantsmen and women and growers set out fresh vegetables, bedding plants, baked goods, seafood and colorful cut flowers on Thursdays through Sundays from the end of April through October. Hours are 10-3.

Information about annual events and festivals may be obtained from the Olympia-Thurston County Visitors Information Center, 1000 Plum Street, Olympia, WA 98501. Telephone (206) 357-3362. And, the Greater Olympia Visitor & Convention Bureau, (206) 357-3370.

Just northeast of Olympia, via Highway 410, the VAN LIEROP BULB FARM gardens greet visitors with acres of luscious yellow daffodils during early spring months. Dormant bulbs and perennials, potted plants, baskets and seasonal cut flowers are available at the farm's retail shop. The address is 13407 80th Street East, Puyallup, WA 98372. Telephone (206) 848-7272. The gardens are open daily February, March, April and part of May. The retail shop is open until the end of June and from mid-September to mid-October.

For an eyeful of those luscious spring blooming rhododendrons plan a visit to STAAB'S DISPLAY GARDEN where you'll enjoy a visual innundation of more than 300 varieties growing in profusion beneath tall native Douglas fir. Staab's is located at 14015 - 113th Avenue Court E., Puyallup, WA 98372. Telephone (206) 848-4082. Hours are 9-5 daily.

Information about annual events, including the DAFFODIL FESTIVAL, may be obtained from the Puyallup Valley Visitors Information Center, 2823 E. Main Street, Puyallup, WA 98371. Telephone (206) 845-6755.

TACOMA ~ GIG HARBOR ~ VASHON ISLAND ~ FEDERAL WAY

To find an elegant Victorian style glass conservatory filled with some 200 species of exotic orchids, ferns, cacti and tree species, plan a stop at the W.W. SEYMOUR BOTANICAL CONSERVATORY located in Tacoma's WRIGHT PARK, near city center. After a stroll through the conservatory you may notice local outdoor sports afficionados nearby engaged in games of lawn bowling or horseshoes.

There are also paths for walking and jogging amid a developing arboretum of ginkgos, paulownias, katsuras and more than 100 other tree species. This lovely city park is located at South 4th and 'G' Streets, Tacoma, WA 98424. Telephone (206) 591-5330. The conservatory hours are 8-4 daily and group tours can be arranged by calling ahead for an appointment.

Located close to Tacoma's downtown area, the 54-acre SNAKE LAKE PARK (named for the lake's shape) is a cool, green reserve readily accessible from the Interstate 5 freeway. Enjoy 2.5 miles of trails, including a short paved section along the lake, and melodious songs and chatter from nearly a hundred species of birds and waterfowl. Some twenty different small mammals, including the nocturnal flying squirrel and the red fox, have been identified by volunteers and staff from the Snake Lake Nature Center.

For information about guided tours, usually the second and fourth Saturdays from 10-noon, contact the Snake Lake Nature Center, 1919 S. Tyler Street, Tacoma, WA 98424. Telephone (206) 591-5939. Park hours are 8 a.m. till dusk daily. From I-5 take the Bremerton-Gig Harbor exit onto State Highway 16 for about 2.5 miles, turning north (right) on 19th, then east (right) on Tyler to the park.

Should you be in the Tacoma area around the end of April, celebrate spring's arrival at PUGET GARDENS annual Garden Party which is cosponsored by several local garden clubs. You may stop by for tea, homemade cookies and special music, all in the company of other garden lovers and friends.

There are shaded paths to stroll and musical waterfalls to hear as well as a visual panorama lush with rhododendrons, azaleas and an extraordinary primrose collection. Meander across footbridges which span several small streams and notice fruit trees, ornamental cherries and roses as well as a host of other unusual plant species.

Puget Gardens was the 20-year labor of love of Clara and John Skupen. The couple worked throughout those years to transform their three-acre marshy hillside into a remarkable garden which is now administered by the Metropolitan Park District of Tacoma. Puget Gardens was dedicated as a city park in 1986, open now for everyone to enjoy and appreciate.

Information about other annual events and yearly public tours of local private gardens (including the Wagner estate, LAKEWOLD GARDENS, near Gravelley Lake) may be obtained from the Metropolitan Park District, 10 Idaho Street, Tacoma, WA 98409. Telephone (206) 591-3690. Puget Gardens is located at 3204 Ruston Way. From downtown Tacoma take Pacific Avenue north, continue onto Ruston Way and turn left on Alder Street to the park, on the left.

To find Tacoma's 700-acre peninsula wonderland, PT. DEFIANCE PARK, ZOO, & AQUARIUM, continue west along Ruston Way as you leave Puget Gardens. Featuring native forests with some 38 tree species, spectacular wide-angle views of Commencement Bay, some 17 miles of trails and paths, and rolling lawns, you'll want to spend time strolling not only the park but the gardens here as well.

See and identify native annuals and perennials in the NATIVE GARDEN, a wide variety of species in the RHODODENDRON GARDEN and nearly 200 varieties of luscious roses in the formal ROSE GARDEN. Walk beneath hundreds of blooming roses trailing over the romantic old-fashioned rose arbor. In the dahlia test gardens gaze at a display of some 85 varieties of the voluptuous hardy perennials which bloom in late summer and early autumn.

Sense the ancient oriental garden tradition of quietness and serenity when you pass through the traditional Torii gate into the JAPANESE TEA GARDEN. There's also a Shinto shrine in the tea garden.

There are places to picnic, a boat launch and boat rentals, a waterfront area, a five-mile loop drive through native Douglas fir, an historic logging and railroad replica, a nursery rhyme storyland for children and the oldest standing building in the state – in Fort Nisqually, the 1850s complex which features a restoration of the former Hudson's Bay Company fur trading post located here.

The Point Defiance Park gardens are located at North Pearl & 54th Streets, Tacoma, WA 98424. Telephone (206) 591-5335. Open 8 a.m. till dusk daily. From downtown Tacoma take Schuster Parkway and Ruston Way to Pearl Street, then right to the park's entrance.

A large variety of native wildflowers and animal life can often be seen along Tacoma's 20-acre green belt, BAYSIDE TRAIL SYSTEM, located between downtown and the Old Town Historic District, along the way out to Pt. Defiance Park. The trail system runs along the bluffs for about 2.5 miles and offers splendid views of salty Commencement Bay and the bustling Port of Tacoma (one of the world's few deepwater ports). A map of the trail system may be obtained from the Metropolitan Park District, 10 Idaho Street, Tacoma, WA 98409. Telephone (206) 591-5300.

If you prefer more undeveloped natural areas, find SWAN CREEK PARK at East Pioneer Avenue (east of I-5 toward Fife) just west of Waller Road where nature trails follow the creek about two miles up the canyon. Only a jogger or two may pass as you stroll and pause to peer at the native plants and wildflowers which thrive here.

Further information about other nearby natural areas for viewing birdlife and wildflowers may be obtained from the Pierce County Parks and Recreation Department. Telephone (206) 593-4176. Ask about the local volksporting groups who plan and conduct walks in the area.

Information about the annual DAFFODIL PARADE and week-long festival held in April may be obtained from the Tacoma-Pierce County Visitors Information Center, 950 Pacific Avenue/Suite 450, (P.O. Box 1933), Tacoma, WA 98401. Telephone (206) 627-2175. Hours are 8-5 Monday-Friday.

For a pleasant excursion to another section of Puget Sound's watery Kitsap Peninsula, take Highway 16 from Tacoma across the Narrows Bridge. On the sparkling waters of Commencement Bay and The Narrows far below, seagulls wheel and dip over the frothy wakes of sleek sailboats and trim motorboats, playing hide and seek with the waves.

On blue-sky days you may see snowcapped 14,410-foot Mount Rainier in your rear view mirror, to the east, and Fox Island and the jagged shoulders of the Olympic Mountains ahead, to the west.

Exit at Gig Harbor (City Center exit) to find FOXGLOVE FARMS, a local herb farm owned and operated by Steve and Mike Burkhart. They are located at 6617 Rosedale Drive, NW, Gig Harbor, WA 98335. Telephone (206) 851-7477. Call ahead for current hours.

From downtown Gig Harbor (where you'll find charming shops, art galleries, quaint boutiques and delis) turn left at the yellow blinking light onto Harbor View one block, then left onto Rosedale to the farm. Information about local annual events and festivals may be obtained from the Gig Harbor Visitors Information Center, 3125 Judson Street (P.O. Box 1245), Gig Harbor, WA 98335. Telephone (206) 851-6865. Hours are 8-5 Monday-Friday.

For another pleasant side-trip, take the 10-minute ferry ride across Commencement Bay (easily accessed from Pt. Defiance Park) to Vashon Island. Motor along Vashon Island Highway (extending some 12 miles between the north and south tips of the island) to find DAISY'S NURSERY and BEALL GREENHOUSES. At Daisy's you'll find an assortment of bulbs and perennials and at Beall's some 1.5 acres of gorgeous potted orchids, all under glass.

From the town of Vashon, turn east at the four-way stop, in .5 mile bear right at the fork for another .5 mile to Beall's which is open 8-4 Monday-Saturday. Telephone (206) 463-9151.

To find Daisy's, head north again on the main highway from Vashon to 156th Street (Glen Acres Road), then head east. Another ferry at the northern tip of the island connects with Fauntleroy Way on the mainland and access to I-5 north or south.

An important stop on the garden lovers itinerary is the RHODODENDRON SPECIES FOUNDATION garden located near the Weyerhaeuser Lumber Company headquarters in Federal Way. You'll see here the largest collection of rhododendrons in the U.S.

On 24 acres there are more than 22,000 plants representing 475 species, some 90% of rhododendrons now cultivated. A selection of the less hardy species can be seen in the conservatory. Pick up a booklet and take your own self-guided walk through this lush wonderland of pastel springtime color.

Among others, you'll want to find "Centennial Celebration," created to honor

Washington State's 1989 Centennial birthday. Dark green, leathery leaves surround flowers that change from deep orchid buds to luscious pale orchid blossoms.

The garden, handicap accessible, is open from about March 25 to May 30 on Sundays and Wednesdays, 10-3. The schedule varies somewhat each year and small group guided tours may be arranged by calling in advance. Nominal fee. An annual Fall Foliage Festival held on the last three Sundays of October includes tours of the garden, a mushroom walk and bonsai demonstrations. Additional information may be obtained from the Rhododendron Species Foundation, P.O. Box 3798, Federal Way, WA 98003. Telephone (206) 927-6960. Exit from I-5 at Highway 18, take 32nd Avenue South, head north and follow signs to the garden.

Plan a visit to the Catherine Montgomery Interpretive Center just east of Federal Way for a refresher course on the Evergreen State's seven biotic or life zones, including exhibits and films about the unique native plants and trees characteristic of each climate zone. The Center is located about 18 miles east of Enumclaw on Highway 410. Telephone (206) 663-2207. **Note:** a brief summary of the Life Zones (which also apply to the entire Northwest and western Canada) is included in the Appendix.

Olympic Peninsula

HUMPTULIPS ~ QUINAULT ~ QUEETS ~ KALALOCH

Those who linger awhile longer on the far northwestern Washington coast via Highway 101 will find not only the coast rhododendron, salal and huckleberry but wild lily of the valley, oxalis, mosses and at least three kinds of low elevation ferns. You'll find also glacier-fed streams and lakes, wildlife (including the curious marmot, frisky western pine squirrels and the magnificent Roosevelt elk), and a variety of bird species.

In addition you may visit several ancient Indian cultures, view an archaeological dig and walk beneath those unbelievable moss-draped canopies of big-leaf maple, alder, cedar and spruce found in the rain forests of OLYMPIC NATIONAL PARK and the OLYMPIC NATIONAL FOREST.

In Humptulips, 22 miles north of Hoquiam on Highway 101, travelers can visit a fish hatchery and learn about the northwest salmon's life cycle. **Note:** motorists are advised to head north with a full tank of gas as facilities are farther apart along this route.

The highway ribbon soon angles around the west end of Lake Quinault and heads seaward again toward Queets and Kalaloch (gas station here). The QUINAULT RAIN FOREST NATURE TRAIL is an easily accessed half mile loop trail into the rain forest which is found on the south side of the lake just off Highway 101. The trail begins near the public parking area.

Winter and early spring rains of some 140 inches coupled with mild temperatures and a low elevation create an environment for growing the enormous trees and lush vegetation seen here. A map of this and other nearby rain forest trails may be obtained from the Quinault Ranger Station, P.O. Box 43, Quinault, WA 98575. Telephone (206) 288-2525. Open 8-5 daily from May through October. The Ranger Station is located a mile or so beyond the trailhead and next door to Lake Quinault Lodge.

The Olympic National Park also staffs a park Ranger Station/Visitor's Center just beyond July Creek Campground on North Shore Road of Lake Quinault, Route 2, Box 76, Amanda Park, WA 98526. Telephone (206) 288-2444. Hours 9-6 daily, Memorial Day through Labor Day. There is parking and a public restroom here.

Because the Olympic National Forest (USDA Forest Service) and the Olympic National Park Service share in managing various sections of this verdant corner of Washington state, you'll find ample and helpful Visitors Information Centers and Ranger Stations along the entire route. There are service stations, restaurants and lodging facilities in Quinault, Kalaloch, Forks, LaPush, Clallam Bay-Sekiu and Neah Bay.

Hidden beyond the lush forest to the west along the route are rock and driftwood-strewn beaches where racoons and bears forage for intertidal marine life and where seals, sea lions and whales can be seen swimming just offshore in the Pacific Ocean. Take any of the roads labeled "to the beach" along Highway 101 as you head north toward Kalaloch to see some of these off-the-beaten-path primitive beaches and wildlife refuge areas which have been protected by the National Park Service since 1953.

Travelers, especially first-time visitors, are advised to stop at the Kalaloch Ranger Station on Highway 101 north of Queets for the helpful "A Strip of Wilderness" guide to the rugged beach areas. Also, discuss with the park rangers current weather and tide conditions, regulations, tide tables and most accessible beaches. The mailing address is Star Route 1, Box 2200, Forks, WA 98331. Telephone (206) 962-2283. Park rangers suggest that travelers have warm parkas, windbreakers, caps and sturdy shoes when venturing onto the beach areas and into the forest.

HOH RIVER RAIN FOREST ~ LA PUSH ~ FORKS

If you're not inclined to venture out on windy, wave-tossed beaches in this rugged coastal region,at the very least treat yourself to the all weather two-lane road just half an hour north of Kalaloch which carries travelers with ease 19 miles into the HOH VALLEY RAIN FOREST.

There is a Ranger Station and Visitor Center here along with rain forest ecology displays, a campground, and picnic areas, all handicap accessible. Guided walks on the SPRUCE NATURE TRAIL are offered during the summer; plan about two hours. The Hoh Ranger Station telephone is (206) 374-6925.

You may take your own easy self-guided loop walks here, including one which is wheelchair accessible, which offer an informative look at the lush rain forest environment. Walk beneath 500-year-old spruce and hemlock and moss-draped big-leaf maples and alder. Notice the tangled undergrowth of salmonberry and salal, sword and lady ferns, and fallen moss-covered "nurse" logs where new growth is nourished. Wonder at masses of spongy moss, lichens, liverworts and wildflowers carpeting mounds and hollows where one may expect to find colonies of elves hiding.

Stand very still, watch shafts of sunlight waft through the misty forest glen, marvel at the cathedral of towering trees whose lacy emerald drapes of moss often trail on the forest floor, and know that this is, indeed, "the forest primeval... standing like Druids of old, with voices sad and prophetic," as penned by poet Henry Wadsworth Longfellow in the late 1840s.

When visiting this incredibly magnificent verdant region it is comforting to know that, in 1981, Olympic National Park (all 900,000 acres of it including more than 130 peaks, 60 active glaciers and the narrow strip of wilderness coast) was awarded status by the United Nations as a World Heritage Site. It is one of only 100 locations in the world (just nine in the U.S.) to be given this special designation as one of those rare places on planet Earth where natural or cultural qualities are so exceptional that the need for their preservation transcends political boundaries.

Heading north again on Highway 101, you may want to plan a stop at the Forks Visitors Information Center located on the highway across from the airport to pick up local information about the annual autumn WILD MUSHROOM SHOW and the Forks Old Fashioned 4th of July Festival. Telephone (206) 374-2531. Hours 10-6 daily May 1 through October 31. Mailing address: P.O. Box 1249, Forks, WA 98331.

A scenic 35 mile side-loop drive from Forks, the OCEAN BEACHES SCENIC ROUTE passes through rain forests in various stages of growth and leads travelers out to a spectacular view of the ocean and James Island. You'll pass through LaPush, an 800 year old Indian fishing village and home of the Quileute Indian Tribe, where there are resorts and campgrounds. The Ranger Station at Mora Campground can provide information about nearby Rialto Beach (one of the safest and most accessible places to hike and picnic), beachcombing regulations and wilderness hikes. Telephone (206) 374-5460. Mailing address: Star Route 2, Box 170, Forks, WA 98331.

CLALLAM BAY ~ SEKIU ~ NEAH BAY ~ CAPE FLATTERY ~ LAKE OZETTE

For another spectacular side loop, detour from Highway 101 at Sappho, about 11 miles north of Forks. On the way plan a stop at the joint Visitors Information Center (about 5 miles north of Forks) for maps and helpful information for the area northwest toward Clallam Bay and Sekiu, Lake Ozette, Neah Bay and the Makah Indian Reservation, and Cape Flattery. Telephone (206) 374-6522 (Forest Service) and 374-5450 (National Park). Mailing address: Star Route 1, Box 185, Forks, WA 98331.

The COASTAL SCENIC ROUTE from Clallam Bay and Sekiu journeys some 20 miles along the sparkling waters of the Strait of Juan de Fuca through deep rain forests and out to Neah Bay and the westernmost point in the continental U.S., Cape Flattery. The area receives over 100 inches of rain a year (mostly in the winter and early spring months!).

Secluded beaches near the cape offer places to see California gray whales (between March and May) on their twice-yearly migration between Alaska and Baja California. The striking black and white Orca whales who live here year around may also be sighted. On nearby Tatoosh Island, you may spot elephant seals and their pups during spring and early summer months. And, just as impressive, an array of deep magenta and red-orange sunsets (the romantic kind) may be enjoyed throughout most the year as well.

Plan to visit the splendid MAKAH MUSEUM in Neah Bay where impressive 500-year-old artifacts from the OZETTE ARCHAEOLOGICAL SITE are displayed. Hand-woven baskets of cedar splints and bear grass, seal and whaling harpoons, canoes and a longhouse are all part of this irreplaceable collection. Information about the non-profit museum association and the university's HOKO DIG near Lake Ozette (open for summer visits) may be obtained from the Makah Cultural and Research Center, P.O. Box 95, Neah Bay, WA 98357. Telephone (206) 645-2711. This fine museum was designed by J.J. Andre who also designed the Provincial

Museum in Victoria, British Columbia.

The Ozette dig was closed in 1981 after 11 years of excavation by instructors and students from Washington State University. If time allows, take the 3.3 mile INDIAN VILLAGE TRAIL through the rain forest on an old-style puncheon boardwalk leading out to Cape Alva and the site. Many of the original crosswise cedar puncheon planks were laid in place by early settler Lars Ahlstrom who lived out on the cape for 56 years.

Well worth the 21-mile bumpy road trip from Highway 101 (access east of Neah Bay near Seiku), find the trailhead near the Ranger Station at the north end of Lake Ozette. A well-written guide, "The Indian Village Nature Trail," contains helpful sketches of the trees, berries, shrubs, flowers and wildlife seen along the rain forest walk. You may want to take along a picnic lunch and beverages. **Note:** Do not drink any water in the park unless boiling it first.

For information about guided Field Seminars in the Olympic National Park, including outdoor classes in the park's natural history, botany and biology, resource management, art and photography, contact the Field Seminar Coordinator, Olympic National Park Headquarters, 600 E. Park Avenue, Port Angeles, WA 98362. Telephone (206) 452-4501, Extension 227.

SOL DUC ~ LAKE CRESCENT ~ HURRICANE RIDGE ~ PORT ANGELES

During a drive through the Olympic Peninsula and an exploration of its many life zones—from lush cathedral-like rain forests and windswept beaches of the western coastal section to the drier north and eastern region dotted with glacier-strewn peaks, high-country lakes and clothed in forests of fir, pine and hemlock—one must seriously consider abandoning a fixed schedule and, for awhile, erase even thoughts of those calendars or datebooks.

In fact, just about now, road-weary travelers may be ready for a comforting soak in the warm, therapeutic mineral waters of SOL DUC HOT SPRINGS.

Located about 14 miles south of Highway 101 (look for signs just before Fairholm and Lake Crescent) and nestled in the Soleduck Valley of enormous old growth Douglas fir, Sol Duc Hot Springs has welcomed travelers since the early 1900s. You'll find here a resort, mineral pools and swimming pool, cabins, a trailer park, grocery store, and restaurant all of which open for the summer beginning Memorial Day weekend.

First, stop at the seasonal Ranger Station near the Sol Duc Campground (about 2 miles before reaching the hot springs) for current information about nearby nature walks and naturalist programs at the campground amphitheater.

Then, lower yourself into one of those warm mineral water pools and relax tired feet and sore muscles for awhile, all at the 1,680-foot level. Information about lodging may be obtained from Sol Duc Hot Springs Resort, P.O. Box 1355, Port Angeles, WA 98362. Telephone (206) 327-3583. **Note:** There is a nominal fee per vehicle for traveling into this section of the park which was reopened in 1988 (the year of Olympic National Park's 50th anniversary) following two years of extensive reconstruction, renovation and improvement (including the vintage resort and mineral pools).

Highway 101, winding east toward Port Angeles and Sequim, soon skirts lovely LAKE CRESCENT and passes rustic Lake Crescent Lodge where a short nature trail may be taken to 90-foot MARYMERE FALLS. The .7 mile trail begins near the lodge and along the way you can observe native plants and wildflowers as well as mushrooms in season. **Note:** The final portion of the trail is mostly uphill.

The Lake Crescent Ranger Station staff can provide helpful information about this trail and the SPRUCE RAILROAD TRAIL as well. This 4-mile trail skirts the lake's north shore at about 600 feet and follows along sections of an old railroad bed which transported spruce logs (for constructing the lightweight World War I airplanes) to mills in Port Angeles. Along the trail you may see old railroad ties and two abandoned tunnel shafts as well as Indian paintbrush, woolly sunflower, silver-back luina and saxifrage (along with many others), especially during May and June.

This park Ranger Station is located just off Highway 101 beyond Marymere Falls and near the lodge. Mailing address: Star Route 1, Box 10, Port Angeles, WA 98362. Telephone (206) 928-3380. **Note:** Sundays are usually best for traveling this route because of fewer logging trucks on the narrow highway.

In Port Angeles (about 20 miles east of Lake Crescent) plan a visit to the OLYMPIC NATIONAL PARK headquarters and PIONEER MEMORIAL MUSEUM & VISITOR'S CENTER. Here you can see colorful displays and dioramas which interpret the geology of the many life zones within the Olympic National Park along with interpretive displays about the wildlife, bird species and native plants of the region. An excellent bookstore offers a fine selection of informative books about the park's natural and geological history and there is also a .5 mile self-guided nature trail which begins at the west end of the headquarter's parking area.

The Visitor's Center is located at 3002 Mt. Angeles Road, Port Angeles, WA 98548. Telephone (206) 452-4501. Call (206) 452-9235 for a recorded report of current and forecasted weather throughout the park. You may want to ask about membership in the museum's non-profit Natural History Association which supports the park's educational programs. Olympic National Park headquarters, museum and Visitor's Center hours are 9-4 daily. Access from downtown Port Angeles via Race Street.

Weather permitting, don't miss the scenic drive from park headquarters about 20 miles up to 5,200-foot HURRICANE RIDGE where you'll have splendid high altitude views of snowy Olympic Mountain peaks and Cascade Mountains to the east and south. To the north are the Strait of Juan de Fuca and Canada's Vancouver Island. On a clear night the lights of Victoria glitter like a jeweled necklace at the southeastern tip of the island.

On the network of paved trails that meander near the rustic Hurricane Ridge visitor's lodge, walk as far as you wish on your own or take a guided walk, during summer months. From June to September an array of alpine wildflowers can often be seen including glacier and avalanche lilies, subalpine buttercups and lupine, American bistort and showy polemonium, smooth douglasia and mats of partridgefoot to mention just a few.

At the visitor's lodge, open from early May through September, there is a deli counter, gift shop, natural history displays and public restrooms. Hours 10-6. The nominal park fee per vehicle collected on the drive up to the ridge allows unlimited visits (for seven days) to any of the park's half dozen fee station entrances. Seniors age 62 and over who are U.S. citizens qualify for a free lifetime entrance pass. **Note:** Daytime temperatures are often cool and crisp at this elevation.

Stop at the ranger station at Heart of the Hills Campground (about halfway up the ridge road) for information about naturalist programs at the campground's amphitheater and about wildflowers along SWITCHBACK TRAIL (three miles from the ridge).

However, if zig-zagging up about 2,000 feet in 1.5 miles to a saddle overlooking

Port Angeles and the Strait seems somewhat strenuous, at least try the first half-mile of the Switchback Trail. Your reward will be visions of shooting stars, dainty white saxifrage, bright yellow monkeyflowers, yellow willow-herb and the violet-like flowers of common butterwort—all appearing around mossy rocks near a small stream along the first section of the trail.

And, just up the trail a short distance you may often see red and yellow Sitka columbine, miniature star-shaped Scouler's harebell, sunny yellow violets and 4-foot spikes of deep purple larkspur. Along the Switchback Trail are some of the best wildflower gardens in this section of the park. Helpful resources and field guides, available at the headquarters Visitor's Center bookstore, include "Wildflowers of the Olympic" by Charles Stewart and "Mountain Flowers" by Harvey Manning.

Deer, mountain goats and inquisitive marmots are often spied along the trails that shoelace in and around Hurricane Ridge as well. The curious marmots can often be seen near the visitor's lodge parking area. Occasionally the elusive Roosevelt elk may be seen although it is often said, especially by those who have explored the region's hinterlands and know the park well, that the animals will most likely spy the unsuspecting traveler first.

While their soft colors blend with the natural vegetation and form a readymade camouflage, our voices and footsteps as well as our brightly colored caps and parkas are immediate signals for those frisky squirrels, wide-eyed marmots, gentle deer, stately elk, and sturdy mountain goats who watch so quietly and intently as we pass by.

Incidentally, those soil-trampling and wildflower-munching mountain goats (not native but released on the peninsula by settlers in the 1920s), are being phased out of the park's delicate ecosystem and taken to other areas of the northwest where they where they can live and be observed in their native and natural habitat.

When you've absorbed several hour's worth of 360-degree mountain wilderness vistas, seen numerous birds and wildlife, and identified scores of alpine wildflowers drive slowly down the asphalt ribbon through the scenery to Port Angeles, the largest city on the northern Olympic Peninsula.

A splendid view of the water, port, and ferry landing may be seen by walking up the LAUREL STREET STAIRS which begin near the cascading fountain and benches in Conrad Dyar Memorial Circle in the center of town. Each of the three levels has a bench for resting.

Visitors also enjoy walking along the promenade decks at CITY PIER PARK (located at the north end of Lincoln Street) which features an observation tower, grassy picnic area, sandy wading beach, short-term moorage for small boats and seaplanes, the Coast Guard cutter Active, the nearby ferry terminal and the ARTHUR D. FEIRO MARINE LABORATORY.

Here you can see a display of local marine life donated by divers and examine a large touching tank filled with sea urchins, sea cucumbers and other marine animals. Volunteers are on hand to answer questions and guided tours are available by appointment. Operated by Peninsula College as a marine laboratory for its fishery technology program, it is open daily, 10-8, from June through Labor Day; winter and spring hours are noon-4 on Saturday and Sunday. Telephone (206) 452-9277.

Among the local bed and breakfast inns which have lovely grounds and gardens are THE TUDOR INN and GLEN MAR BY THE SEA. Both are open just to inn guests but may be seen on a walking tour. Information about annual events and festivals, and a city map may be obtained from the well-stocked Port

Angeles Visitors Information Center, 121 Railroad Avenue, Port Angeles, WA 98362. Telephone (206) 452-2363. Open 8-9 daily during summer months and 10-4 Monday-Friday during fall and winter.

Port Angeles is also a major port-of-entry to and from Canada, with the *M.V. Coho* ferry plying the Strait of Juan de Fuca on its four daily 90-minute roundtrips to Victoria. Cost is about $22 for car and driver, $5.50 for adult passengers and walk-ons, and $2.75 for children ages 5-11. One of the best options, especially during heavily traveled peak summertime runs, is to park the car in Port Angeles and ferry over for the day as a foot passenger. See the Victoria B.C. section which begins on page 122.

SEQUIM ~ DUNGENESS SPIT & WILDLIFE REFUGE

Often called the banana belt of the Olympic Peninsula, the pastoral Sequim ('Skwim')-Dungeness Valley receives dramatically less rainfall than the rain forests just visited. Those water-soaked clouds rolling in from the Pacific Ocean drench the low coastal western region first, just as they're siphoned upward and over the Olympic Mountains—leaving just 10-18 inches of moisture to fall in the Sequim area on the far northeast corner of the peninsula.

Before early settlers dug irrigation ditches to bring fresh water from the Dungeness River, the prairie grew cactus and grasshoppers rather than lush fields of hay, berries, vegetables and tree seedlings. Motoring along the 14-mile DUNGENESS SCENIC LOOP allows wide-angle views of the lush irrigated fields with snowy Olympic peaks a stunning backdrop.

From the center of town head north on Sequim Avenue which becomes Sequim-Dungeness Way as it winds out to this section of the Strait of Juan de Fuca and Dungeness Bay, along which you'll find the DUNGENESS NATIONAL WILDLIFE REFUGE, Dungeness Spit and the vintage Dungeness lighthouse. You may want to pick up a copy of the Wildlife Species List which details birds as well as upland and marine animals found on the eight different habitats here—coniferous forest, shrub, grassy meadow, salt marsh, sand spit, tideflats, inner bay and marine.

To obtain the list, contact the Dungeness Wildlife Refuge, c/o Nisqually National Wildlife Refuge, 100 Brown Farm Road, Olympia, WA 98506. Telephone (206) 753-9467. Or, stop at the Sequim Visitors Information Center located on Highway 101 on the outskirts of town, to the east, which usually has ample copies of the helpful booklet.

Over 200 bird species have been recorded at the refuge including loons, grebes, cormorants, herons, swans, teals and wigeons as well as plovers, sandpipers, snipe, dowitchers, gulls, terns and puffin—in addition to numerous raptors and passerines. To walk a short distance out onto the 6-mile spit, find the well-maintained .4 mile trail through a wooded area, just beyond the campground and Spit trail parking area.

The hike out to the lighthouse at the end of the spit is *long* and best taken at low tide, allowing at least two hours each way. Lighthouse tender Chris Berns will conduct tours on request. Telephone (206) 683-5544. Oldest of all the lighthouses north of the Columbia River, the Dungeness Spit lighthouse was built in 1857 and opened about one week earlier than the Tatoosh Island lighthouse (off Cape Flattery, near Neah Bay).

If you haven't time for the drive out to the wildlife refuge and spit, meander out as far as the historic McALMOND HOUSE which is surrounded by well-tended perennial gardens and stately old trees. Built in 1861 and now on the

Historic Register, the house is considered one of the finest on the peninsula and the first constructed of sawed lumber in the county. The McAlmond House is not open to the public but you may stop along the road to see the grounds from a distance. Turn right just beyond the bridge which spans the Dungeness River, then left onto Twin View and look for the large house on a rise away from the road, on the right.

At the SEQUIM NATURAL HISTORY MUSEUM visitors may see lifelike dioramas which contain the birds and wildlife found in each of the peninsula's natural environments—beginning at the saltwater beach you'll progress along to the marshlands, the deciduous and coniferous forests, and finally to the sub-alpine Olympic Mountains. You'll see the endangered Trumpeter swan as well as Cooper's hawk, belted kingfisher, bufflehead, saw-whet owl, osprey, great-horned owl and the Canada goose along with some 75 other birds and animals most of which were preserved by taxidermist Mark Hanson.

The museum is located at 503 N. Sequim Avenue, Room 4 of the Peninsula Cultural Arts Center. Hours are noon-4 Saturday, Sunday and Wednesday; closed December to mid-February and holidays. A helpful guide to other museums and historic sites may be obtained from the Clallam County Heritage Association, Fourth & Lincoln Streets, Sequim, WA 98382. Telephone (206) 452-7831, extension 364.

Located just south of town, off Highway 101 toward the foothills, peninsula travelers may find CEDARBROOK HERB FARM located on 12 acres of lush farmland watered by a freshwater creek which bubbles down from the Olympic Mountains. The historic BELL HOUSE, built here some 100 years ago, provides the herb-growing McReynolds family a natural place for both their work area and giftshop.

Wander through the gardens surrounding the old farmhouse, especially in June when nearly everything is in glorious bloom. Poke into the greenhouse and sniff over 150 varieties of culinary, medicinal and fragrant herbs. Walk through the farmhouse gift area where you may often spy aromatic and colorful bouquets and bunches of everlastings and flowers hanging from the old rafters in the work room.

The family harvests, throughout July and August, everything from Baby Breath, Bee Balm, Catnip and Comfrey to Rosemary, Sorrel, Statice and Yarrow. Freshly cut Basil is always available from July through September and Elephant Garlic can also be found at the farm. In the gift area herbal vinegars and fragrant potpourris share shelf-space with rose petal beads and lavender wands. A selection of books on growing herbs is also on hand.

Cedarbrook Herb Farm is found at 986 Sequim Avenue South, Sequim, WA 98382. Telephone (206) 683-7733. Spring and summer hours, daily 10-5, March 15 through September. Fall hours 10-4, Monday-Saturday, October through December. A yearly mail order list is also available.

If you're in the area during May plan to head 40 miles south on Highway 101 to see the outstanding collection of rhododendrons and azaleas at WHITNEY GARDENS & NURSERY, located in Brinnon along the west side of HOOD CANAL. The 7-acre nursery and gardens are a festival of color and fragrance, with peak blooming around Mother's Day. For the early blooming hybrids and species stop by from March through the middle of April.

In this extraordinary garden you may see over 3,000 plants and species ranging from Asia, Europe, Australia and New Zealand as well as the eastern and western U.S. Some of the eldest rhododendrons are massive, growing to heights of 20 feet or more. Notice the giant pastel pink rhododendron guarding the entrance to the self-guided garden paths, like a wizened emperor overseeing a floral harem of the most elegant and beautiful species in the kingdom.

What began as a retirement hobby for George and Anne Sather (they acquired the garden from original owner Bill Whitney some 20 years ago) evolved into a full-time nursery business. Now, Anne and her daughter Ellie are carrying on the work and continuing to incorporate design changes in the nursery area as well as maintaining and adding to the original gardens. A considerable number of Whitney Gardens hybrid rhododendrons have been selected for parks, gardens and arboreta throughout the world, including the Great Park at Windsor, England.

Find Whitney Gardens & Nursery just 12 miles south of Quilcene on Highway 101. The address is P.O. Box F, Brinnon, WA 98320. Telephone (206) 796-4411. Nursery hours 10-5:30 daily and garden viewing hours 9-dusk daily.

A pleasant spot to picnic and camp is nearby Dosewallips State Park, just north of the gardens. Along this side of the peninsula are many places to see myriads of wild rhododendrons, Washington's state flower, which also bloom in May. Their pastel pink blossoms brighten dense Douglas fir and deciduous forests along long and narrow Hood Canal, one of the saltwater fingers projecting south of Port Townsend and the Strait of Juan De Fuca.

To discover the many paths and trails in the area, along which may be found many native wildflowers as well as the luscious wild rhododendrons, stop at the Olympic National Forest Ranger Station in Quilcene, just north on Highway 101, P.O. Box 280, Quilcene, WA 98376. Telephone (206) 753-3368. Ask about the MOUNT TOWNSEND TRAIL in the Buckhorn Wilderness, a 5-mile hike through forests blooming with beadlily, foamflower, vanilla leaf and rhododendrons to open meadows of Indian paintbrush, Columbia lily, lupine and Sitka valerian. Subalpine buttercups, mountain sandwort, saxifrage, long-plumed avens, spreading pholx and others hug the wind-swept ridge.

If the high mountain trails don't tempt you, try the easy drive up through spring-blooming rhododendron to the splendid MOUNT WALKER VIEWPOINT where you'll see, on a clear day, wide-angle views of the canal, the Olympic Mountains and the Cascade Mountains. Find the turn-off just 6 miles or so north of Dosewallips State Park as you're heading toward Quilcene. Drive up the steep and winding 5-mile paved road to the twin viewpoints or park at the base and enjoy a 2-mile hike through virgin forests and past craggy basalt walls, wild rhododendrons and native wildflowers.

If you elect to head south on Highway 101 toward Eldon, Lilliwaup, Hoodsport, Shelton and Olympia you may want to stop at the joint Olympic National Park/National Forest Ranger Station in Hoodsport to inquire about wildflowers blooming along the easy forested trails near Lake Cushman and Staircase National Park Ranger Station.

The joint Ranger Station address is P.O. Box 68, Hoodsport, WA 98548. Telephone (206) 877-5254. Lake Cushman and Staircase are about 16 miles from Highway 101 at Hoodsport; as the crow flies this is almost directly east of Lake Quinault and the rain forest on the low Pacific coast side of the park.

PORT TOWNSEND ~ KEYSTONE FERRY

Located about 25 miles north of Mount Walker and Quilcene, a tiny community known for its oyster production, travelers enjoy the Victorian seaport community of Port Townsend and its lovely CHETZEMOKA PARK. Found on the upper section of town, on Jackson Street, you may enjoy not only a splendid panoramic

. (Continued on page 83)

Color Photographs

Note: All photographs taken by the author from 1981-1988 on travels throughout the region.

Discover
A PRIVATE
GARDEN...

1

2

3

4

VISIT
HERB
GARDENS
AND
NURSERIES...

5

6

7

8

STROLL THROUGH RHODODENDRON AND PERENNIAL GARDENS...

9

10

Discover many oriental gardens...

ENJOY A
FORMAL
GARDEN...

11

12

13

Walk through an alpine garden next to the sky. . .

Visit
Historic
Monuments
and
Their
Gardens...

14

15

F<small>IND</small>
GARDENS
FOR
FAMILIES
AND
FOR
LEARNING...

16

17

18

DISCOVER THE REGION'S NATURAL SCENIC AREAS...

19

20

21

22

23

A ND A
PLETHORA
OF
NATIVE
PLANTS
AND
WILDFLOWERS. . .

24

25

26

27

28

29

30

31

32

33

34

35

36

(Continued from page 65)

view of Admiralty Inlet, Mt. Baker and the Cascades to the northeast, but a stroll through the lovely rose arbor and grounds as well. Bring a deli picnic and sit in the wide old-fashioned wooden swing for one of the best views.

From the park, named for Chief Chetzemoka who was an Indian friend of the city's first settlers, you can walk on the sandy beach south to the boat basin at Pt. Hudson and the east end of Water Street or north (the longer walk) to Fort Warden State Park.

On Lawrence Street, near the park, stop by the ABUNDANT LIFE SEED COMPANY where you can browse through and purchase packets of wildflower seeds harvested from local roadsides, fields and meadows.

Near the downtown waterfront area you may find the TYLER STREET STAIRWAY directly behind two of the many renovated Victorian commercial buildings—Captain Tibbals Building and the Loren Hastings Building—near Tyler and Water Streets. The trees were planted by Port Townsend Kiwanians who also planted many other trees along the city's streets. Notice the elegant tree, Chinese Tree of Heaven, to the west of the stairway which was a gift to the seaport city from the Emperor of China in the 1860s.

Find the TAYLOR STREET TERRACE nearby, at Water and Taylor Streets, another landscaped stairway to the upper residential area where many historic and renovated Victorians are open to bed & breakfast travelers. At the base of the stairway you'll see the Haller Fountain which features a delicate Grecian mythological sea nymph, Galatea. The fountain was presented to the city in 1906 by Theodore N. Haller in memory of early pioneers who settled the area.

As you walk up the landscaped stairway, turn at the upper landing to see the grand view of Water Street and the downtown area, the Quincy Street ferry dock, and boats bobbing in Port Townsend Bay—all against that verdant and often snowy mountain backdrop.

It is said that, during the 1800s when rowdy seamen swarmed off trading ships and frequented the Water Street bars and dance halls, no self-respecting Victorian lady would dare to go shopping downtown, even in broad daylight. So a second business area was built atop the bluff, on Lawrence Street, with the stairs later connecting the two areas.

At the ROTHSCHILD HOUSE, downtown on Taylor between Jefferson and Franklin Streets, you may find an intimate, well-tended ROSE GARDEN and restored HERB GARDEN. Just 50 by 200 feet in size, you're visiting one of Washington's smallest state parks.

Additional information, including dates for the annual RHODODENDRON FESTIVAL and Historic Victorian Homes and Garden Tours, may be obtained from the Port Townsend Visitors Information Center. Ask about binocular birdwatching at PROTECTION ISLAND and the new lagoon park trail (for spying many seabird species) at nearby KAH TAI LAGOON. The Visitor's Center is located at 2437 Sims Way, Port Townsend, WA 98368. Telephone (206) 385-2722. Hours 9-5 Monday-Friday, 10-4 Saturday, and 11-4 on Sunday.

After visiting Port Townsend you may want to board the Keystone ferry, at the Quincey Street dock, for the short ride across Admiralty Inlet to Whidbey Island and points north, toward LaConner and Anacortes, or south toward Langley and the Mukilteo ferry to the mainland north of Seattle, near Everett. Whidbey Island is included in the North Coast section beginning on page 91.

Seattle & King County

KENT ~ MAPLE VALLEY ~ FALL CITY ~ CARNATION

Heading north from Federal Way toward Seattle, consider an optional loop through Kent, Maple Valley, Fall City and Carnation to visit several botanic surprises somewhat off the beaten path but within easy driving distance to and from the Seattle metropolitan area.

In Kent, located just east of I-5 at DesMoines, herb-lovers may want to detour to DIANA'S HERBS at TALL FIRS HERB FARM. You may call ahead for a schedule of classes on growing and using herbs and for an appointment to take a self-guided tour of the theme gardens. Diana's gift shop is filled with delectable herb products. The address is 26824 108th Avenue S.E., Kent, WA 98031. Telephone (206) 854-4664. Open March through December, Tuesday-Saturdays, 10-4 and to 7 on Thursdays.

If you're in the area on a weekend plan also to take in the KENT SATURDAY MARKET located near Second and Fourth Avenues where artists, farmers and nurseymen and women gather to sell paintings and pottery, fruits and vegetables, flowers and herbs from 9-4 on Saturdays from early spring through fall.

Located near Maple Valley, accessed via Highway 18 east of Kent, travelers may find the SOUTH KING COUNTY ARBORETUM at S.E. 248th Street and Witte Road. Open 9-4 daily the arboretum offers native and exotic tree and shrub species along with a collection of rainbow-colored perennials.

To find another herb-lovers paradise, THE HERBFARM, continue north on Highway 18 to I-90 then west to Exit 22, Preston-Fall City. Follow signs through the village of Preston, at the 'y' turn left across bridge about .5 mile to The Herbfarm entrance.

You'll want to plan an hour or so to wander through the Zimmerman family's lovely herbal theme gardens which feature a Shakespeare Garden, Salad Garden, Succulent Garden, Silver Foliage Garden and Fragrance Garden; look through the selection of some 400 herb plants for sale; poke through the well-stocked gift shop (offering scented potpourris, herbal wreaths, homemade vinegars and preserves); check the menu at the Herbfarm restaurant; and, enjoy the masses of colorful shade-loving annuals and perennials which bloom beneath stately walnut trees surrounding the farm and greenhouses.

From April through Christmas The Herbfarm offers a 6-course luncheon which features regional foods delicately seasoned with herbs. Offered Friday-Sunday the luncheon begins with a guided garden tour. Cost is about $20 and reservations are a must. Contact The Herbfarm, 32804 Issaquah-Fall City Road, Fall City, WA 98024. Telephone (206) 784-2222. The Herbfarm is open Monday-Friday 9-5 and Saturday-Sunday 9-6, from mid-March through early October. Call for hours during late fall and winter months. An informative catalog is available.

Continue north on Highway 203 from Fall City through Carnation and follow the signs to discover a little-known gem, the CARNATION RESEARCH FARM GARDENS. Find the stone steps leading to the gardens just beyond the large statue of Segis Pietertje Prospect. This cow, affectionately known as Possum Sweetheart, broke a world's record in 1920 when she produced 37,381 lbs. of milk.

At the top of the stone steps find first the lovely fountain and sweeping tree-shaded lawn with a view across the Snoqualmie Valley toward the Cascade Mountains. Pioneer businessman E.A. Stuart built his world-renowned dairy farm by reclaiming the swampy valley floor below where the first set of barns was constructed. Later new barns and research areas were built on the hillside location where the lovely formal and informal gardens were also planted.

Towering over the garden hedges are hemlocks and native cedar, pine and fir. Flower beds bordering the wide expanse of lawn are reminiscent of an English informal garden with tall clumps of perennials lush with both colorful blooms as well as textured leaves and stems.

Walk beneath a vine-covered pergola and around low boxwood hedges for a nostalgic stroll through the elegantly sculptured formal rose garden beds which contain old scented favorites as well as newer varieties. The stately home in the gardens, called the "Bungalow," was build by owner E.A. Stuart in 1914 as a summer retreat for his family.

Stroll up toward the Friskies Feline Care & Research Center and greenhouses, along more beds of annuals, then return down the driveway (near the bungalow) and notice the stunning collection of fibrous and tuberous begonias which thrive along with colorful fuschias in shady areas beneath towering Douglas fir.

This is, indeed, a garden gem not to be missed. The Carnation Research Farm Gardens are open to the public March-October, Monday-Saturday 10-3 and there is no charge. The gardens are closed Sundays, holidays and winter months. Telephone (206) 788-1511. Visitors may also take a self-guided tour of the farm's museum, calf nursery, maternity barn and milking parlor.

Travelers may backtrack a few miles to Interstate 90, connecting at the Fall City-Preston entrance heading west toward Issaquah, Bellevue and across the Mercer Island bridge into Seattle, or north via I-405 toward Kirkland and Woodinville.

ISSAQUAH ~ BELLEVUE ~ KIRKLAND ~ WOODINVILLE

From Issaquah head south a few miles toward Renton to find EMRICK'S FUCHSIAS & BEGONIAS and SQUAK MOUNTAIN GREENHOUSES. Emrick's, which offers the luscious shade-loving fuchsias and begonias in every conceivable variety and color is located at 7303 Renton-Issaquah Road, Issaquah, WA 98027. Telephone (206) 392-6779. Open daily 7-6, except Wednesdays. Squak Mountain Greenhouses, offering a variety of colorful annuals and perennials, is located at 7600 Renton-Issaquah Road, Issaquah, WA 98027. Telephone (206) 392-1025. Open daily from 9-4.

Further information about other nurseries in the area, as well as annual events, may be obtained from the Issaquah Visitors Information Center, 155 N.W. Gilman Boulevard, Issaquah, WA 98027. Telephone (206) 392-7024. Hours are 9-4 daily Memorial Day through Salmon Days in early October. The Center is near the quaint Gilman Village shops.

You may also want to plan a mouth-watering stop at the EASTSIDE PUBLIC MARKET near Crossroads Mall at N.E. 8th Street in Bellevue where flowers, vegetables and herbs from local farms are offered for sale along with fresh fish and ready-to-eat foods displayed under some 36,000 square feet of covered space. This delectable and friendly market is open Monday-Friday 10-6 and on Saturdays noon-5 from early spring through fall months.

Located near Kirkland bird-watchers may want to plan a sidetrip to JUANITA BAY PARK. Nestled along a sheltered cove on Lake Washington's northeastern shore, find the .4 mile wooden footbridge and walk safely right out on the marsh for a close-up view of more than 20 species of migrating waterfowl during spring months and again in the fall.

You may see beaver dams and lodges and also spy the tracks of raccoons, muskrats, opossum and deer in shallow muddy areas below the footbridge. The bridge was once a section of main road between Kirkland and Juanita and the 65-acre park was a golf course many years ago. On the first Sunday of each month you may join an interpretive walk with volunteers and staff from the Kirkland Parks and Recreation Department. Call for current times and meeting place. Telephone (206) 828-1218. Access Kirkland from Bellevue via I-405.

Just a few miles north of Kirkland, off I-405, are two possbilities for your floral itinerary. The beautifully landscaped grounds and picnic area at the CHATEAU STE. MICHELLE WINERY surround an elegant French chateau-style winery and tasting room. After strolling the grounds (the Autumn colors are especially vibrant), you may take a guided winery tour, offered hourly from 10-4:30. The winery is located at 14111 N.E. 145th Street, Woodinville, WA. Telephone (206) 488-1133.

MOLBAK'S GREENHOUSE offers two acres of luscious indoor plants and 700 varieties of trees. From African violets and gardenias to cyclamin and poinsettias some 1,000 different annuals and perennials are available here. Guided group tours are available, by appointment, or take your own self-guided stroll between 9:30-6 daily and until 9 on Fridays. The greenhouse is located at 13625 N.E. 175th Street, Woodinville, WA. Telephone (206) 483-5000. Access from I-405 at Exit 23 (Monroe-Wenatchee) to Highway 522, then continue on Highway 522 to Woodinville exit, right to 175th and left about 3 blocks to the parking area.

Information about annual events and festivals may be obtained from the East King County Visitors Bureau, 515 - 116th Avenue N.E., Suite 111, Bellevue, WA 98004. Telephone (206) 455-1926. Hours 10-4 daily Memorial Day to Labor Day, 8:30-5 Monday-Friday during the remainder of the year.

SEATTLE

In downtown Seattle, between 6th and Seneca Streets, find the lovely FREEWAY PARK GARDENS and a cascading fountain which provide a pleasant backdrop for frequently scheduled noontime concerts. The container gardens are maintained by the Department of Parks & Recreation, 100 Dexter Avenue North, Seattle, WA 98109. Telephone (206) 625-4671.

Nearby you may find the romantic PARSONS GARDENS, often used for weddings, located at 7th Avenue West and West Highland Drive. This lovely garden of roses and annuals is maintained by the Seattle Parks Department.

Located high atop Capitol Hill just east of the downtown area, plan a stop at the SEATTLE PARK CONSERVATORY in which are displays of palms, cycads and tropical flowers along with the ANNA CLISE ORCHID COLLECTION (begun in 1919). The Victorian style conservatory, constructed in 1912, is similar in style to the elegant London Crystal Palace.

Located in VOLUNTEER PARK (off 15th near Prospect), the Seattle Park Conservatory is open daily 9-5. Telephone (206) 625-4043. For information about membership in Friends of the Conservatory, write to P.O. Box 33103, Seattle, WA 98133.

Also, drive around to the west side of Volunteer Park to see a panoramic view of Seattle and the Space Needle, especially grand at sunset. The park and Conservatory may be accessed from I-5 at Exit 166, right on E. Olive to E. John and left onto 15th Avenue to the park.

Nearby, just off East Madison and Lake Washington Boulevard East, is the premier WASHINGTON PARK ARBORETUM which needs to be on everyone's travel itinerary. Also included in the arboretum is the JOSEPH A. WITT WINTER GARDEN, the WOODLAND GARDEN and the JAPANESE TEA GARDEN, all located at the southwest corner of the University of Washington campus.

This vast 200-acre arboretum began as a small collection of trees planted on the campus by Professor Edmond S. Meany in 1894. In 1935 a cooperative agreement between the University and the Seattle Parks Department created the Washington Park Arboretum, fulfilling the professor's lifelong dream. The Arboretum Foundation was formed later that year and now helps support the arboretum's educational and horticultural programs.

Containing more than 5,000 plants and trees, begin your exploration of this wooded wonderland by strolling down AZALEA WAY, the Arboretum's main walkway, where you'll be surrounded in mid-May by a kaleidoscope of color from hundreds and hundreds of blooming azaleas.

Walk along other trails within the arboretum including one along a pond which features semi-acquatic plants. See unusual specimens of Nootka-cypress and an Elm hybrid, 'Ice-cream Tree,' along with flowering cherries, crab-apples, dogwood, camellias, California lilacs, hollies, 23 different kind of vines and many other types of trees.

The Arboretum changes dramatically with each season, providing a tranquil and inviting year round oasis. The first weeks in May are usually best for walking through the RHODODENDRON GLEN, followed by the blossoms along Azalea Way during mid-May. During summer months see a massive hydrangea collection and colorful rock roses, followed by glorious fall colors in mid-September through October and often into November. In December greens, wreaths, swags, garlands and cones from the arboretum are offered for sale.

Stop by the Donald Graham Visitors Center, built by funds raised by The Arboretum Foundation, for information about guided walks, classes, seminars and horticultural programs at the Arboretum and Japanese Tea Garden. Information about membership in the foundation may be obtained from The Arboretum Foundation, c/o University of Washington, XD-10, Seattle, WA 98195. The Visitors Center is located at 2300 Arboretum Drive East. Telephone (206) 543-8800.

In the early 1960s the Arboretum's JAPANESE TEA GARDEN was constructed on 3.5 acres surrounding a traditional pond. Enormous boulders, some 11 tons of them, were brought from the Cascade Mountains near Snoqualmie Pass (east of Issaquah via I-90) and carefully placed throughout the terrain. Then, thousands of native and non-native plants were selected to represent diverse natural scenes found in Japan and arranged according to designer Juki Iida's carefully drawn landscape plan.

Pick up an illustrated brochure and horticultural plant list at the entrance booth and take your own self-guided tour of this serene oasis. From ten different vantage points, gaze at a miniature world of mountains, forests, a koi-filled lake, tableland and village, streams and waterfall, each with its own quiet message.

An authentic Tea House, a delicate pagoda and 10 ancient lanterns located in various sections of the garden all contribute to the peacefulness and tranquility here as well. Chado (The Way of Tea), an ancient ceremony conducted by a certified Tea Master from the Sheseikai Tea Club, may be seen on the third Sunday of each month at 2 and 3. It is said that, served with a sincere and respectful heart and received with gratitude, a bowl of tea satisfies both physical and spiritual thirst.

Now supporting the garden both physically and financially, the nonprofit Japanese Garden Society was formed under the guidance of the Seattle Parks and Recreation Department and the Prentice Bloedel Unit of the Arboretum Foundation. Information about society membership and special events may be obtained by contacting the Horticulture Section, Seattle Department of Parks and Recreation, 5201 Green Lake Way North, Seattle, WA 98103. Telephone (206) 625-4671. Tours of the Japanese Garden may be arranged by calling the entrance booth several days in advance—telephone (206) 625-2635. There is a nominal admission fee for visiting the garden.

Those who are particularly interested in Oriental gardens may also want to arrange a visit to KUBOTA GARDENS located at 9727 Renton Avenue S., Seattle, WA 98118. Telephone (206) 725-4400. This privately owned garden may be visited by appointment only.

And, IKENOBO GARDENS which are located at 23025 N.E. 8th Street, Redmond, WA 98053. Telephone (206) 885-BANA. The gardens, located east of 228th Avenue N.E. and the corner of N.E. Inglewood Hills Road, are open by appointment only from April 20 to October 20. Garden tours, arranged two to three weeks in advance, take about two hours. The $4 admission fee aids the Ikenobo Ikebana Society's scholarship fund. Group luncheons may be arranged at a nearby country club.

Located on the University of Washington campus, the MEDICINAL HERB GARDEN is easily found south of Drumheller Fountain along Stevens Way. In 1984 a group of educators and students, pharmacists, herbalists and garden enthusiasts formed the Friends of the Medicinal Herb Garden to help maintain this comprehensive and colorful 2-acre collection of medicinal herbs.

By May the garden blooms with old roses, European redbuds, and Johnny jump-ups but you'll see the most color in June. By July and August fennel, thistle, Joe Pye weed, pokeweed, loose-strife and goldenrod tower high over visitor's heads. You'll also see those busy pollinators—leafcutter bees, honeybees, skippers, ants, butterflies and moths. In September and October the colors soften and you'll spy fascinating seed pods like teasel, love-in-a-mist, cardoon and shoo-fly plant. Also, watch for blooming autumn crocus.

The Garden Friends weed and prune the garden, collect and clean seed for exchange with other botanical gardens around the world, and provide horticultural tours. Although the ancient "physick" or medicinal gardens are somewhat rare on the West Coast, this internationally known Medicinal Herb Garden offers a 'living library' of over 600 species of medicinal and useful plants and is the largest collection of its kind in the Western Hemisphere.

For membership information contact Friends of the Medicinal Herb Garden, Botany Department KB-15, University of Washington, Seattle, WA 98195. Telephone (206) 543-1126 (leave message). Access the campus from Washington Park Arboretum via Montelake Bridge, along Montelake Boulevard N.E. to Whatcom Lane and Gate 3 for a campus map and directions to the garden. The campus may also be accessed from Interstate 5 from the N.E. 45th-50th Street exits and bearing to the east on N.E. 45th to 15th, then right to Gate 5.

The University of Washington Visitor Information Center is located at 4014 University Way N.E., Seattle, WA 98105. Telephone (206) 543-9198. Hours 8-5 Monday-Friday.

For monthly horticultural events, classes and tours of local public and private gardens contact the CENTER FOR URBAN HORTICULTURE, located just north of the Washington Park Arboretum. From visits to a private fern garden and lectures on Chinese ferns for a Fern Festival to classes on pruning roses, vegetable garden planning and raising perennials, the Center offers an eclectic selection of interesting horticultural events every month of the year, all designed for the particular needs of garden lovers who live in large cities.

The Center can also provide information about tours and events open to the public offered by the Northwest Horticultural Society, the Washington State Federation of Garden Clubs, and other local horticultural organizations. The Center for Urban Horticulture is located at the southern edge of the university campus, at 3501 N.E. 41st Street, Seattle, WA 98105. Telephone (206) 545-8033.

You might also want to inquire about dates for the annual Northwest Flower and Garden Show which is held in February. Throughout the show, which usually runs for four days at the Convention and Trade Center, well-known Northwest horticultural experts give lectures and demonstrations. Guest experts from other regions are also on the full agenda of horticultural activities—including herbalists, floral designers, perennial experts and tree species authorities.

Travelers may also plan to visit the HERBAN RENEWAL HERB GARDEN & NURSERY where guided tours are often offered during an early spring Open House, usually the first weekend in April. The garden is located at 10437 - 19th Avenue S.W., Seattle, WA. Hours 9-5 and tours at 11 and 3. Call ahead for specific dates. Telephone (206) 243-8821.

Located just a few blocks north of the university campus, rose-lovers may want to add the WOODLAND PARK ROSE GARDEN to the travel itinerary, This formal garden, established in 1922, is an official test garden of the All-American Rose Selection Committee. You'll find here over 5,000 plants which represent some 190 varieties of new and old roses. The Rose Garden, open daily from dawn to dusk, is located at 50th and Fremont Avenue North.

While you're visiting the Rose Garden you may want to allow time to visit also the splendid WOODLAND PARK AVIARY & ZOOLOGICAL GARDENS, a 1,000 animal zoo set amidst temperate, tropical and semi-tropical plants. In the AVIARY you'll see an entire tropical forest. Hours are 8:30-6 daily May-September, 8:30-5 October-December, and 8:30-4 January-April.

Just west of Woodland Park are the CARL S. ENGLISH JR. GARDENS, located among seven landscaped acres along the banks of the HIRAM CHITTENDEN CANAL & LOCKS in Ballard. Among the stately trees in the arboretum, which was founded in 1917, are species from China, Burma, and India. The Greater Seattle Fuchsia Society FUCHSIA TEST GARDEN can be found in front of the Chittenden Administration Building. When you have an eyeful of luscious fuchsias—from the splashy tropical-looking blossoms of 'Texas Longhorn', the candy-cane red and white of 'Swingtime', to the snowy white of 'Marshmallow', along with many other favorites—take a gander at the colorful parade of pleasure boats heading in and out of Puget Sound via the system of locks which deposit all those boat-lovers into Lake Washington.

Find the Carl S. English Jr. Gardens just off N.W. 54th at 32nd Avenue N.W. Hours 7:30-9 daily; Visitor Center 11-8 daily, June 15-September 15; 11-5 Thursday through Monday during the rest of the year. There is wheelchair access. Telephone (206) 783-7059. From Woodland Park Rose Gardens head west on North 50th to N.W. Market, following Market about a mile to the locks.

For a brochure and helpful map showing the general location of all the Seattle parks, including those mentioned plus DISCOVERY PARK (for a taste of Puget Sound's natural coastline), MAGNOLIA DRIVE, and SCHMITZ PARK FOREST PRESERVE (for a sampling of northwest primeval forest), and others, write to Friends of Seattle's Olmsted Parks, P.O. Box 15984, Seattle, WA 98115.

This brochure/map also explains how the Olmsted Brothers, renowned landscape architects from Brookline, Massachusetts (the firm developed the design plan for New York's Central Park) were hired by the Seattle Parks

Department in 1903 to fulfill parks superintendent E.O. Schwagerl's dream of a system of parks and parkways linking the city's beautiful bodies of water— Lake Washington, Green Lake and Puget Sound. Parks, parkways and playgrounds designed by John Charles and Frederick Law Olmsted, Jr. kept the firm busy in Seattle from 1903 to 1934 and the city now has one of the largest and best preserved Olmsted park systems in the U.S.

Information about annual events and festivals, including the Rhododendron Festival and Cherry Blossom Festival, may be obtained from the Seattle/King County Visitors Information Center, 666 Stewart Street, Seattle, WA 98101. Telephone (206) 447-4240. An Information Center at Seattle Center, adjacent to the Space Needle, is open 10-6 daily Memorial Day through Labor Day. Telephone (206) 447-4244.

Additional outdoor recreation information may be obtained from the USDA Forest Service/National Park Service/Washington State Parks Information Center, 1018 First Avenue, Seattle, WA 98104. Telephone (206) 442-1070. Hours 8-4:30 Monday-Friday.

BAINBRIDGE ISLAND

Before leaving the Seattle area, plan a ferry excursion to nearby Bainbridge Island to stroll forested paths, shady glens, a bird refuge, and special gardens in THE BLOEDEL RESERVE, former estate of the Bloedel family. About 84 of the 150 acres are second-growth forest and the remaining 66 acres were developed, over a period of some 35 years, into an integral and natural series of gardens, ponds, meadows and wildlife habitats.

Opened to the public in 1988, you may visit this private reserve and enjoy THE GLEN, with its spring and summer blooming rhododendrons and plethora of perennials, bulbs and wildflowers which bloom among thousands of gorgeous cyclamens; the JAPANESE GARDEN designed by Fujitaro Kubota which invites visitors to look outward to many vistas; the MOSS GARDEN, with its hushed and quiet spaces; the REFLECTION GARDEN, where earth and trees and sky refect in majestic simplicity; the WOODS, lush evergreens and undergrowth undisturbed except for footsteps; and, the BIRD REFUGE, transient homes among native sedges, ferns and cattails for swans, geese, ducks and red-winged blackbirds.

Reservations are required to tour the reserve and may be made by telephoning (206) 842-7052. The address is 7571 N.E. Dolphin Drive, Bainbridge Island, WA 98110. To reach The Bloedel Reserve, motor from Winslow, at the ferry landing, out Highway 305 to Seabold, then onto Dolphin Drive to the entrance. Access the Bainbridge Island ferry from downtown Seattle, following signs to the waterfront and pier shops.

Information about annual events may be obtained from the Bainbridge Island Visitors Information Center, 153 Madrone Lane N., Winslow, WA 98110. Telephone (206) 842-3700. Hours 9-5 Monday-Saturday.

For an optional route north, continue on Highway 305 through Poulsbo, a charming Scandinavian community, to Port Gamble and Kingston (at the northern tip of the Kitsap Peninsula) where a short ferry ride deposits travelers at Edmonds, on the mainland, connecting with Interstate 5 north and south. Or, from The Bloedel Reserve, retrace your route to Winslow and take the ferry there to Seattle. Ferry information may be obtained from Washington State Ferries, Pier 52, Colman Dock, Seattle, WA 98104. Telephone (206) 464-6400.

North Coast

WHIDBEY ISLAND ~ GREENBANK ~ COUPEVILLE ~ OAK HARBOR

You may want to plan a short detour to Whidbey Island before heading further north up Washington's north coast toward the Canadian border. Whidbey may be accessed from Port Townsend, on the Olympic Peninsula side, and from Mukilteo which is just north of Edmonds, off Interstate 5. Incidently, downtown Edmonds is a veritable garden of sunshine-hued blooms bursting from planters and containers at ground level as well as overflowing in pots of flowers and greenery hanging from lamp posts and storefronts.

From Mukilteo the 15-minute ferry deposits travelers at the southern tip of Whidbey Island where you may head directly north on Highway 525 or detour through Langley, a picturesque village with interesting shops and boutiques overlooking Saratoga Passage. The island also offers travelers an abundance of fine bed & breakfast inns, many with lovely perennial gardens and wide water views.

One of the best times to visit Whidbey is during the month of May when the 53-acre MEERKERK GARDENS are ablaze with over 1,500 native and hybrid species of blooming rhododendrons. Islanders Max and Ann Meerkerk have devoted countless years developing their lovely wooded oasis near Greenbank. The gardens, about 15 miles north of Langley and Freeland, are open to the public during April and May on weekends, from 10-5. Weekday visits may be arranged by appointment. The Meerkerks may be contacted at P.O. Box 154, Greenbank, WA 98253. Telephone (206) 321-6682.

Just north of Greenbank, stop at GREENBANK FARM for a tour of the largest loganberry farm in the U.S. You may picnic on the spacious grounds, have a sample of the farm's delicious loganberry liqueur, and see acres of lush loganberries under cultivation in this scenic pastoral section of the island. There are also photos and displays of early island history and gourmet picnic fixings in the retail shop. Hours are 10-4:30 daily. Telephone (206) 678-7700. Turn right on Wonn Road about .4 mile north of Greenbank to the farm's entrance.

More luscious rhododendrons, native specimens, are seen in full bloom at 160-acre RHODODENDRON PARK, located off Highway 525 and Highway 20 near the Victorian village of Coupeville. GRASSER'S HILL, on Skyview Meadows Road, is one of the best spots to find blooming wildflowers. Follow Madrona Way from Coupeville past Grasser's Lagoon to the turn-off. Also, in the village are a number of cafes and delis offering wide-angle views of the lagoon along with their tasty meals.

In Oak Harbor, the island's largest community, find lovely HOLLAND GARDENS at 500 Avenue West at 30th N.W., easily spotted because of its picturesque blue and white Dutch-style windmill. Friendly Dutch provincial flags wave merrily over thousands of blooming tulips and daffodils and nearly all of Oak Harbor bursts with these colorful flowers during the spring HOLLAND HAPPENINGS festival.

Information about other parks and nature trails on Whidbey Island may be obtained from the Greater Oak Harbor Visitors Information Center, 5506 Highway 20, P.O. Box 883, Oak Harbor, WA 98277. Telephone (206) 675-3535. Hours are 9-5 Monday-Friday and, during summer months, 10-5 on Saturday, 11-6 Sundays.

Information about South Whidbey may be obtained from The Langley Visitors Information Center, 220 First Street, P.O. Box 403, Langley, WA 98260. Telephone (206) 321-6765. Hours are 11-3 Monday through Friday.

SNOHOMISH ~ EVERETT ~ MARYSVILLE ~ STANWOOD

In historic Snohomish, just east of Mulilteo and Interstate 5, the Snohomish Garden Club usually sponsors a tour of private gardens in the area, often in early August. Those travelers interested in summer dates and details may contact the garden club for the current schedule. Telephone (206) 568-8256.

For those who love the elegant and stately peony, that herbaceous plant that goes so well with rhododendrons, iris and other spring bloomers, the A & D PEONY NURSERY may also be discovered near this historic dairy community. The address is 6808 - 180th Street S.E., Snohomish, WA 98290. Telephone (206) 668-9690. Call ahead for current hours and best time in the spring to see the luscious blooming plants.

A list of other Washington specialty nurseries may be obtained by writing for the Specialty Nursery Guide, WSU Cooperative Extension, 600-128th Street S.E., Everett, WA 98208.

Although these nurseries are often hidden in out-of-the-way places and require some persistance to locate, you may be rewarded with meeting those dedicated plantsmen and women who've often spent years and years cultivating and propagating their favorite species. You may also want to fill a basket with gourmet goodies for an impromptu picnic on these serendipitous side-trips. Delicatessens and bakeries may be found in nearly every North Coast community.

In fact, for another of those sumptuous and genial open air northwest markets, head just a few miles north of Mukilteo's ferry landing via Interstate-5 to the EVERETT PUBLIC MARKET where you may replenish that picnic basket with fresh-baked goodies, fresh fruits and vegetables as well as marvel over an eclectic assortment of local arts and crafts and fresh flowers. Open for business from 10-5:30 Monday-Saturday, the market is located at 2804 Grand Avenue in Everett.

Information about events and festivals, including the annual Salty Sea Days, may be obtained from the Everett Visitors Information Center, 1710 W. Marine View Drive, Everett, WA 98201. Telephone (206) 252-5181. Hours are 9-5 Monday-Friday. The Visitors Center is located near Everett Marina Village, a waterfront cluster of eateries and shops, all within view of Puget Sound and the boat-filled marina.

If time allows, ask directions to the north section of town – especially Colby Avenue, Grand Avenue and Rucker Street – where plum, crabapple, cherry and hawthorn trees bloom along many residential streets from late February through May. You might also inquire about the EVERETT AREA ARBORETUM, a tree-filled oasis located in Legion Park at Alverson Boulevard with remarkable colors and textures during all four seasons.

At Jennings Memorial Park in Marysville you may visit the PILCHUCK FUCHSIA SOCIETY TEST GARDEN. Walk along a shaded lath display area to view the splendid lush-blooming perennials. The garden is located at 7027 - 51st Avenue N.E. Information about the Pilchuck Fuchsia Society may be obtained from Jennings Memorial Park, City of Marysville, 514 Delta, Marysville, WA 98270. Telephone (206) 659-8477. From I-5, take exit 199 east one mile to the park.

Another small test garden may be found in Stanwood, about 20 miles north of Marysville. The NORTH CASCADES FUCHSIA SOCIETY TEST GARDEN is located in Church Creek Park just across from the high school on Highway

532. From I-5 head west from exit 212 to the park.

MOUNT VERNON ~ LA CONNER

The fertile Skagit Valley bursts into broad patchwork carpets of blooming DAFFODILS about March 15-April 15, then colorful TULIPS from about April 1-May 10, and lastly, elegant IRIS from about May 15-June 15.

Travelers hasten from throughout the northwest to see this eye-catching 1,500-acre springtime spectacle in enormous cultivated fields near Mount Vernon and LaConner. At SKAGIT VALLEY BULB FARMS you may find picnic facilities and areas to walk into the blooming fields. Telephone (206) 424-8152 for current field location. At ROOZENGAARDE, a division of WASHINGTON BULB COMPANY (the largest grower of bulbs in the U.S.), flower-lovers may find a DISPLAY GARDEN and gift shop. Open daily and located at 1587 Beaver Marsh Road. Telephone (206) 424-8531.

You can also visit WESTSHORE ACRES BULB FARM at 956 Downey Road where a large 1.5 acre DISPLAY GARDEN surrounds a stately 1886 Victorian home. Telephone (206) 466-3158. And, SKAGIT GARDENS located at 1695 Johnson Road also welcomes visitors. Telephone (206) 424-6760. The LACONNER FLATS DISPLAY GARDEN is located at 1598 Best Road. Telephone (206) 466-3821 (there is a nominal admission fee).

For the helpful SKAGIT VALLEY TULIP FESTIVAL Map & Activity Schedule, which shows clearly the current blooming field locations, write to P.O. Box 1007, Mount Vernon, WA 98273. Telephone (206) 428-8547. The schedule is crammed with interesting events— from Cleave's Greenhouse U-Pick Tulip Fields (take Exit 225 from I-5 onto Old Highway 99 South), a Tulip Festival Quilt Show, and "A Taste of Skagit" Food Fair to a "Tulip Pedal" Bicycle Ride, the Mount Vernon Kiwanis Salmon Barbecue, and Burlington's Berry Dairy Days—to mention just a few. **Note:** If you want to avoid the heavy weekend crowds and long traffic lines on narrow country roads, plan to visit during the early part of the week.

If you want to leave the colorful frenzy and fellow daffodil-tulip-iris field watchers and photography buffs for awhile, stroll through the miniature ORIENTAL GARDEN located in HILLCREST PARK in Mount Vernon. Open daily, dawn to dusk, find this quiet oasis away from the crowds at 13th and Blackburn Streets. At EDGEWATER PARK, along the Skagit River, a SCENTED GARDEN for the blind has been cultivated.

Housing more than one hundred years of nursery memorabilia, consider a visit to TILLINGHAST SEED COMPANY while you're exploring the Skagit Valley. Founded in 1885 (as Puget Sound Seed Gardens) the museum features turn-of-the-century seed bins, printing presses and seed processing equipment. From the covered porch to original wood plank floors, you'll find yourself transported into a nostalgic and charming kaleidoscope of vintage yesterdays. Find the Tillinghast Seed Company and museum at 623 Morris Street, LaConner, WA. Telephone (206) 466-3329. Hours are 9-5:30 Monday-Saturday and 11-6 Sundays, year round.

Further information about the area may be obtained from the Mount Vernon Visitors Information Center located in the Mount Vernon Mall, 325 E. College Way, Mount Vernon, WA 98273. Telephone (206) 428-8547. Hours are 8:30-5:30 Monday-Friday.

Bird-lovers may want to ask about the Skagit River Eagle Reserve, located between Marblemount and Rockport (off Highway 20 east of Sedro Woolley and Concrete). It's one of the five largest wintering bald eagle spots in the country.

Highway 20, the North Cascades Highway, is a particularly impressive drive during October's fall color spectacular. **Note:** The highway section from Ross Dam to Mazama is closed with snow during the winter months. Information about day hikes into mid-summer wildflower meadows may be obtained from North Cascades National Park headquarters, 2105 Highway 20, Sedro-Woolley, WA 98284. Telephone (206) 856-5700.

ANACORTES ~ SAN JUAN ISLANDS

Located just west of Mount Vernon, both picturesque LaConner (nestled along the Swinomish Channel) and Anacortes, about 10 miles west, serve as gateways to both Fidalgo Island and the San Juan Islands.

Those verdant island jewels are scattered like large and small emeralds between Haro Strait and British Columbia's Vancouver Island, to the west, and between Rosario Strait and Washington's north coast mainland near Bellingham, to the east. At the Anacortes ferry terminal you may drive aboard one of those wide green and white Washington State ferries for one of the best and most scenic voyages in all of the Northwest. And, the price is right as well.

Stand along the railing outside, on the sunny side, or watch from wide windows on the inside with a steaming cup of coffee or hot chocolate. Allow those madrone and oak-clothed islands, the tangy salt air and cool ocean breezes, along with the cry of sweeping gulls and other waterbirds, to seep into one's travel-weary frame. Relaxing both mind and body becomes an appealing alternative on a one-hour journey to Lopez and Orcas Island, thirty minutes farther to San Juan Island, or another hour to Sydney, B.C. on Vancouver Island.

On Orcas you may enjoy the old-fashioned Victorian gardens which surround the renovated turn-of-the-century Orcas Hotel, located just up the hill from the ferry landing. In MORAN STATE PARK, near Eastsound, you can drive to the top of Mount Constitution for a superb view of the islands which is especially memorable at sunset. Within the park are easy hiking trails through quiet green forests which skirt native plants, small streams and icy lakes.

On San Juan Island you may drive from the ferry landing at Friday Harbor (lots of shops and eateries here) out winding country roads along which grow profusions of pink wild roses and lush blackberries during summer months. You may visit English Camp and American Camp and see interesting historical displays about the island's early history. At English Camp notice the enormous, old broadleaf maples which shade the Visitor Center. Genial rangers can offer information about local wildflowers, native plants and good bird-watching areas.

You can also ask about places to whale-watch for those striking black and white Orcas who swim and play in San Juan waters all year. If time allows, plan to visit the interesting Whale Museum in Friday Harbor, near the ferry landing.

Pastoral Lopez Island also offers those nostalgic country roads with water views as well as the friendly folks who live there – everyone waves on Lopez. Information about private nurseries and rhododendron gardens on the islands, as well as annual events and festivals, may be obtained from the San Juan Islands Tourism Cooperative, Box 65, Lopez Island, WA 98261. Telephone (206) 468-3663. The staff will gladly provide information about all of the major islands in the San Juans.

Ferry information may be obtained from the Washington State ferries office in Anacortes, telephone (206) 293-3832. There are more frequent sailings from Memorial Day through Labor Day. Island-hoppers will want to pay close attention to the daily ferry schedule – most island travels, visits and activities are determined and scheduled by the ferries' arrivals and departures and the lines are longest on busy summer weekends. If possible, travel to and from the San Juan Islands during the first part of the week. The friendly and professional staff load and unload motorists and foot passengers quickly, with not a moment to spare.

Additional information may be obtained from the Anacortes Visitors Information Center, 1319 Commercial Street, Anacortes, WA 98221. Telephone (206) 293-3832. Hours are 8-5:30 daily from June through August and 9-5 Monday-Friday September through May.

BAYVIEW ~ EDISON ~ CHUCKANUT DRIVE ~ BELLINGHAM

Consider abandoning busy Interstate-5 for awhile and meandering north to Bellingham on one of the most picturesque back roads in western Skagit and Whatcom Counties—historic CHUCKANUT DRIVE.

First, head north from La Conner and Highway 20 on Bayview-Edison Road which skirts the eastern shore of Padilla Bay. At the BREAZEALE-PADILLA BAY INTERPRETIVE CENTER you may walk an .8 mile UPLAND TRAIL with self-guided learning stations where you'll learn about the unique salt and freshwater estuary environment, its native vegetation and the birds of the area.

In the massive 7500-acre seagrass 'meadow' nourished by Padilla Bay tides, many species of fish, shellfish, and invertebrates thrive. Large numbers of wintering waterfowl may be seen among the marine grasses in the bay as well as in the salt marshes along the shore. In the Interpretive Center visitors may have close encounters with friendly starfish, barnacles, crabs, sea anenomes and other creatures who inhabit the estuary. The Breazeale Interpretive Center is located at 1043 Bayview-Edison Road, Mount Vernon, WA 98273. Telephone (206) 428-1558. Hours are 10-5 Wednesday through Sundays.

Head north toward Samish Bay, veering to the right through Edison to Chuckanut Drive (Highway 11). If the Rhododendron Cafe is still open you may want to stop in for a luscious dessert. As you continue north on cliff-hugging Chuckanut Drive with its panoramic views of Samish Bay, Lummi Island, and Orcas Island (in the far distance), you'll soon pass through the Fairhaven Historic District on the southern edge of Bellingham.

You may also want to stop at FAIRHAVEN PARK to visit the lovely ROSE GARDEN located there. Hours are dawn to dusk, daily. The park is located at 107 Chuckanut Drive. For a walking tour guide of the nearby historic area which dates back to the 1880s, contact the Old Fairhaven Association, P.O. Box 4083, Bellingham, WA 98227. Telephone (206) 671-7573.

In a spectacular setting which overlooks Bellingham Bay and the San Juan Islands to the west and Mt. Baker to the east, you may stroll the scenic footpaths of 165-acre SEHOME HILL ARBORETUM, maintained jointly by the City of Bellingham and Western Washington University.

Designated a native plant arboretum some twenty years ago, visitors may access the hillside through the south entrance of the campus, off the Bill McDonald Parkway. Enjoy wide-angle panoramic views from the 40-foot sheltered observation tower atop the hill. An appointment for a group tour may be arranged by contacting the Arboretum coordinator, Western Washington University, Haggard Hall - 351, Bellingham, WA 98225. Telephone (206) 676-3627. Pick up a brochure which contains a trail map and information about the arboretum's geology, wildlife and plants at the local Visitors Information Center.

Another rose collection may be viewed at CORNWALL PARK ROSE GARDEN located at 3424 Meridian Street. Hours are dawn to dusk, daily. Further information about the area's parks and gardens, as well as the arboretum, may also be obtained from the City of Bellingham, Parks and Recreation Department, 210 Lottie Street, Bellingham, WA 98225. Telephone (206) 676-6985.

At BIG ROCK GARDENS & NURSERY visitors may stroll the landscaped grounds and nursery area filled with a large selection of annuals and perennials. An annual Japanese Garden Tour is held on the Sunday following Mother's Day and group tours of the gardens and nursery may be made calling ahead several days. Open early April through mid-October, Wednesday through Sundays. The address is 2900 Sylvan Street, Bellingham, WA 98226. Telephone (206) 734-4167.

Information about annual events and festivals, along with a copy of the Sehome Hill Arboretum map, may be obtained from the Bellingham/Whatcom County Visitors Information Center, 904 Potter Street, Bellingham, WA 98226. Telephone (206) 671-3990. Hours are 9-6 daily Memorial Day through Labor Day and 8:30-5:30 daily during the remainder of the year.

MOUNT BAKER

Those flower-lovers exploring the North Coast region during mid to late summer may want to plan a wilderness wildflower sidetrip to Mount Baker, Washington's northernmost crown in the Cascade Mountain's volcanic chain of high snowcapped peaks. Driving on Highway 542 from Bellingham, stop at the Glacier Public Service Center about 25 miles northeast of Deming for maps and information about the most accessible day hikes into wildflower meadows near Mount Baker and Mt. Shuksan. The Center's address is Glacier, WA 98244. Telephone (206) 599-2714.

Ask here about areas along the scenic Canyon Creek Road where you may picnic with Mt. Baker, Coleman Glacier and Mt. Shuksan looking over your shoulder. Or, weather permitting, follow Highway 542 as it winds high along the northeast flank of Mt. Baker to a spectacular panoramic viewpoint and the ski area, at road's end.

You'll be driving into some of the most remote areas of the North Cascades where forest giants of western red cedar, hemlock and Douglas fir clothe deep valleys, where tangled growths of vine maple, stinging nettles and devil's club hide along old Indian trails and where glacier crevasses, permanent snowfields and sheer-walled cliffs of ice still challenge the mountaineer. A list of natural history books, helpful maps and native plant and wildlife pamphlets about the North Cascades may be obtained from the North Cascades National Park headquarters, 2105 Highway 20, Sedro-Woolley, WA 98284. Telephone (206) 856-5700. Hours are 8-4:30 Sunday-Thursday and 8-6 Friday-Saturday.

FERNDALE ~ EVERSON

One of the most unique experiences on your North Coast horticultural itinerary may be the TENNANT LAKE NATURAL HISTORY INTERPRETIVE CENTER and HOVANDER HOMESTEAD PARK, located near Ferndale. Stop first at the historic NEILSEN HOUSE to enjoy the well-tended annual and perennial garden which nestles along the picket-fenced entrance to this early home which now serves as the interpretive center for the environment in and around Tennant Lake.

After feasting your eyes on the lovely perennial beds, stroll the handicap accessible paved pathway which meanders through the nearby FRAGRANCE GARDEN. From aromatic Angelica, herbal Comfrey, licorice-flavored Fennel and scented Lavender to peppery tasting Nasturtium, minty Penny Royal, lemon-scented Southernwood and sweetly scented Wooly Lambs Ear, the Fragrance Garden plantings are the dedicated cooperative project of both the Chuckanut

District Garden Clubs and the Whatcom County Park and Recreation Board.
Next, find the grassy path out to the Tennant Lake boardwalk, just beyond the old-fashioned wooden observation tower (good spot to bird-watch). The sturdy boardwalk zigzags in a .5 mile loop out onto the shallow lake and along its marshy shore, allowing plenty of opportunity to observe close-up the fascinating marsh and plantlife growing in this natural habitat. Fat-leaved pond lilies, willows and other water-loving native plants thrive in thick clusters on both sides of the boardwalk and there are good places to see some of the nearly 200 species of birds who rest here on their twice-yearly migration along the Pacific Flyway.

And finally, when you head out of the parking area back toward Ferndale, take the first left and drive west on the narrow paved drive into the historic Hovander Homestead Park. A bed of old-fashioned late summer dahlias blooms near the entrance to this 60-acre farm developed by Hakan and Louisa Hovander at the turn of the century. The family emmigrated from Sweden and were among the second generation of pioneers to settle the river valleys and cedar forests surrounding Puget Sound.

Master gardeners from the Ferndale area now cultivate and maintain a large vegetable garden which can be seen along the north side of the well-preserved Victorian style home built by the Hovanders (Hakan was an architect). The home is now on the Historic Register. Wander the grounds and enjoy also the old-fashioned flower garden on the south side of the house. Often you can see the farm's horses over by the huge red barn. Trails meander down to the banks of the Nooksack River and there are both sunny and shady places to picnic in this lovely place.

Long serving as the Hovander family home, son Otis passed ownership of the homestead to the Whatcom County Park and Recreation Board in 1971 for complete restoration as a county park and living history farm. For further information about annual events and festivals contact Hovander Homestead Park, 5299 Nielsen Road, Ferndale, WA 98248. Telephone (206) 384-3444. The house and grounds open in May of each year.

Information about guided bird walks at Tennant Lake may be obtained from the park manager, Whatcom County Park and Recreation Board, 3373 Mount Baker Highway, Bellingham, WA 98226. Telephone (206) 733-2900 or (206) 592-5161.

Access the Tennant Lake Nature Area, Nielson House Intrepretive Center, Fragrance Garden and Hovander Homestead from Hovander Road, turning left just beyond the railroad underpass (toward city center) and following signs to both areas.

Information about other annual events and festivals may be obtained from the Ferndale Visitors Information Center, 5640 Riverside Drive, Ferndale, WA 98248. Telephone (206) 384-3042. Hours are 8-5 daily from June through August and 10-3 Monday-Friday during the remainder of the year. Access Ferndale from I-5 at exit 262. The visitor's center, located in the log cabin to the west of the freeway, will also have information about the Mount Baker Wilderness to the east.

In nearby Everson, just east of Ferndale, iris-lovers may want to search out INGERSOLL IRIS GARDEN located at 4288 Deming Road. You'll find over 450 different kinds of irises in this lovely private garden-nursery. Call ahead for current hours, directions and prime bloom times, usually in mid-May to mid-June. Telephone (206) 592-5800.

BIRCH BAY ~ BLAINE ~ PEACE ARCH PARK

Heading north again on Interstate 5 toward the Washington-Canadian border you may want to plan a bird-watching stop at TERRELL CREEK ESTUARY, located near the south entrance of Birch Bay State Park. In 40 acres of shallow marsh flourishing with beach grass are the watery hiding places of many beaver, opossum and muskrat families. Along the .4 mile nature trail you may also spot some 300 bird species, including the great blue heron which often stands guard within sight of the binoculars.

Semiahmoo Indian families once lived in this area as well, gathering shellfish, waterfowl and edible plants from the shores of Birch Bay and the marsh. A botanist with Captain George Vancouver's 1792 expedition into Puget Sound gave the bay its present name. Those who visit the park may enjoy crabbing, clamming, shore fishing, beachcombing and picnicking, just as did those early Indian families who lived here long before pioneers headed west and settled the area, in the 1850s. The Terrell Creek Estuary and Birch Bay State Park may be accessed from I-5 at exit 266. Head west on Grandview to Helwig, then right to Birch Bay State Park, 5105 Helwig Road, Blaine, WA 98230.

Weather permitting plan a horticultural-picnic stop at the Washington-Canadian border, taking exit 276 at Blaine along Second Street to PEACE ARCH STATE HERITAGE AREA. Here you may lunch and stroll among the luscious roses, rainbow-colored perennials, sunshine-bright annuals, graceful trees and sweeping lawns of this stunning border park.

Choose from many scenic picnic spots, most with panoramic views of Drayton Harbor, the Semiahmoo Light House, Boundary Bay, and the Strait of Georgia beyond. In fact, the best wide-angle views are seen from this U.S. section of the border park. Atop the massive white Peace Arch, which was built by pioneer businessman Sam Hill, fly the U.S. and Canadian flags. The massive arch reaches skyward silhouetted against the sparkling waters to the west, reflecting a gesture of love and friendship to all who pass.

The Peace Arch State Heritage Area Park is open daily from dawn to dusk. Further information may be obtained from Washington State Parks and Recreation Commission, 7150 Cleanwater Lane, KY-11, Olympia, WA 98504. Telephone (206) 753-2027. Picnic makings may be obtained from local delis and bakeries in Ferndale or Blaine.

However, if time doesn't allow and you're heading into Canada during the busy summer months, move into the long lines which inch north toward the Customs stations. Everyone except the driver can walk through the marvelous gardens, then rendezvous at the Customs station or parking area beyond.

The 20 acres of combined gardens, including the lovely Canadian PEACE ARCH PROVINCIAL PARK, are filled with thousands of colorful annuals, shrubs and trees. You'll notice especially the more formal plantings in the Canadian section of the park. To picnic on the Canadian side take the second left after going through customs and drive about a block back to the park entrance.

Travelers may continue north to Vancouver, B.C., or detour west on Highway 17 to Tsawwassen and the 90-minute ferry to Swartz Bay and Victoria, on Vancouver Island. Ferry information may be obtained from the Blaine Visitor Information Center, 900 Peace Portal Drive, P.O. Box Q, Blaine, WA 98230. Telephone (206) 332-4544. Hours are 9-5 daily.

Cascades and Central Region

WALLACE FALLS ~ SKYKOMISH ~ STEVENS PASS

For a close-up encounter with the rugged and scenic Cascade Mountains, along the route to several botanic areas in the high central and eastern regions of the Evergreen State, head east on Highway 2 from Everett. You'll pass by lowland towns like Snohomish, Monroe, and Sultan before reaching the foothills communities of Startup and Gold Bar.

Consider a brief stop at Wallace Falls State Park, about two miles east of Gold Bar, for a panoramic view of the verdant Skykomish Valley from high atop 300-foot WALLACE FALLS. The trail to the top of the falls climbs about 1,200 feet but the hike is worth it for the breathtaking wide angle views of the southern section of Snoqualmie National Forest. To the north are the rugged Glacier Peak Wilderness and North Cascades National Park.

About 10 miles further, SUNSET FALLS can be seen near a 1,024 foot fishway which allows the watery creatures to safely navigate around the scenic but treacherous falling water. Access from Highway 2 at the sign for the fishway about 10 miles east of Gold Bar. To the south notice wispy Bridal Veil Falls about half way up the sheer north face of craggy 5,979-foot Mt. Index.

Along the drive to the top of 4,061-foot Stevens Pass you may see white water rafters bobbing on the Skykomish River and eagles soaring high over second-growth Douglas fir forests. Near Skykomish, a mountain timber community, you may want to plan a picnic stop at DECEPTION FALLS. For picnic fixings, plan a stop before heading into the mountains, perhaps at the Cadyville Bakery & Deli in Snohomish, just east of Everett. Or, stop at the vintage hotel in Skykomish (constructed in 1904) which has a restaurant and lounge. Telephone (206) 677-2345.

Continue uphill on the wide Highway 2 asphalt ribbon where you'll soon view a section of the 7.8 mile long Cascade railroad tunnel, a massive project which was completed in 1929; then, on up toward the timberline to the top of 4,061-foot Stevens Pass.

If it's late in the day, you may notice elongated shadows moving across the forested mountains, hills and valleys drenched with old sol's late afternoon golden hues. Driving into the Cascade Mountains is an unforgettable experience regardless of the season and similar high mountain panoramas can be seen via Highway 20, to the north, and Interstate 90 and Highway 12 to the south.

Those mint-green and misty Springs, warm dark green Summers, yellow and orange-hued Autumns, or crystal-white snowy Winters show off Mother Nature at her high altitude, alpine best.

LEAVENWORTH ~ CASHMERE

Drop down another 20 miles or so through scenic Tumwater Canyon to Leavenworth, at an elevation of 1,164 feet. This charming Bavarian-style community, cradled by forested mountains, is virtually filled with lush hanging flower baskets and over flowing window boxes from early spring into late fall — from colorful petunias and geraniums to alyssum and daisies, along with an assortment of trailing ivys and other greenery. Leavenworth metamorphosed from a dying lumber and railroad town, in the early 1960s, into a friendly and attractive flower-filled tourist community — greeting "Wilkommen" to thousands of visitors from all over the world to its year round festivals.

Enjoy strolling the picturesque downtown area – along gable-roofed storefronts sporting Bavarian-style colors and old-fashioned stencilling and lettering (along with all those colorful flowers), past delectable delis and bakeries, and into shops offering an assortment of exquisite glassware, toys and gifts from Germany, Austria, Scandanavia and Switzerland.

During the summer months artists and craftsmen and women display their wares in Central Park and often you may hear Bavarian melodies played by costumed musicians gathered in the park's old-fashioned gazebo. During special celebrations both friendly locals and visitors alike can be seen dancing the Polka and Waltzing in the streets.

Information about local events and festivals may be obtained from the Leavenworth Visitors Information Center, 703 U.S. Highway 2 (P.O. Box 327), Leavenworth, WA 98826. Telephone (509) 548-5807. Hours 9-5 Monday through Saturday. Ask about nature walks and wildflower and photo treks into Tumwater Canyon and Icicle Canyon which are often offered during the summer months. A lovely picnic spot may be found at Waterfront Park, near 8th and Main Street. It nestles alongside the Wenatchee River, with a view of nearby Blackbird Island. Icicle Creek joins the river just south of the park.

In nearby Cashmere an Early American theme prevails in the picturesque downtown area. The folks here, often seen dancing in the streets during their local festivals as well, wear long gingham dresses or jeans and cowboy hats in contrast to the alpine Bavarian dress worn by the Leavenworth folks.

A canopy of pink and white blossoms fills the rich farmland between Cashmere and Leavenworth during early spring – from long rows of apple and pear trees as well as apricot and peach trees. You'll find friendly growers, like those at Duncan Orchards, Prey's Fruit Barn and Bob's Apple Barrel offering tree-fresh fruit, honey and dried fruits as well as natural juices, cider, syrups, jams, butters and Washington wines. Discover them near Cashmere.

Visitors may also tour the local commercial kitchen of Aplets and Cotlets, that fruit and nut confection produced for over 60 years in the Evergreen State. You'll also get to taste a scrumptious fruity sample, freshly made. Hours 8-12 and 1-5 Monday-Friday and 10-4 most weekends from June to December. Telephone (509) 782-2191. And, chocolate lovers may watch the making of sumptuous old world-style chocolates at Suswarren Bavarian Chocolatiers, also located in Cashmere. Telephone (509) 782-4218 for current hours.

WENATCHEE ~ ROCKY REACH DAM ~ LAKE CHELAN

The lush forested Cascade Mountains give way to the high desert of Central Washington, revealing rugged brownish-tan hills clothed in sagebrush, juniper and other arid native plants and trees. Water from the Columbia River nourishes thousands of acres of fruit orchards in the valley and Wenatchee is referred to as the "Apple Capitol." There is even a local historical museum devoted to the crunchy fruit and its history, including ingenious turn of the century contraptions for harvesting and squeezing juices.

On a sagebrush-covered rocky hill near Wenatchee, early orchardist Herman H. Ohme one day surveyed his hilltop domain with its superb view of the valley and decided to create an alpine garden next to the sky. The year was 1929. Working on weekends and after hours from the orchard business over the next 10 years, the family hauled tons of rocks, dug out scores of sagebrush, fashioned pools and ponds, laid out paths and steps and planted hundreds of trees, ferns and alpine plants.

By 1939 Herman and Ruth Ohme, along with two small sons, had created a two-acre alpine garden atop their rocky hill. Herman built a log picnic shelter, a wishing well and a stone lookout. Interested friends and community members urged the Ohmes to allow visits to their alpine paradise and soon the gardens were officially opened to the public. When Herman passed away in 1971, son Gordon and his wife along with Ruth, continued the planting and the gardens expanded another five acres under his direction. A carefully engineered automatic sprinkling system was installed to water the gardens at night.

Some fifty years later travelers still flock to OHME GARDENS, Herman's lush and green alpine garden next to the sky. From atop the Ohme's perpendicular basalt outcropping you may have the widest views of the lush, irrigated Wenatchee Valley and sparkling Columbia River as well as those sagebrush-covered tan and ochre hills in the distance.

With sturdy shoes you can easily walk the stepping stones and narrow flagstone paths which shoelace in and around shady fern-lined pools, large ponds reflecting sky and clouds, and immense boulders which shelter low-growing alpine plantings and assymetrical sweeps of green lawn.

In addition to more than 15 varieties of native evergreens gathered from the Cascade Mountains, you may see many varieties of sedum (dragon blood and yellow sedum predominate in the upper garden section), lavender creeping thyme, white and pink creeping phlox, alyssums, dianthus and many species of fern planted near pools shaded by western red cedar, mountain hemlock, grand fir, Douglas fir and alpine fir.

There are quiet, contemplative places to sit and survey Herman Ohme's hilltop kingdom. Perhaps words best describing a unique and beautiful alpine garden such as this may be those from O. Sitwell in The Garden Book, "Green is the clue to creating a garden. . .the most beautiful gardens in the world show few flowers. They depend for their beauty on trees, stone and water, and on the prospect which their terraces frame. . .created for rest in cool surroundings, for idleness and sauntering and imaginative thought, for love and a sense of mystery."

Find these special gardens located at 3327 Ohme Road, Wenatchee, WA 98801. Hours 9-dusk daily from April 15 through October 15. Nominal admission fee. Access from Highway 2 about three miles north of Wenatchee, near the junction of Highway 97. The gardens are not wheelchair accessible and visitors are advised to wear sturdy shoes.

Also near the junction you may want to plan a stop at the Washington Apple Commission Visitors Center where you'll see interesting exhibits, visual displays, and films about the apple industry. You can also select your own fresh juicy apple as a welcome gift to munch or add to the picnic basket. From Golden Delicious, Red Delicious and Winesap to Rome Beauty, Newton and Granny Smith, nearly one-half of all the fresh apples grown in the U.S. come from the fertile valleys of the Evergreen State. The Visitors Center is located at 2900 Euclid Avenue (P.O. Box 18), Wenatchee, WA 98807. Telephone (509) 663-9600.

Information about annual events and festivals, including the APPLE BLOSSOM FESTIVAL, may be obtained from the Wenatchee Area Visitors Information Center, 2 South Chelan Street (P.O. Box 850), Wenatchee, WA 98801. Telephone (509) 662-4774. Hours are 9-5 Monday through Friday.

If time allows continue about 10 miles north on Highway 97 to visit the ROCKY REACH DAM GARDENS. The sunny picnic area overlooks immaculate sweeping lawns, children's play area and a lush PERENNIAL GARDEN. Baskets of colorful flowers hang from the eaves of the community building. On PETUNIA ISLAND over 5,000 of the dainty pastel-hued annuals are planted each year in a formal though lush sculptured design surrounding the fish ladders.

In the DAHLIA GARDEN thrive over 180 varieties of the striking flowers from around the world. And, the garden's most striking planting, the American flag — OLD GLORY GARDEN — gracefully unfurled in the lawn above the Perennial Garden in red, white and blue annuals. Actually, the best view of the garden flag is from the ladder attached to the children's slide. Plan a picnic at Rocky Reach Dam Gardens if time allows along with an hour or so to stroll and enjoy this lovely oasis alongside the Columbia River.

The gardens are maintained by the Chelan County Public Utlity District with offices in Wenatchee. The 4,800 foot long dam has a spillway of 750 feet. Eleven generators produce over a million kilowatts of power for Wenatchee Valley area residential and commercial consumers. The grounds and gardens at Rocky Reach Dam are among the finest of any utility visited in the entire Northwest.

A pleasant side excursion from Lake Chelan, some 28 miles north of the dam, is the 12-mile MANSON SCENIC DRIVE which meanders through some of the region's finest golden and red delicious apple orchards, around three small lakes and past an old Indian burial ground. The trees blossom around the end of May and harvest takes place during Indian summer, in the fall.

For one of the best inland lake trips into the eastern portion of rugged North Cascades National Park, ask about the 55-mile boat trip on Lake Chelan into remote Stehekin. This is wildlife and birdlife watching at its most convenient — from the decks of "Lady of the Lake." The season runs from April 15 to October 15 and the all-day trip departs from Chelan at 8:30 and returns around 6 p.m. The nature trails and hikes into alpine wildflower meadows from Stehekin are fairly long and more rugged than in other parts of the state. A brochure, Day Hiking in Stehekin, is available from the Ranger Station in Chelan.

You may also fly in a floatplane the 55 miles into Stehekin, soaring with the eagles, but there are no roads into this wilderness area. Chelan Airways may be contacted at (509) 682-5555. Actually, the Campbell House (now a restaurant) in Chelan was a stagecoach stop for early travelers heading to primitive cabins and resorts up the lake in the early 1900s. They arrived by stagecoach following a steamboat trip up the Columbia River, then waited for the final day-long leg of the trip — another boatride up the lake to Stehekin.

For those nature-lovers who want to get way off the beaten path and experience the primitive scenic beauty, native plants, wildflowers and birdlife of the remote Chelan National Recreation Area and southern section of North Cascades National Park, a well-coordinated guided pack trip from Stehekin may be an appealing option. Information may be obtained from Stehekin Valley Ranch, Box 36, Stehekin, WA 98852. There is no telephone service into Stehekin but messages may be left at the ranch's answering service. Telephone (509) 682-4677. The season runs from April 15 to October 15.

The natural and geologic history of Lake Chelan has its roots in the Ice Age when glaciers gouged this 1,500-foot deep narrow fiord-like finger some 55 miles into the heart of the northern Washington wilderness. It is one of the nation's deepest freshwater lakes.

Information about annual events and festivals may be obtained from the Lake Chelan Visitors Information Center, 102 East Johnson (P.O. Box 216), Chelan, WA 98816. Telephone (509) 682-2022. Hours are 8-5 daily.

Information about natural areas north of Chelan and Pateros may be obtained from the Oroville/Washington State Visitor Information Center, 1728 Main Street, Oroville, WA 98844. Telephone (509) 476-2739. Hours are 9-5 daily about May 19 through October 1. Ask about BIG TREE BOTANICAL AREA near Lost Lake which offers an easy 15-minute walk to large specimens of native Western larch, often called tamarack. This elegant ladylike conifer has needles which turn lime-yellow in the fall and drop to the forest floor. The tamarack's iridescent autumn hues constrast vividly with the darker green Ponderosa pine, Lodgepole pine and manzanita which often grow in the same climate zone.

VANTAGE ~ ELLENSBURG ~ YAKIMA ~ TRI CITIES

To the south, about 30 miles from Wenatchee via Highway 28, you may walk an interpretive trail at GINKGO PETRIFIED FOREST and explore an interesting Interpretive Center near Wanapum State Park. One of the most unique fossil forests in the world, and similar to Lava Cast Forest near Bend in Central Oregon, the trees here were entomed and petrified in molten lava eons ago. In addition to petrified ginkgo, you'll see petrified hickory, fir, sycamore, oak and pine. Located near Vantage, the park is also near the Columbia River and offers both camping and picnicking areas. Telephone (509) 856-2700. Hours are 10-6 daily from May 13 through September 15.

In the Yakima Valley area travelers may cruise winding country roads through thousands of acres of blooming apple trees in the spring. Or, take a guided tour of the area from a restored 1906 vintage automobile. Join a tour into the Yakima River Canyon led by local rockhounds to learn about the geological formations and native plants and wildflowers of the valley. Try Indian fry bread and buffalo burgers at the restaurant located on the 7-acre Yakima Nation Cultural Center in nearby Toppenish. And, tree-lovers will want plan a stroll through both the YAKIMA AREA ARBORETUM in Yakima and the CENTRAL WASHINGTON UNIVERSITY ARBORETUM in Ellensburg.

Information about annual events and festivals may be obtained from the Yakima Valley Visitors Information Center, 10 North 8th Street (P.O. Box 124), Yakima, WA 98907. Telephone (509) 575-1300. Hours are 8-5 Monday-Friday and 9-1 on Saturdays, Memorial Day through Labor Day. Nature lovers may want to ask directions to MOXEE BOG, a spring-fed nature preserve near the Yakima River where a rare Monarch butterfly species may be seen. **Note:** Add also to your Yakima area itinerary from the Columbia River Gorge section, page 36.

Helpful information may also be obtained from the Ellensburg Visitors Information Center, 436 North Sprague Street, Ellensburg, WA 98926. Telephone (509) 925-3137. Hours are 8-5 Monday-Friday.

In the Tri-Cities area herb-lovers may want to investigate the miniature herb garden at PERSEUS GOURMET PRODUCTS where two sisters produce and sell dried herbs and herb and fruit vinegars. They are located at 1426 E. Third Avenue, Kennewick, WA 99335. Telephone (509) 582-2434. Hours are 7-4 weekdays.

Information about local nurseries, Farmer's Markets, and wineries may be obtained from the Tri-Cities Visitors Information Center, 6951 Grandridge Boulevard, Kennewick, WA 99336. Telephone (509) 735-8486. Hours are 8:30-5 Monday-Friday.

Eastern Region

CHENEY ~ SPOKANE

Heading east toward the Spokane area you may want to plan a bird-watching stop at the TURNBULL NATIONAL WILDLIFE REFUGE located near Cheney. The refuge is a fine example of an area reclaimed from draining and development which was undertaken in the early 1920s. Through the efforts of naturalists, sportsmen and interested community members the lakes and marshes have been restored much as they were originally.

Before the early 1900s settlement, thousands of ducks, geese and water-birds both nested here or stopped to rest on their twice-yearly Pacific Flyway journey. Native Spokane Indians came to the lakes and marshes to collect roots and herbs such as purple camas, wild onion, bitteroot, kouse and kinnikinick.

The refuge is managed so that all types of birdlife and wildlife can again live harmoniously in this special place. You'll see ducks, geese and tundra swans with offspring in tow during the spring. Diving ducks like Redheads, Canvasbacks and Scaup busily paddle and search for marsh tidbits. The large Canada geese who stop to rest strut about as well.

Stop at the refuge headquarters for a helpful map which pinpoints the PINE CREEK AUTO TOUR ROUTE and several self-guided paths and trails. PINE LOOP TRAIL and HEADQUARTERS TRAIL are easily accessed from the visitor's center. A photoblind may be used near the Kepple Overlook. There are areas open to horseback riding as well.

Additional information may be obtained from the Refuge Manager, Turnbull National Wildlife Refuge, Route 3, Box 385, Cheney, WA 99004. Telephone (509) 235-4723. Access the refuge from Interstate 90 via Highway 395 or from Spokane via Highway 195, both toward Cheney.

Another good bird-watching area may be found at LITTLE SPOKANE NATURAL AREA just north of Spokane on Highway 291. A large heron rookery comes alive during April and can be spied with binoculars from the easy two mile trail along the river's north bank. Audubon Society volunteers are often on hand to point out good viewing areas, through April.

In downtown Spokane visitors enjoy strolling through RIVERFRONT PARK which skirts the bubbling Spokane River. The 100-acre park was the site of the 1974 World Exposition. Ride the vintage Carrousel constructed at the turn of the century which, until 1968, resided in Spokane's Natatorium Park. There are numerous places to see the cascading river and observe birdlife, walk through grassy meadow-lawns and see attractive garden displays of colorful summer annuals as well as baskets of flowers hanging from old-fashioned lamp posts. For a safe high-altitude view of the park and Spokane Falls try the Gondola Sky-ride.

Information about events and activities in the park may be obtained from Riverfront Park, North 507 Howard Street, Spokane, WA 99201. Telephone (509) 456-5512. Riverfront Park Fun Phone (509) 456-5511. The park is located between Monroe and Division Streets in the downtown area, with parking areas along Spokane Falls Boulevard and Mallon Street.

Near the downtown area the lovely JOHN A. FINCH ARBORETUM offers a quiet respite from the bustling activity at Riverfront Park. The arboretum was planned in 1907 when the Spokane Park Board designated a mile long strip along

Garden Springs Creek and eventually purchased the property from early pioneer businessmen John A. Finch and D.H. Dwight.

Some of the oldest trees in the Arboretum were planted by Dwight around his summer cottage, "Brookside." In 1949 planting began in earnest, with 49 specimens comprising 10 genera and 23 species. You may now see over 2,000 labeled trees and shrubs representing over 600 species.

Early spring brings Arboretum visitors to LILAC LANE, a luscious collection of over 75 varieties in varying shades of lavender, lilac, purple, pink and white. Then, walk up along the creek through the glorious magnolias and dogwoods to the FLOWERING CRABAPPLE SECTION and the COREY RHODODEN-DRON GLEN. Stroll the quiet paths through the glen which meander along Garden Springs Creek where colorful rhodies and azaleas bloom in bright patches among native trees and shrubs.

You may also enjoy the Hawthorn Section, the Conifer Section, the Maple Section and the TOUCH & SEE NATURE TRAIL designed for those who are visually impaired.

The John A. Finch Arboretum may be accessed from downtown Spokane by heading west on Second Avenue to Sunset Highway, then on Sunset past Government Way to the entrance, just before 'F' Street. The address is West 3404 Woodland Boulevard, Spokane, WA. Telephone (509) 747-2894. Hours dawn to dusk daily. A helpful map is available at an information stand near the parking area.

In spite of eastern Washington's higher altitude, icy cold winters and short growing season, one of the most elegant garden collections in the region may be found in Spokane's MANITO PARK. Maintained by the City of Spokane Park and Recreation Department, Manito Park offers four separate gardens and a glass conservatory.

The lovely ROSE HILL GARDENS are situated on a four acre hill area overlooking the other gardens. Formal beds of 1500 bushes, representing over 150 varieties, are cared for by the Parks Department in cooperation with the Spokane Rose Society. You'll also see informal beds and borders of old-fashioned scented roses.

Walk down the path to the JOEL E. FERRIS PERENNIAL GARDEN, a three-acre oasis of lawns and large perennial beds. From yellow and white Yarrows, creamy white and pink Astilbes, towering Shasta daisies, cheery Coreopsis with their large yellow flowers, and mounds of long-stemmed red, orange and yellow Geum to rosy purple Liatris, magenta blossomed Lychnis, old-fashioned spiky clumps of red and pink Lythrum, and Veronicas in shades of pinks and reds and bluish-purples.

You may also wander past striking borders of golden and coppery-orange blossoming heleniums; colorful hellebores, solidagos and cosmos; salvias, poppies, spiky liatris and phlox; daisy-like pink echinacea, aconitum and vibrant basket-of-gold; and, textured Hostas, bright-eyed daisies, phlox, and lacy Thalictrum.

When you've had an eyeful of the luscious perennials, wander over to the DUNCAN FORMAL GARDENS just opposite GAISER CONSERVATORY. The best sweeping view of this symmetrically balanced three-acre garden are from atop the stone steps next to the conservatory. Sculptured beds of colorful annuals placed in broad sweeps of lawn are bisected by a formal walkway leading to a circular central planting and a formal fountain just beyond. Well-clipped rounded shrubs and conifers clipped into formal cone shapes march along both borders.

Along the west perimeter of this elegant 18th century-style garden tall and stately stalks of deep purple, blue and white delphinium formed a long eye-catching border which constrasted with more than a dozen dark green Douglas fir towering protectively just beyond.

Next, stroll through the Gaiser Conservatory for a look at large tropical plants and trees growing in the center dome area. In the two adjoining wings you can see cyclamen, fuchsias, and begonias as well as poinsettias, chrysanthemums and spring flowering bulb displays.

And lastly, find the NISHINOMIYA JAPANESE GARDEN just beyond the LILAC GARDEN and the OLD-FASHIONED ROSE GARDEN, below Rose Garden Hill.

Symbolizing a friendship between Spokane and its Sister City, Nishinomiya, this lovely oasis is cared for and maintained jointly by the Spokane Nishinomiya Japanese Garden Association and the City of Spokane Parks and Recreation Department.

Influenced by Eastern philosphies, a Japanese garden is considered a creative art form which grows as an intimate reminder that nature can inspire both peace and tranquility in the viewer. The stones, water, plants, statues, pagodas, lanterns and sitting spaces are used by the landscape artist to develop the overall garden space.

All objects in the garden are set either singly, in two's, or in odd numbers. Usually one large shape is balanced with two smaller objects. The garden landscape artist prunes, places and manipulates the garden elements always with an asymmetrical rather than a formal balance as the ultimate goal.

Notice the three vertical stones in the central pond; they suggest cranes or ships at sea. The large flat stone may be a tortise or an island. According to ancient legends, the crane (said to live for 1,000 years) and the tortise (said to live for 10,000 years) together represent long life and eternal youth.

The bright vermillion curved bridge over the pond is borrowed from the Chinese who often used it as a central architectural feature. Ceremonies were often performed on or paraded over the Ceremonial Bridge. The small waterfall flows from the rising sun, in the East, to the setting sun, in the West, and is said to be purified in this east-west journey.

Considered a living work of art, visitors enjoy a quiet and contemplative stroll along the self-guided path of this lovely Japanese garden.

Manito Park, which also offers picnic areas and a children's playground, is located at 4 West 21st Avenue and there is no admission charge. The gardens are open to the public 8-dusk daily from May to November. Further information may be obtained from the City of Spokane Parks and Recreation Department, West 4 - 21st Avenue, Spokane, WA 99203. Telephone (509) 456-4331. Department staff can also provide a contact number for the annual summer tour of local private gardens which is sponsored by the Associated Garden Clubs of Spokane. It's usually offered on the second Sunday in July.

Information about annual events and festivals, including the annual LILAC FESTIVAL, may be obtained from the Spokane Regional Visitors Bureau, West 926 Sprague Avenue, Spokane, WA 99204. Telephone (509) 747-3230. Hours are 8:30-5 daily during summer months. You may want to ask about times and dates for the local Farmer's Open-air Market held near Riverside Park during summer months.

IDAHO

A Sampling

f time allows on your trek into eastern Washington, there are several botanic and horticultural surprises as well as natural areas worth a place on your excursions into nearby Idaho, the Gem State. This is a region of rugged mountains, rushing rivers and high alpine lakes and meadows as well as rolling farmland, small cities and towns offering tree and flower-filled parks, arboreta and gardens.

COEUR D'ALENE ~ SANDPOINT

First, head northeast of Spokane and Coeur d'Alene on Highway 95 to Sandpoint, a distance of about 52 miles. Just outside of Sandpoint, which nestles on the northern shore where the Pend Oreille River meets Lake Pend Oreille, a private herb garden jewel is found tucked away like a vintage gem hidden in grandmother's cedar chest.

THE PEACEABLE KINGDOM is one of those pleasant horticultural surprises one finds only by being in the right place at the right time. Surrounding the house and workshop areas are the most wonderful herb gardens, including the Shakespeare Garden, a Pioneer Culinary Herb Garden, the Butterfly and Bees Garden, and the large Vegetable Garden.

The master gardener and queen of this peaceful, hidden domain near Rapid Lightening Creek is Lois Wythe. She and her helpful gardening friends offer, among other things, "Wednesdays at the Farm" from May through August.

In these gardening workshops planned especially for beginners, eager students may learn about planting methods for annual herbs, perennial herbs, vegetables, berries and orchard crops. They learn about permaculturing, polyculture and edible landscaping. Later, they study gathering, preserving and using the fresh bounty. And, finally, participants learn how to prepare the garden for the winter season (which comes early in northern Idaho).

Other workshops at the farm during the spring, summer and early fall months may cover such topics as making berry and herbal vinegars, "all you ever wanted

The Peaceable Kingdom Herb Garden, Sandpoint, Idaho

to know about growing, drying and using everlasting flowers plus edible flowers and their culinary uses," gathering seeds, and using pods, cones, lichens, mosses and other natural materials for home decorations, crafts and gifts.

All sorts of marvelous herbal surprises and dried flowers can be ordered from Lois' newsy quarterly newsletter. Hopefully two new herb teas will continue to be available – 'Autumn Raspberry,' a blend of hibiscus flowers, spearmint and raspberry leaves and 'Citrus Soother' which combines lemon verbena, chamomile, orange peel, cloves and cinnamon. To get on the mailing list send your request (along with a small donation for postage) to The Peaceable Kingdom, 8375 Rapid Lightning Creek Road, Sandpoint, ID 83864. Telephone (208) 263-8038. Call ahead to make an appointment to visit this special private garden.

Information about annual events and festivals in the area, and the local Farmer's Open Air Market, may be obtained from the Greater Sandpoint Visitors Information Center, P.O. Box 928, Sandpoint, ID 98964. Telephone (208) 263-2161.

LAKE COEUR D'ALENE ~ HARRISON ~ ST. MARIES

Within just minutes of Coeur d'Alene are two scenic drives worth considering for your eastern Washington and northern Idaho itinerary. Pick up picnic or snack fixings in Coeur d'Alene first, then head east on Interstate 90 to exit 22 to access the LAKE COEUR D'ALENE SCENIC ROUTE along Highway 97. You'll meander along the eastern shore of Lake Coeur d'Alene toward Harrison and St. Maries. The narrow winding asphalt ribbon hugs craggy forested basalt bluffs on the one side while offering wide views of the lake on the other, especially grand at sunset.

For spring wildflowers, through April and May, find the 2.8 MINERAL RIDGE TRAIL which begins at the BLM picnic area on Beauty Bay, about two miles along the scenic route. Pick up a booklet at the trailhead which helps identify about a dozen of the 100 native plants which thrive on the ridge. The trail winds up among tall cinnamon-barked ponderosa pines to a ridgetop shelter overlooking Wolf Lodge Bay.

From Harrison, a small resort community of about 260 persons, you may climb up and away from the lake into rolling rural countryside where yellow moth mullen, cramy white ocean spray, white daisies, and hot pink fireweed bloom and wave along the roadside.

At an elevation of 2,128 feet, you'll spot the St. Joe River near St. Maries. The highest navigable river in the world, its tree-lined channel actually flows between Round Lake, Chatcolet Lake and Benewah Lake. The St. Joe empties about 18 miles downstream into Lake Coeur d'Alene. During early spring the waters of Round Lake turn to a sea of white – some 1,000 swans detour here from the Pacific Flyway for about three weeks.

Osprey families nest nearby during spring and summer before returning to Mexico for the winter and in the fall, the Canadian geese and wood ducks appear. For many years there were no roads to St. Maries and folks traveled to and from Coeur d'Alene by riverboat. Furniture, machinery and other goods came by barges pushed up the river by tugboats. The area has also been long known for its delicious wild rice.

Information about activities in this colorful revitalized frontier and riverboat community may be obtained from the St. Maries Visitors Information Center, 905 Main Street (P.O. Box 162), St. Maries, ID 83861. Telephone (208) 245-5106.

MOSCOW ~ SCENIC ROUTES SOUTH ~ BOISE

From St. Maries you may continue along the WHITE PINE SCENIC ROUTE,

Highway 3, meandering through the St. Joe National Forest toward Moscow.

In Moscow take time to stroll the grounds of the University of Idaho where a number of impressive conifers have been planted by such well-known figures as Theodore Roosevelt and Harry S. Truman in the area known as PRESIDENT'S GROVE. Near the grove is the entrance to the SHATTUCK ARBORETUM which is in the process of being reclaimed by the recently formed Arboretum Associates. Information about membership may be obtained from Arboretum Associates, P.O. Box 3391, University Station, Moscow, ID 83843.

South of Moscow, toward the southern section of the Gem State, travelers may choose from three additional scenic routes – the PAYETTE RIVER SCENIC ROUTE along Payette River and Payette Lake in the Boise National Forest, the PONDEROSA PINE SCENIC ROUTE northeast of Boise, and the SALMON RIVER SCENIC ROUTE along the Salmon River just north of the Sawtooth National Recreational Area.

In addition, the SAWTOOTH SCENIC ROUTE extends south toward Ketchum and Sun Valley, the TETON SCENIC ROUTE is found on the far eastern border in the Targhee National Forest, and the THOUSAND SPRINGS SCENIC ROUTE meanders along the Snake River near Twin Falls, southeast of Boise.

Detailed maps and specific information about each of the scenic routes may be obtained from The Idaho Travel Council, Room 108, Statehouse, Boise, ID 83720. Telephone (208) 334-2470. Toll free outside of Idaho, (800) 635-7820.

In and around Idaho's capitol city, Boise, nature lovers will find several notable horticultural and natural areas to include on the travel itinerary. First, find the IDAHO BOTANICAL GARDEN which is located at 2355 Old Penitentiary Road. In May a tour of five or six private gardens in the area is offered, ending at the botanical garden with light refreshments. For information contact the Idaho Botanical Garden. Telephone (208) 343-8649.

Next, visitors may enjoy two lovely public parks near the revitalized downtown area. ANN MORRISON MEMORIAL PARK offers both formal and informal gardens of annuals and perennials. Situated along the Boise River, this 153-acre park also offers visitors an impressive tree-lined mall and a large reflecting pool with cascading waters. Hours 6-midnight. The gardens are found near Royal Boulevard, Americana Boulevard and University Drive.

And, JULIA DAVIS PARK which is located at 700 S. Capitol Boulevard, also nestles alongside the river and offers formal plantings as well as a small rose garden. Hours 6-midnight daily. There are picnic areas at both parks and handicap access at Julia Davis Park. Further information may be obtained from the Boise Parks and Recreation Department. Telephone (208) 344-5515 or (208) 384-4240. Ask about the GREENBELT APPRECIATION DAY which honors those early settlers who planted a plethora of trees along the Boise River. The celebration takes place during autumn's spectacular show when rainbow colored leaves wave 'goodbye' to summer.

Collect picnic makings at any of the bakeries and delis in the restored Eighth Street Marketplace or in the nearby Basque Neighborhood Marketplace, both located near Julia Davis Park, the Zoo, Art and Historical Museum, and the State Capitol building and landscaped grounds.

For a spring wildflower hike check with the Boise Ranger Station about the WILLIAM H. POGUE NATIONAL RECREATION TRAIL which is located about 45 miles east of Boise via Highway 21 and past Lucky Peak Dam. Ranger Station hours are 7:30-4:30 weekdays. Telephone (208) 343-2527. The lower section of the trail, about 2.5 miles, offers a look at an old mining flume and a good picnic spot, near the pack bridge which crosses Sheep Creek.

Another easy nature trek, MORES MOUNTAIN NATURE TRAIL, may be found at the Shafer Butte Recreation Site just 20 miles from Boise, at a spectacular 4,000 feet above the scenic Boise Valley. The nature trail is a fairly level two mile loop affording several grand wide-angle views of the valley and the Sawtooth Mountain Range to the east. For current information contact the Boise Ranger Station. Telephone (208) 343-2527. Ask about a list of wildflowers, trees, and birds of the area and for local contacts with Native Plant Society members who offer occasional guided tours in the area.

HILL CITY ~ LITTLE CITY OF ROCKS

Wildflower and bird-lovers may want to check out the HILL CITY WILDLIFE MANAGEMENT AREA located about an hour and a half southeast of Boise, via Interstate 84 and Highway 20 from Mountain Home to Hill City. The wildflowers usually begin blooming in April (depending on the weather and spring snow melt), with buttercups and starflowers, but the grandest show are the large patches of native blue camas so well known to early Indian families.

You'll see scores of migrating ducks such as pintails, widgeons and mallards as well as busy shorebirds like curlews, willets and avocets. Colonies of graceful tundra swans may also be spied as well as the resident Canada geese, sandhill cranes and wood ducks. For current information on wildflowers, bird populations, road conditions and specific directions contact the state fish and game regional office in Jerome. Telephone (208) 324-4359. The Sawtooth Scenic Route may be accessed just to the east of Hill City via Highway 20. **Note:** This is rugged high mountain country with cool days and crisp night-time temperatures; take along those sturdy shoes, windbreakers, caps, water and picnic or hearty snack fixings.

For an easy natural history sidetrip, detour from Highway 20 onto Highway 46 and head south toward Gooding to the turnoff labeled LITTLE CITY OF ROCKS (about 12.5 miles north of Gooding), then about one mile northwest on a dirt road. The intriguing canyons of eroded volcanic tuffs are similar to those found on the high desert of Central Oregon. You'll hear meadowlarks singing their easily-identified melodies, you can spy many native plants and you may also find blooming the sweetly scented wild mock orange or syringa, the Gem State's official flower.

The month of June is syringa's usual bloom time but just to make sure, contact the Bureau of Land Management's district office, 400 West 'F' Street (Box 2B), Shosone, ID 83352. Telephone (208) 886-2206. The staff will gladly answer questions about weather and road conditions as well. A map of the area is also available.

KETCHUM ~ SUN VALLEY ~ STANLEY

Heading north again, on the Sawtooth Scenic Route (Highway 75) toward Hailey, Elkhorn Village, Ketchum and Sun Valley, you may continue north into the rugged and spectacularly scenic Sawtooth National Recreational Area to Stanley, then access the equally scenic Ponderosa Pine Scenic Route (Highway 21) which loops up to 7,056 Banner Summit and back down to Boise. For a helpful packet of information, including a map of the area and pamphlets on day-hiking, wildlife, bird and wildflowers, contact the Sawtooth National Recreation Area, Star Route, Ketchum ID 83340. Telephone (208) 726-8291. Travelers may also stop at the Stanley Ranger Station when driving through. There are campgrounds, resorts, inns and cafes sprinkled along the routes.

Victoria's Inner Harbour, British Columbia

WESTERN BRITISH COLUMBIA

A Sampling

lessed with a mild maritime climate and superb setting of mountains, straits, sounds, bays and inlets, Western British Columbia is a garden and nature lover's paradise. Vacationers may visit and learn from a plethora of fine public gardens and natural areas—enough to fill one's itinerary for many weeks on the mainland and on Vancouver Island as well.

Greater Vancouver Area

RICHMOND ~ VANCOUVER

After visiting the stunning formal gardens at PEACE ARCH PROVINCIAL PARK, head north on Highway 99 toward Richmond and British Columbia's largest city, cosmopolitan Vancouver. If you cross the border sometime between May 1 through May 25, THE GLADES WOODLAND GARDEN near Richmond may be open to the public.

Owned and developed by the Hill family, almost all of the rhododendrons were grown from seed ordered from British estates such as Exbury. Some of the older rhododendrons tower as high as 25 feet, much the same as those grown by Rae Selling Berry in her early Portland garden (now the Berry Botanic Garden). Paths lead visitors through cloisters of blooming 'rhodies,' into shady groves of Western red cedar and dawn redwood, through a bog filled with enormous water-loving plants, around a koi-filled lily pond, and out into sunny meadows.

To find this private garden take Eighth Avenue exit from Highway 99 about a mile north of the border, head east to 172nd Street and right to the entrance, parking along the road shoulder. Hours are noon-7 about May 1-25. Nominal admission fee.

On nearby Westham Island one of the finest waterfowl refuges in North America may be a good destination in early spring and again in the fall. The

GEORGE C. REIFEL WATERFOWL REFUGE may be accessed from Highway 99 at the Ladner cut off, driving west to the Westham Island Bridge and following the signs to the refuge. Further information may be obtained from the refuge manager. Telephone (604) 946-6980.

Just beyond the Massey Tunnel a large commercial garden, VANDER ZALM'S FANTASY GARDENS, is located within a short distance of Highway 99. Through the colorful windmill entry you'll find a quaint European-style village with gift shops, bakeries and eateries — many with small tables and chairs set about for eating and people-watching. There is no charge for visiting the village shops.

To the rear is the garden entrance where visitors may stroll past elegant beds of annuals draped about a pond of water lilies, a Gazebo Teahouse surrounded by hundreds of roses, a quiet and serene Biblical Garden, a tiny Wedding Chapel and a lovely Crystal Conservatory filled with orchids and tropical plants. The spring display of tulips, in every conceivable hue, is stunning and when the Christmas Lights are turned on in December, the gardens are transformed into a sparkling fantasy world.

Vander Zalm's Fantasy Gardens are located at 10800 No.5 Road, Richmond, B.C. Telephone (604) 271-9325. Hours are 9-dusk daily. General admission fee about $5. Seasonal lunches and afternoon teas are offered in the garden and a Sunday brunch is also available, with reservations suggested. The garden is wheelchair accessible.

Nature buffs may want to plan a visit to the RICHMOND NATURE PARK, a 110-acre natural sphagnum moss bog where you may walk several self-guided nature trails amid shore pines, labrador tea shrubs, bog blueberries and the miniature sundew which digests its insect meals. You may spy hummingbirds, red-tailed hawks, Canada geese and, if you're quite lucky, the great horned owl. Easily found at 11851 Westminster Highway, Richmond, B.C., the park also features the Richmond Nature House. Telephone (604) 273-7015. You may join a free guided walk on Sundays at 11 and 3 year round and on Wednesdays at 1:30 during July and August. General hours are 10-6 during summer months, 10-5 during the remainder of the year.

To visit one of Canada's most comprehensive horticultural collections, plan several hours to stroll the wheelchair accessible paths and trails of the VAN DUSEN BOTANICAL GARDEN. An intertwining network of self-guided paths meander around several man-made lakes and lead visitors through 39 different botanical areas — from the Children's Garden, The Formal Rose Garden, Meditation Garden, Sino-Himalayan Garden, Heather Garden and Fragrance Garden to stunning collections of Perennials, Hydrangeas, Rhododendrons and Camellias, Japanese Azaleas, Magnolias, Hollies, Bamboos, Ornamental Grasses, Viburnums and Ginkgos.

There are sections for Herbs, Native Ground Covers for various climate zones (displayed in miniature settings), a Home Demonstration Garden, the Stanley Smith Rock Garden, the Canadian Heritage Garden Site, and an intriguing garden Maze as well.

Enter the garden through the latticed entry which deposits visitors inside the Garden Pavilion and Sprinklers Restaurant area. This fine botanical garden, carved from a former golf course, is maintained by the Board of Parks and Recreation of Vancouver with devoted assistance from the Vancouver Botanical Garden Association. There are both guided tours as well as wide variety of classes, workshops (including offerings for children) and floral shows offered throughout the year, all staffed by friendly and helpful garden volunteers.

The address is 5251 Oak Street, Vancouver, B.C. V6M 4H1. Telephone (604) 266-7194. Open daily. Nominal admission fee. Access the Van Dusen Botanical Garden by veering from Highway 99 onto Oak Street after crossing the Oak Street Bridge.

For the next stop on your horticultural tour of Vancouver proceed just a few blocks east via 41st Avenue to everyone's favorite family experience, QUEEN ELIZABETH PARK. Cultivated in a former rock quarry of 130 sloping acres (similar to the Butchart Gardens in Victoria) the garden is located at Vancouver's geographical center.

Two separate sunken gardens, one on the western perimeter and the other on the sunset east side, offer velvety lawns etched with elegant sculptured beds of lush rainbow-hued annuals and perennials. Lush plantings of dwarf snapdragons and old-fashioned zinnias make splashes of sun-bright color while blue-violet ageratum, stately cannas and huge-leafed Gunnera chilensis often form lush background plantings.

A gravel path atop the sunset garden offers superb wide-angle views of Burrard Inlet and English Bay to the north and the mountains beyond. Some 500 feet below, children and adults stroll around the flower beds and bubbling stream or sit in friendly groups about the lawns.

Towering above the vine-draped quarry walls, the BLOEDEL FLORAL CON-SERVATORY is a 70-foot high triodetic dome of nearly 1500 plexiglass bubbles. Inside this giant dome you may walk through over 15,000 square feet of lush tropical palms, ferns, orchids, bromelaids and banana trees—collections of some 500 species and varieties of plants from deep jungle to desert climates. Colorful Brazilian cardinals, parrots, doves and macaws fly freely in one section of the dome. Hours are 10-9 during summer months and 10-5 during the winter. Telephone (604) 872-5513. There is an admission fee for the visiting the Conservatory.

Next to the Bloedel Floral Conservatory find the lovely fountain plaza with enormously wide sections for wading and strolling which both children and adults of all ages find irresistible. Around this inviting watery piazza are benches for sitting and a latticed area from which hang extraordinary overflowing planters of perennials, ivy and other lush greenery.

Queen Elizabeth Park is located at Cambie Street and 33rd Avenue, Vancouver, B.C. Open daily dawn to dusk. There is also a restaurant on the grounds. The park is particularly busy during summer weekends, with large tour buses vying for parking spaces. Mid-week is generally a quieter time to visit and early in the day or sunset are particularly good for photo buffs.

Near Vancouver's downtown area the DR. SUN YAT-SEN CLASSICAL CHINESE GARDEN offers an intriguing look at an intimate garden modeled on the classical style developed in the City of Suzhou during the Ming dynasty, 1368-1644. The first full-scale classical garden constructed outside of China, the garden reflects the Taoist philosophy of yin and yang.

Shadow is balanced by sunlight, smoothness contrasts with texture, small objects balance with large ones—all elements of the garden are placed to remain in perfect equilibrium. Craggy rocks (most were shipped from China) beckon one to look beyond and seek the quiet waters of a large green pond, and the pebbled path urges guests past blooming iris, flowering fruit trees, graceful willows and clipped conifers across a small bridge to the Yun Wei Ting—"Colourful and Cloudy Pavilion"—a large classic-shaped viewing gazebo.

The Dr. Sun Yat-Sen Garden is located at 578 Carrall Street, Vancouver, B.C. V6B 2J8. Telephone (604) 689-7133. Hours 10-8 daily. Admission fee about $4.

Information may be obtained about special tours, exhibitions, lectures and cultural events which take place throughout the year.

Easily accessible from the bustling downtown area, Vancouver's emerald jewel— STANLEY PARK— is situated on a partially forested 1,000-acre peninsula which was originally destined for a military reserve. The park was officially opened in 1889 but the protective seawall around the perimeter was completed just ten years ago. Jutting into Burrard Inlet on the northeast, with English Bay to the west, enjoy the maximum amount of scenery from the six-mile STANLEY PARK SCENIC DRIVE around the peninsula's perimeter.

Then, park the car and enjoy a stroll across acres of rolling lawns beneath towering maples and fir and find the lovely ROSE GARDEN as well as striking beds of annuals and perennials, further on and near the Ferguson Point Tea House.

One of the park's hidden treasures is tiny BEAVER LAKE, a miniature couterpart to the larger LOST LAGOON (which is also a Bird Sanctuary). At quiet Beaver Lake fish hide beneath fat lily pads, ducks paddle about with downy youngsters in tow, turtles often snooze on sunny flat rocks, and birds twitter busily about the lush marsh grasses.

The only intrusion along a quiet self-guided walk around the lake may be an occasional jogger or two. Muffled city sounds seem far away. Offering benches for sitting as well, find Beaver Lake just beyond the Children's Petting Zoo and Miniature Railway.

Stanley Park also contains a large zoo, children's playground, cricket field, an aquarium, snack bars, and picnic areas. The Rose Gardens are located on Pipeline Road, just inside the main park entrance. Hours dawn to dusk, daily. Access from the downtown area via W. Georgia Street, bearing to the right onto Stanley Park Scenic Drive.

For take-along beverages and picnic fixings, before leaving the downtown area, try the Granville Island delis, bakeries and public markets — easily accessed from W. 6th Avenue, beneath the Granville Bridge. The Public Market hours are 9-6 daily during summer months and 9-6 Tuesday through Sunday during winter months.

Incidentally, the scenic paved walk around False Creek is easily accessed from Granville Island and affords spectacular seawall views of Vancouver's skyline and marinas. Well used by local families, couples, children and leashed pets, it's one of the best daytime as well as sunset walks in the entire area.

Another set of gardens located on the spacious grounds of the University of British Columbia, out on the tip of Point Grey, can easily emcompass a satisfying day-long visit. First, stop at the Visitors Information Office at 6501 N.W. Marine Drive to pick up helpful maps of THE UBC BOTANICAL GARDENS and the NITOBE MEMORIAL JAPANESE GARDEN.

The Nitobe Memorial Garden is within easy walking distance from the Office and parking area adjacent to the Museum of Anthropology. The 2.5 acre garden was designed to use native species trained in traditional Japanese fashion. Pines are carefully pruned to show the form and structure of the trunk as well as the individual branches.

Visitors are invited to walk the self-guided pathways that surround the garden's small lake, featuring a waterfall and miniature mountain, and connect also with the tea garden and moss garden areas. As transient visitors in this type of strolling garden, we're encouraged to follow the pathways in our own time, stopping to ponder and appreciate the vistas which open as we cross a bridge or catch a glimpse of a graceful willow, lantern or stone across the serene water.

The Tea Garden is essentially a path to and from the Tea House and is intended, according to Buddhist tradition, as a place for quiet reflection and self-illumination. We're invited to keep in mind that the overall purpose of the garden is to refresh the spirit and deepen one's understanding of the many cycles of life—an hour, a day, a week, a lifetime.

In the spring you may see varieties of Japanese Iris in shades of purple, blue and white—usually at their best during the second and third weeks of June. In addition to the pastel colors of April, May and June, the more vivid colors may be seen in the fall during September, October and November. The maples provide a variety of tans and yellows, the cultivated cherries add splashes of orange and red, and two native species—the Red huckleberry and Bitter cherry—add their own bright colors against the velvety deep green of the pines, firs and cedars.

In 1969 the Nitobe Memorial Garden Council was formed to assist in the garden's continuity of development. The garden was opened in 1960 and dedicated to Dr. Inazo Nitobe, a Japanese scholar, educator, publicist, and international diplomat whose personal goal was "to become a bridge across the Pacific."

The Nitobe Memorial Garden is located opposite 6565 N.W. Marine Drive and opens at 10. There is a nominal admission fee. Telephone (604) 228-4208.

Next, and hopefully with a picnic, drive along S.W. Marine Drive around to the UBC BOTANICAL GARDEN which offers eleven different garden sections to visit, study and enjoy. Stop at the Main Garden Centre for a helpful map and basic information. The Centre also offers horticultural books, gifts, seeds and plants in season.

Walk first through the E.H. LOHBRUNNER ALPINE GARDEN, a 2.5 acre hillside plot located just below Thunderbird Stadium. You'll spy Edelweiss and blue Gentians from Europe along with saxifrage, sedum, creeping phlox, and more than 12,000 other plants from all the continents and most of the world's mountain ranges.

Next, enjoy strolling through the 16th century-style PHYSICK GARDEN. You may inspect a labeled collection of traditional medicinal and culinary herbs, 37 of which were grown from seeds obtained from England's famous Chelsea Physic Garden. Twelve formal brick-lined beds are arranged about a large working sun dial.

A traditional English yew hedge encloses this intimate garden and there is a shaded bench for sitting as well. Developed in 1976, the Physick Garden was a cooperative research project between Friends of the Garden, university staff members, and included a consultation with Mr. Allen Paterson, the Director of the Chelsea Physic Garden in London.

Next, stroll through a large arbour with its trailing vines and find the half-acre FOOD GARDEN. This garden was introduced in 1983 to provide a demonstration and display plot for those interested in developing and caring for various kind of fruits and vegetables. Many newer varieties are introduced each year, including watermelon, canteloupe and at least two varieties of pumpkin—Jack O'Lantern and Atlantic Giant, the world's largest pumpkin.

You'll see luscious berries and fruit trees (both standard and espaliered), nuts, vine fruits and grapes as well as a healthy, well-tended collection of vegetables in raised beds. Ample harvests from the Food Garden are traditionally distributed to the local Food Bank. The development of this garden was assisted by a grant from the Garden Club of Vancouver.

Although it's easy to overlook the path just beyond the Food Garden, walk through a short tunnel (under the road) and through the vermillion Chinese Moon

Gate where you may walk soft paths through the 30-acre ASIAN GARDEN. Amid this quiet coastal forest you're greeted with meandering beds of nodding Primulas in the early spring, surrounded by drifts of blue Himalayan poppies (Meconopsis) later in the season, and later still many colorful varieties of the lily family. A collection of species rhododendrons and elegant Magnolias bloom in secluded areas.

Exotic trees and shrubs laced with vines (like clematis and kiwi) and climbing roses form a lush overhead canopy which envelops the visitor in a dozen or more shades of verdant greens. From pale chartreuse and minty medium hues to lively emerald, subtle jade and deep blue-greens, ribbons of sunlight stream through leaves and branches bathing the garden in an ethereal light, much like a stage set for Midsummer Night's Dream.

A treasure trove to garden lovers, plantsmen and horticulturalists, the Asian Garden may have the largest collection of woody Asian plants on the American continent. Because this is a species garden, no man-made hybrids are included.

Those who happen upon this wooded glen in the fall may experience a kaleidoscope of autumn hues with those sunlight ribbons creating yet another mood. The Asian Garden is one not to be missed.

Just above the Food Garden and the Alpine Garden follow another path, this one leading to the B.C. NATIVE GARDEN where you may walk the interconnecting self-guided trails through an aromatic woodland and meadow, past a peat bog, brook and pond.

Walk through the meadow during the spring to see blue Camas, Fawn and Mariposa lilies, Shooting Stars and Lady Slippers nodding near the native rhododendrons. The wildflower parade continues during summer months with many shades of Phlox, Columbines, Mountain Avens, Indian Paintbrush, Ceanothus and sweetly scented Honeysuckles, all displaying their traditional colors in the alpine garden area.

In the fall Asters, Goldenrod and Bluebells splash bright color against the golden larches and red and yellow maples. At the end of the growing season seeds are collected for the garden's gene and seed bank which is maintained to help replace plants in nature when species and sites are destroyed.

Dedicated in 1978, the Native Garden was named in honour of John Davidson, the first director of the UBC Botanical Garden.

Near the sweeping lawn area next to the Food Garden and Main Garden Centre, you may see the CONTEMPORARY GARDEN which emphasizes recently introduced hybrids and new flowering perennials in colorful beds. Notice also the lush basket-containers, so typical of the British Columbia gardens, hanging near the entry gift area—often dripping with delicate pastel impatiens, trailing nasturtiums, bright red geraniums, graceful fuchsias and long drapes of glechoma.

The Main Garden is located at 6250 Stadium Road, near 16th Avenue and S.W. Marine Drive. Hours 10-dusk. There is a nominal admission fee. For horticultural information telephone (604) 228-5858. Visitors may also obtain information about membership in The Davidson Club, established in 1982 to help provide both operating and endowment support for the UBC Botanical Garden.

The Main Office of the UBC Botanical Garden is located a short distance from the Nitobe Memorial Garden — at 6501 N.W. Marine Drive, Vancouver, B.C. V6T 1W5. Telephone (604) 228-4208.

If you retrace your route on Marine Drive from the Main Garden toward the Nitobe Memorial Garden, stop to see and sniff the old-fashioned roses in the

ROSE GARDEN just next door to the Faculty Club. It's just beyond the Botanical Office and Museum of Anthropology (where there is usually plenty of visitor parking).

Access the University of British Columbia campus from downtown Vancouver via 4th Avenue, turning onto MARINE SCENIC DRIVE near Chancellor Boulevard. There are no formal picnic areas in the botanical areas on the campus but visitors may sit on the grass most everywhere. Other UBC botanical areas worth investigating include the MALCOLM KNAPP RESEARCH FOREST in Maple Ridge (about an hour's drive east via Highway 7). Telephone (604) 463-8148. And, the ALEX FRASER RESEARCH FOREST, a 9,000 hectare forest with eight lakes which offers summer camping and picnicking in the interior, near Williams Lake, B.C. Telephone (604) 392-2207.

Information about annual events and festivals may be obtained from the Greater Vancouver Visitors Information Centre, Royal Centre Mall, 1055 West Georgia Street, Vancouver, B.C. V6E 4C8. Telephone (604) 682-2222.

And, from Tourism British Columbia, c/o Parliament Buildings, Victoria, B.C. V8V 1X4. In the U.S., Tourism British Columbia, P.O. Box C-34971, Seattle, WA 98124.

NORTH VANCOUVER

From Stanley Park it's an easy drive across Lions Gate Bridge over First Narrows (which connects English Bay with Burrard Inlet) to North Vancouver. At CAPILANO REGIONAL PARK you may enjoy lovely gardens of colorful annuals and perennials as well as nature trails and a frothy 200-foot waterfall. Nearby, you may also walk across a 455-foot bridge of wire rope and wood decking which suspends 230 feet above the cascading Capilano River. As you peer below there may be canoes, kayaks or rafts-full of folks enjoying a close-up encounter with the river.

The 15-acre park nestles amid towering Douglas fir, western red cedar and other native deciduous trees which clothe the steep Capilano River canyon. The Capilano Suspension Bridge and Park is located at 3735 Capilano Road, North Vancouver, B.C. Telephone (206) 985-7474. Summer hours 8-dusk, winter 9-5. Access from downtown Vancouver from Georgia Street through Stanley Park, across Lions Gate Bridge to Marine Drive, left on Capilano Road 1.7 miles to the entrance. There is a nominal admission fee.

If you'd like a high altitude view of the greater Vancouver area, continue to the end of Capilano Road and take the aerial skyride to the top of 3,700-foot GROUSE MOUNTAIN. At the top you may enjoy a brisk walk along the trail around BLUE GROUSE LAKE, a ride up the Peak Chairlift (it carries skiers during the winter), or just browsing through the gift shop and enjoying the view from inside the cafeteria and restaurant.

There is a nominal fee for the aerial skyride and information and dinner reservations may be obtained by calling ahead. Telephone (604) 984-0661. The high altitude after-dark view of Vancouver's lights sparkling like scattered diamonds below is spectacular.

Nearby, LYNN CANYON PARK may be a good place to rest and picnic, next to Lynn Creek. A naturalist is on hand at the Nature House (during summer months) and you may stroll across another suspension bridge as well as meander the nature trails up into the pines. The address is 3663 Lynn Valley Park Road, North Vancouver, B.C. Telephone (604) 987-5922. There is a small snack shop on the grounds. Access from Marine Drive heading east and follow signs to the park.

After several years the PARK AND TILFORD GARDENS have reopened as part of the new Park and Tilford Centre, offering large and small shops, bakeries, delis and eateries on the site of the Park & Tilford Distilleries. Closed in 1984, the distillery created the spectacular 2.5 acre gardens many years ago. There is a rose garden, including lovely trellised and old-fashioned climbing roses, and a small oriental garden as well as a fine collection of rhododendrons, native trees and ornamental shrubs. Lavish displays of colorful annuals brighten walkways, fountains and sitting areas.

The new retail centre, which opened in the fall of 1988, reflects a garden theme throughout and special floral events are planned for each of the four seasons of the year. The Park & Tilford Centre gardens are located at 1200 Cotton Road, North Vancouver, B.C. Hours 8-11 daily. Access from Marine Drive to 3rd Street, then onto Cotton, just east of the North Vancouver Seabus terminal.

Perched on a hill near the north end of the Second Narrows Bridge and surrounded by verdant forests and a profusion of blossoming spring wild- flowers, the CAPILANO COLLEGE grounds are well known for scenic paths and flower-lined walkways. Access just east and north of the Park & Tilford Gardens.

Those heading back to Vancouver may want to add the WEST VANCOUVER MARINE SCENIC DRIVE to the itinerary. This scenic drive skirts English Bay as it heads west toward LIGHTHOUSE PARK and Horseshoe Bay. In the park are not only some of the largest trees in British Columbia but panoramic wide-angle views of Vancouver, to the east, as well. You'll find accessible nature trails for conducting self-guided walking tours of all this outdoor scenery overlooking English Bay and Vancouver to the east and the Strait of Georgia and the Gulf Islands to the southwest. Access Lighthouse Park at Beacon Lane.

If time allows continue north on the SEA TO SKY HIGHWAY (Highway 99) which winds past vertical rock cliffs with views of glacier-capped mountains and alongside fjord-like Howe Sound toward Shannon Falls Park, Squamish, Garibaldi Provincial Park, Brandywine Falls, Whistler-Blackcomb and Pemberton Valley.

In this high altitude section of British Columbia you'll find the air crisp and fresh, the scenery more off the beaten path and more ruggedly spectacular and the native wildlife and birdlife spied more often. You'll see native plants and wildflowers bloom later in the summer, and autumn colors splashing an earlier palette of reds, yellows and oranges as well. The best time to drive back from Whistler-Blackcomb via the Sea to Sky Highway is about 45 minutes before sunset when you'll often see the waters of Howe Sound and the Strait of Georgia turn a shimmering orange, gold and copper against the verdant Gulf Islands and steep snow-capped mountains. It's a sight not to be missed.

Travelers heading west to Vancouver Island may access the British Columbia ferries at Horseshoe Bay, just north of Lighthouse Park. Information about ferry schedules to Vancouver Island (Nanaimo), Bowen Island, and the Sunshine Coast may be obtained from the British Columbia Ferry Corporation. Telephone (604) 669-1211. For recorded information: Vancouver (604) 685-1021; Nanaimo (604) 753-6626.

BURNABY ~ NEW WESTMINSTER ~ SURREY

Burnaby may be accessed from North Vancouver across the Second Narrows Bridge which spans Burrard Inlet's mid-section on its watery way east and north where it then becomes Indian Arm.

At BURNABY MOUNTAIN PARK visitors enjoy a series of lovely coastal native gardens and nature trails. There are picnic areas in this mountain setting—among colorful, carved totem poles. Near Simon Fraser University, access the park from Hastings Street (Highway 7A).

Nearby, at BURNABY LAKE REGIONAL PARK, easy nature trails skirt the large lake and marsh areas where waterfowl and muskrat families live. This also is a good spot to observe those scores of bird species who migrate on the Pacific Flyway in the spring and fall. The well-staffed Nature House offers helpful displays, bird and wildflower lists, and nature talks during summer months. The park is located at 5216 Glencarin Drive, Burnaby. Telephone (604) 526-7275. Access from Gaglardi Way which meanders south from Burnaby Mountain Park.

Plan a visit to BURNABY CENTURY GARDENS on miniature Deer Lake, just next to the Burnaby Village Museum (where you can stroll a turn-of-the-century street scene which includes an apothecary shop, general store, log cabin, church and soda parlour). The gardens feature more than 200 varieties of rhododendrons and formal plantings on rolling terrain which edges a winding stream. This is a small jewel not to be missed by springtime travelers. Access via Kensington Avenue from Burnaby Lake Regional Park.

In nearby New Westminster garden lovers may add QUEENS PARK and the JAPANESE FRIENDSHIP GARDENS to the horticultural itinerary. In a luscious setting of over 10,000 annuals and perennials in well-tended formal beds, Queens Park also features a lovely Rose Garden. You may catch a summer Sunday performance at the bandshell and there is also a children's zoo and playground. The park is located at 1st Street and 3rd Avenue, near the Royal City Museum and Irving House (a stately well-preserved Victorian built in 1882). Telephone (604) 524-9796.

Several blocks away, and too easily missed, is the Japanese Friendship Garden, a western interpretation of a classic oriental garden. Designed in the 1960s and dedicated to Moriguchi, New Westminster's sister city, this intimate 2.5 acre garden features one hundred Yoshino cherry trees which bloom in pastel profusion in the spring. There are also fine collections of black bamboo, gunnera and many native plants. Graceful weeping willow branches drift over a pond filled with bright orange goldfish. A traditional vermillion bridge frames the distant shoreline. This garden jewel is located at Royal Avenue near City Hall, New Westminster. Hours are dawn to dusk daily.

Just across the Pattullo Bridge which spans the Fraser River, WOODLAND GARDEN offers an arboretum of flowering cherry trees and stately magnolias grouped about several ponds. The collection of old rhododendrons are especially colorful around Mother's Day. The Woodland Garden is located in Surrey. Telephone (604) 536-9282. Hours are dawn to dusk, daily. There is a nominal admission fee.

LANGLEY ~ ALDERGROVE ~ BRADNER ~ ROSEDALE

From New Westminster or Surrey head east on Fraser Highway 1A toward Langley where you may find SENDALL GARDENS. Stroll the network of garden paths, along with stately peacocks, and explore luscious roses, luxuriant beds of colorful annuals and a selection of native and ornamental trees. The gardens are located just off 200th Street toward Campbell Valley Regional Park, Langley, B C. Telephone (604) 534-4014.

Follow Highway 1A east from Langley toward Aldergrove and Bradner where you may feast your eyes on acres of blooming tulips and daffodils in the early spring. Just beyond Aldergrove join Highway 1, the Trans-Canada Highway, heading east toward Rosedale.

Information about peak bloom times and annual events and festivals may be obtained from the Aldergrove Visitors Information Center, 27030-B Fraser Highway (P.O. Box 332) Aldergrove, B.C. V∅X 1A∅. Telephone (604) 856-8382.

Ready yourself for a spectacular visual experience at the MINTER GARDENS, an extraordinary collection of ten different gardens located about an hour and a half east of Vancouver, near Rosedale. Meander through the scented Fragrance Garden, notice surrounding mountains reflected in the lovely Lake Garden and stroll through a Rose Garden, a Hanging Basket Bower and an 18th century-style Formal Garden as well.

There are also fine collections of azaleas and rhododendrons, flowering Japanese cherry and plum as well as enchanting ferns and alpine heathers. You'll see thousands of annuals sculptured as graceful ballgowns on floral 'Southern Belles' and an enormous floral Canadian flag as well. Tropical birds chorus in the aviary near an old-fashioned water wheel.

After strolling the magnificent well-tended gardens you may enjoy brunch, light lunch or tea and dessert in Bloomers Restaurant. Or, browse through the Garden and Gift Shop and the Greenhouse. On Father's Day visitors take a gander at some 150 vintage automobiles displayed by local Rotarians. The Minter Gardens are just as gorgeous when clothed in the rich hues of Autumn as well.

The gardens are located at 52892 Bunker Road, Rosedale, B.C. Telephone (604) 794-7191. The mailing address is P.O. Box 40, Chilliwack, B.C. V2P 6H7. Hours are 9-dusk daily from April through October. Off-season telephone (604) 792-3919. The gardens are wheelchair accessible. Access from Highway 1 at the Harrison Hot Springs exit, about 75 miles east of Vancouver. There is an admission fee.

Information about flower festivals and annual events may be obtained from the Tourism Association of Southwestern British Columbia, 304-828 West 8th Avenue, Vancouver, B.C. V5Z 1E2. Telephone (604) 876-3088.

From here you may continue your scenic natural area and horticultural tour north toward Harrison Hot Springs, east toward Manning Provincial Park and points east, or double back to Vancouver via scenic Highway 7 which meanders along the scenic Fraser River through Dewdney, Silverdale and Maple Ridge.

Victoria & Vancouver Island

From quaint English tea rooms to gourmet fish and chips eateries, from Scottish tartans to English porcelains and Victorian style gardens, both its English roots and British heritage are reflected throughout this charming city. Located at the southeastern tip of Vancouver Island, Victoria is also blessed with that mild marine climate which nurtures the lush gardens so characteristic of western British Columbia and the northwest U.S.

Actually, getting to British Columbia's capital city is half the fun because it involves another of those ferry excursions—from Port Angeles or Seattle on the U.S. mainland, or from Tsawwassen and Horseshoe Bay, across the Canadian border.

Begin your horticultural tour of Victoria at the picturesque Inner Harbour, near the venerable ivy-draped Empress Hotel. A sweeping floral 'Welcome to Victoria' is spelled out in beds of bright annuals along the harbour, framing the stately Parliament Buildings in the background. From Victorian lamp-posts around the entire harbour area hang baskets of colorful flowers and lush greenery—bluish-purple lobelia, white alyssum, pink petunias, dark green ivy and other trailing vines.

Stroll the walkways about the spacious Parliament grounds along which are often planted bright red geraniums and colorful annuals. You'll have a superb view of the harbour, the Empress and the Royal British Columbia Museum as well. The GOVERNMENT HOUSE GARDENS include a 7-acre sunken Rose Garden, a lily pond and fountains. The grounds are open daily and are wheelchair accessible. You may also enjoy the NATIVE PLANT GARDEN just across the way at the Museum which features trees, shrubs and flowers from throughout the Province.

The nearby CRYSTAL GARDEN is a Victorian style glass-roofed conservatory which dates back to 1925 when it contained an enormous saltwater swimming pool. Restored and refurbished, the Crystal Garden now overflows with lush tropical palms, banana trees, ferns and exquisite tropical flowers, and colorful exotic birds.

Offering a festival of shops as well as a stroll through the lush garden accompanied by those colorful parrots, macaws and flamingos, visitors may also enjoy a leisurely English tea served on the Promenade overlooking all this tropical finery under glass. The Crystal Garden is open daily from 8am-11pm. There is an admission fee. Telephone (604) 381-1213. Access directly behind the Empress Hotel on Douglas Street.

Among other lovely flower and plant-filled places to have a very British cup of tea, along with those scrumptious scones and crumpets, are the Empress Hotel, the James Bay Tea Room, The Blethering Place, Adriennes's Tea Garden at Matticks Farm (5325 Cordova Bay Road) and The Gazebo, at 5460 Old West Saanich Road. Inquire at the Visitors Information Centre near the harbour for current hours and directions to Victoria's delectable tea shops.

In nearby BEACON HILL PARK, just a few blocks from the Inner Harbour Walkway area, you may stroll pathways around duck ponds and a formal Rose Garden, meander around large beds of colorful perennials and annuals as well as stand beneath ancient oaks and cedars. Profusions of wild daffodils, blue Camas, spring Crocus, and blossoming fruit trees greet visitors during the spring and summer. Victoria's 154-acre downtown park is located at Douglas Street and Marine Drive. You may also enjoy a walking tour of the surrounding residential area where well-tended yards bordered with colorful annuals and perennials may be seen from the sidewalk.

You may want to inquire about the grand ANNUAL GARDEN TOUR of more than a dozen private gardens in Victoria and Saanich offered during April, in support of the Victoria Conservatory of Music. During the three day event garden lovers may see Rock & Alpine Gardens, Rhododendron Gardens and Herb Gardens as well as informal New England-style Gardens, charming Door-Yard Gardens and the formal stylized Parterre Gardens. Information about dates and cost may be obtained from the Conservatory Office, 839 Academy Close, Victoria, B.C. V8V 2X8. Telephone (604) 386-5311.

At historic POINT ELLICE HOUSE, on nearby upper harbour, you may enjoy one hundred year old holly, redwood and arbutus trees as well as sniff a lovely collection of old scented roses. You can even play a game of croquet on the lawn where it's been played since colonial days. Located at 2616 Pleasant Street, near Bay Street Bridge, the house and gardens open around June 1. Telephone (604) 385-3837 or (604) 387-3067. You may also inquire and obtain information about other Provincial historic homes with gardens in the local area, such as Helmcken House and Craigflower Farmhouse & Schoolhouse.

Among the 17 outdoor parks in the Capital Regional District, the FRANCIS/ KING PARK is a particular favorite among nature lovers. A network of gentle trails weaves throughout and the ELSIE KING TRAIL offers a wheelchair accessible cedar boardwalk through vintage oaks, alder and maple. An especially lovely walk during the spring, you may see early wildflowers like trillium and fawn lilies as well as shooting stars and blue camas hidden here and there. Or, enjoy a crisp autumn day stroll with splashes of red and gold leaves adorning the slender alder and tall maples.

Collect picnic makings in Victoria markets and delis before heading out to the park areas, then enjoy lunching with friendly chattering squirrels, buzzing bees, hammering woodpeckers and other native birds species. Access Francis/King Park from Douglas Street onto Burnside West, then Prospect Lake Road to the park entrance. For recorded information about nature programs at the Francis/King Nature House (1710 Munn Road) telephone (602) 474-PARK.

In the other Regional District outdoor parks located with 20 to 30 minutes of Victoria, wildflowers, native trees and wildlife and bird sounds may also be enjoyed along nature trails and in more remote outdoor picnic areas. Rugged wind-swept coasts, serene lakes, lush rainforests, bird-filled marshes and lagoons and jagged mountaintop vistas – all carved by ancient glaciers – await nature lovers visiting Vancouver Island.

You may visit places where native Indian families once trapped migrating salmon, hunted elk and dug blue camas bulbs. You may see where these Coast Salish people crafted baskets, canoes and clothing from the cedar tree and moved quietly through the four seasons. English settlers from the Hudson's Bay Company bought the Saanich Peninsula and Metchosin area from the Salish tribe for about 140 (British pounds) worth of woolen hats and blankets. Especially fine carvings, baskets and exhibits may be seen at the UBC Museum of Anthropology on the UBC campus in Vancouver.

For a trek in one of the more primitive seacoast parks, drive into the Metchosin area toward Sooke on Highway 14 from Victoria about 20 miles to EAST SOOKE PARK. Hike through forest, marsh and field; see the windswept arbutus with its clusters of pinkish-white flowers clinging to coastal headlands; find ancient Coast Salish petroglyphs hidden in this wild and magnificent place where the forest meets the sea. **Note:** The trails here are fairly challenging and the coastline is rugged. There are regularly scheduled guided nature treks by park naturalists. Telephone (604) 474-PARK for current information, dates and times.

A helpful map showing all 17 Capital Regional District parks may be obtained from Capital Regional District Parks Department, 490 Atkins Avenue, Victoria, B.C. V9B 2Z8. Telephone (604) 478-3344. Ask about wildflower bloom times at MILL HILL PARK (near Francis/King Park), the nature house and bird lookout with wheelchair access at WITTY'S LAGOON PARK (out Metchosin Road), and the wildflowers and mushrooms (plus hilltop views of the Gulf Islands and Georgia Strait) at NORTH HILL PARK (near the Sidney ferry landing).

You may find an easy, well-maintained 15-minute walk through a misty rain forest at CHINA BEACH, a day-use Provincial park about 20 miles northwest of Sooke via Highway 14. And, a wheelchair accessible walkway at FRENCH BEACH, a large campground and park located 12 miles west of Sooke on the way to China Beach.

For those who want to lunch indoors, you may want to call ahead for reservations at SOOKE HARBOUR HOUSE located on Whiffen Spit. Surrounding the inn are lovely annual and perennial gardens framing wide-angle views of the Strait of Juan de Fuca, the Washington mainland and those craggy, snow-shrouded Olympic Mountains – all to the south. You may notice such floral edibles as nasturtiums, honeysuckle, winter pansies and English daisies garnishing your tasty salad or entree. The flowers and herbs used all come from the inn's sumptuous gardens. Sooke Harbour House is located at 1528 Whiffen Spit Road, R.R.4, Sooke, B.C. VØS 1NØ. Telephone (604) 642-3421. Reservations are suggested.

Information about annual events and festivals may be obtained from the Sooke-Jordan River Visitors Information Centre, P.O. Box 18, Sooke, B.C. VØS 1NØ. Telephone (604) 642-6112.

As you retrace the route via Highway 14 toward Victoria, consider a visit to the elegant gardens at ROYAL ROADS MILITARY COLLEGE. The grounds and baronial Hatley Castle were developed at the turn of the century by Scotsman James Dunsmuir, heir to a Vancouver Island coal mining fortune. His father, Robert Dunsmuir, built the impressive Craigdarroch Castle in Victoria in 1887 (now maintained as an historic house and museum).

First, stop at the entrance gate where the genial guard will direct you to the public parking area and offer directions to the Hatley Castle ITALIAN GARDEN. The castle itself is open to the public only on special occasions but you can imagine its oak and mahogany panelled rooms, baronial fireplaces, teak floors and glittering chandeliers.

During Dunsmuir's time the rooms were filled with flowers grown in the Conservatory. At one time, the Conservatory was also filled with exotic white orchids imported from India and a large banana tree grew under the dome. Over a hundred men were employed by James Dunsmuir to tend the gardens and grounds at the castle he built for his wife, Laura.

Just beyond the castle, walk through the vine-draped arbour gate into the intimate walled Italian Garden which is filled with luscious begonias, fucshias, daisies and other colorful annuals and perennials. From the columned, shady portico you'll have a good view of the castle and its 82-foot high turret, both draped with long festoons of ivy. Stroll the boxwood-lined lawns and paths which separate the formal beds and dramatize the statuary placed about. There are benches for sitting and enjoying this intimate and romantic space.

Walk through the wrought iron gate onto the broad sweep of lawn which offers a fine view of Esquimalt Lagoon, then through a small wooded area just to the right find the JAPANESE GARDEN landscaped about a traditional pond. Meander the quiet paths and enjoy this meditative space framed with tall firs and pine.

The only sounds to disturb one's reverie may be the twittering birds, stately peacocks, paddling ducks and the young men running to and from their classes and athletic pursuits. They're in training at the college for the Canadian Armed Forces.

You'll want to plan an hour or so to enjoy this exceptional, historic place. The gardens and grounds are open to the public from 10-4 daily and there is no admission fee. Royal Roads Military College is located on Highway 14 (Sooke Road) in Colwood. From Victoria via Highway 1 and 1A, follow signs for Fort Rodd Hill, taking the Colwood exit from Highway 1 about one mile to the entrance gate.

Another horticultural experience not to be missed are the teaching & learning gardens at the HORTICULTURE CENTRE OF THE PACIFIC. Located on some 136 acres, the Centre was incorporated as a non-profit society in 1979. In 1983, members and volunteers from Vancouver Island garden clubs cleared the six acres of the present Demonstration Garden, paths and picnic areas.

Stroll graveled pathways which interlace the well-labeled beds of more than 185 different perennials, an extensive collection of old roses in the circular Rose Garden, the Rhododendron Garden, the Doris Page Winter Garden and a Kiwi Arbor and greenhouse. You'll see one of the most complete collections of Michaelmas daisies in the northwest—more than 50 varieties of the sun-loving perennial.

Other specialties include well-labeled collections of chrysanthemums and dahlias, lilies and Oriental poppies, heathers and ferns. In the semi-circular Old Rose Garden you may see "Old Blush" (1752), "Mme Alfred Carriers" (1879), "Souvenir de la Malmaison" (1843) and "Stanwell Perpetual" (1838) as well as more than 25 other old roses from the early and mid 1900s. At least three of the roses date to the 1500s—"Jacobite Rose," "White Rose of York," and "Austrian Copper." Try to visit on a sunny day when the old roses emit their sweetest scents—you'll feel surrounded by a Victorian potpourri.

In the Annual Garden you'll identify old favorites like Snapdragons in white, yellow, pink and red; Bachelor's Button (or Cornflower) in blues, pinks and white; Larkspur in tall spikes of white, blue and pink; Annual Coreopsis in shades of yellow to red; scented Pinks in white, pink and red; and Strawflowers, Sweet Peas and colorful Zinnias as well.

As you meander the paths friendly garden volunteers and garden trainees are on hand to help with questions about the garden and its philosophy of demonstrating organic gardening techniques. Also, don't miss the shaded display of luscious begonias and fuchsias—some in hanging baskets and others in enormous wooden tubs. Visitors may find a selection of dried flowers and seeds from the garden for sale in the gift shop along with information about gardening classes and workshops.

The Horticulture Centre of the Pacific is located at 505 Quayle Road, Victoria, B.C. V8X 3X1. Telephone (604) 479-6162. Hours are 8-dusk daily. Admission fee $1. A yearly membership in support of the Centre is $10 and members are sent an informative quarterly newsletter along with special invitations to Tea & Chat's, Workshops, July Evening Cake & Coffee and September Sunday Afternoon Tea. Take along a picnic and access the gardens via Highway 17 about 5.5 miles north of Victoria, taking the Royal Oak Drive exit. Turn left .5 mile to W. Saanich Road, right .8 mile to Beaver Lake Road and left to the end; then, left about .4 mile to the entrance and parking area.

Located just north, off Royal Oak and SCENIC MARINE DRIVE, the FABLE COTTAGE ESTATE offers 3.5 acres of theme gardens and animated floral displays on a former estate. Open for tours, the residence was built in the style of an enchanted cottage. Surrounding the fairytale cottage-estate visitors may stroll through several theme gardens—a romantic Orchard Garden, the Wishing Gardens, and a colorful Foral Valley filled with luscious flowering begonias, petunias, ferns, nasturtiums, geraniums and enormous hanging baskets of flowers and trailing vines. The Fable Cottage Estate is located at 5187 Cordova Bay Road, Victoria, B.C. V8Y 2K7. Telephone (604) 658-5741. Hours are 9:30-dusk. There is an admission charge.

For another stroll among several elegant theme gardens, plan a visit to THE BUTCHART GARDENS, also located north via Highway 17, toward Sidney and

Swartz Bay. The gardens were developed just after the turn of the century in a worked-out limestone quarry site on the 130-acre estate of the R.P. Butchart family, pioneers in the manufacture of cement. First a project of Jennie Butchart, the work of developing these magnificent gardens became a family commitment to horticulture and visitors have been welcomed to the gardens for more than 80 years.

From the latticed display of hanging baskets dripping with elegant begonias stroll paths through a charming English Rose Garden, an intimate and serene Japanese Garden, a formal Italian Garden, and the immense Sunken Garden. From mid-May through September the gardens are also lighted at night, including an impressive fountain lighting display at the Ross Fountain which borders the sunken garden.

Visitors may enjoy a fireworks display on Saturday evenings during July and August and a musical stage show on summer weeknights. Have dinner in the Dining Room Restaurant, located in the former Butchart home; luncheon or tea in The Greenhouse Restaurant which is located in the flower-filled greenhouse and patio area; or, a snack at The Coffee Bar. There is also a Gift Shop which offers momentos and gifts as well as a variety of seeds packaged from the gardens.

The Butchart Gardens are located on Keating Road about 15 miles north of Victoria, off Highway 17. The mailing address is Box 4010, Postal Station "A". There is an admission charge. The gardens are wheelchair accessible. Recorded information (604) 652-5256. Telephone during business hours (604) 652-4422. Access from Highway 17 at the Brentwood-Butchart Gardens turn-off, then 5.5 miles to the entrance. **Note:** To avoid the summer throngs, visit quite early in the day or late in the afternoon or early evening.

Information about annual events and festivals as well as other helpful maps may be obtained from the Greater Victoria Visitors Information Centre, 812 Wharf Street (across from the Empress Hotel), Victoria, B.C. V8W 1T3. Telephone (604) 382-2127.

DUNCAN ~ LADYSMITH ~ NANAIMO

If time allows, plan another side trip up-island via Highway 1 to visit several notable parks, arboreta and nature areas. At GOLDSTREAM PROVINCIAL PARK you may amble along a bubbling stream to the Nature House, explore a delta marsh area, and enjoy a picnic nestled beneath 600 year old Douglas fir. For hardier outdoor buffs, the invigorating trail up Mt. Finlayson will reward with carpets of wildflowers as you climb from the rain forest floor to the sub-alpine ridges.

Near Duncan, called the "City of Totems," the B.C. FOREST MUSEUM offers a fascinating look at the history of logging in the Province from a vintage steam train which circles the 100 acre park through farmland, forest and out on a trestle over Somenos Lake.

Continuing up-island stop at Ladysmith (which was laid out as a township by Scotsman James Dunsmuir) to visit the CROWN FOREST INDUSTRIES ARBORETUM and MUSEUM where a collection of native trees grow tall among exotic species from around the world. The Arboretum and Logging Museum hours are 10-4:30 daily, with no admission charge. Telephone (604) 754-3206. There is a picnic area nearby, at picturesque Transfer Beach Park.

Visitors are also welcomed at HARMAC ARBORETUM located between Ladysmith and Nanaimo. Established in 1956, the arboretum features exotic tree species which can thrive in this northern latitude and a section of native forest as well. Hours 7:30-4 daily with no admission charge. Telephone (604) 753-1112.

The Harmac Arboretum is located about 7 miles south of Nanaimo.

PARKSVILLE ~ PORT ALBERNI ~ TOFINO ~ PORT HARDY

Continue north on Highway 1 and detour west on Highway 4 at Parksville for a side trip to ENGLISHMAN RIVER FALLS and LITTLE QUALICUM FALLS where you may hike scenic nature trails and find picnic areas near the frothy falls. Then, wind along the shore of Cameron Lake into CATHEDRAL GROVE, a magnificent stand of virgin Douglas fir forest with some trees more than 600 years old.

If time allows continue west on Highway 4 from Port Alberni to explore the outdoor wonders in PACIFIC RIM NATIONAL PARK, the rugged WEST COAST TRAIL and picturesque Tofino. Heading north on Highway 1 you'll wind along the Strait of Georgia toward Courtenay and Comox, Campbell River, STRATHCONA PARK, and on north to the end of the paved road at Port Hardy and the B.C. ferry terminal for the overnight sailing up the inside passage to Prince Rupert. Helpful maps and information about the up-island parks and natural areas may be obtained from BC's ISLAND PARKS, 2930 Trans-Canada Highway, RR#6, Victoria, B.C. V8X 3X2. Telephone (604) 387-4363.

Helpful information may also be obtained from the Northern Vancouver Island Visitors Information Centre, Regional District of Mount Waddington, P.O. Box 729, Port McNeill, B.C. VØN 2RØ. Telephone (604) 956-3301 or (604) 956-3161. For helpful information about natural areas in the GULF ISLANDS, telephone (604) 382-3551.

For ferry information from British Columbia ports, contact the Ministry of Transportation and Highways. Telephone (604) 387-3996. Recorded information may be obtained from Vancouver at (604) 685-1021; from Victoria at (604) 656-0757; or from Nanaimo at (604) 753-6626. **Note:** Ferries leave every hour on the hour all summer — arrive **early** and generally expect a two sailing wait.

The Victoria Clipper offers 2.5 hour passenger service to and from Seattle. Telephone (604) 382-8100 in Victoria and (206) 448-5000 in Seattle.

❧

Appendixes

1.0 NORTHWEST LIFE ZONES

Each LIFE ZONE of the Northwest and western British Columbia is characterized by a dominant tree as well as typical understory or ground vegetation—shrubs, native plants and wildflowers, lichens and mosses. There are also specific bird and wildlife species who typically inhabit each Life Zone. These continually evolving communities are influenced by elevation, rainfall and soil development all of which are uniquely different in each zone.

On your floral, horticultural and nature treks though the northwest and western Canada you may use this general guide to help identify the various Life Zones through which you travel. This helpful information is provided by the North Cascades National Park and Mt. Baker-Snoqualmie National Forest headquarters staff, Sedro-Woolley, WA.

1.1 HUMID TRANSITION ZONE

The western regions, from sea level to about 1,500 feet are characterized by dense Douglas fir and western hemlock forests. Streamside vegetation includes maple, alder, cottonwood and dogwood. The understory is dominated by ferns, mosses, mushrooms and flowering native plants such as Oregon grape, salal and salmonberry. This zone receives the most moisture from the Pacific Ocean and is home to the region's ancient old-growth and rain forests.

Birds of the Humid Transition Zone include spotted, barred and great horned owls; ruffed grouse, band-tailed pigeon and Vaux's swift; pileated woodpecker, Stellar's jay and other species of passerines; hundreds of songbird species; and, the hundreds of species of shorebirds, ducks, geese and gulls.

1.2 CANADIAN ZONE

A gradual change in vegetation types may be observed as you enter this zone from 1,500 to 4,500 feet elevation. While the wet western slopes are dominated by western hemlock, western red cedar and silver fir, the dominant trees of the drier eastern sections include lodgepole pine, Douglas fir and Engelmann's spruce. Birds of this zone include Barrow's goldeneye, red-breasted sapsucker, Stellar's and gray jays, mountain chickadee, red-breasted nuthatch, winter wren, dipper, varied thrush, MacGilivray's warbler, Lincoln's sparrow and red crossbill.

1.3 HUDSONIAN ZONE

From 4,500 feet to timberline you'll observe mountain hemlock, subalpine fir and white barked pine as well as more sparse ground vegetation such as mountain huckleberry and manzanita. Though no bird species are confined to this zone, you may identify blue grouse, rufous and calliope hummingbirds, three-toed woodpecker, Clark's nutcracker, Townsend's solitaire, hermit thrush, Townsend's warbler, fox sparrow and white-winged crossbill.

1.4 ARCTIC-ALPINE ZONE

On the windswept treeless ridges above 4,500 feet elevation lie alpine meadows of heather interspersed with luetkea, huckleberry, Labrador tea and a plethora of native wildflowers which show their colors in mid to late summer. The landscape is dominated by snowfields, volcanic rock and ice. The few hardy bird species using this zone include white-tailed Ptarmigan, black swift, common raven, horned lark, water pipit and rosy finch.

1.5 ARID TRANSITION ZONE

Descending the eastern slopes of the Cascade Range onto the drier High Desert regions, you encounter tall, cinnamon-barked ponderosa pine and a ground cover of Oregon grape, snowberry, wildcurrants and sagebrush. In other sections of the High Desert you'll pass into the zone of junipers and, further east, into sagebrush country. This zone is home to the western screech-owl, common nighthawk, Hammond's and dusky flycatchers, pygmy nuthatch, house wren and Cassin's finch.

2.0 GENERAL INFORMATION/ORGANIZATION RESOURCES

Information may be obtained about membership, services, native plants, birds, wildlife and conservation/preservation issues.

2.1 THE NATURE CONSERVANCY

1205 N.W. 25th Avenue
Portland, OR 97210
Telephone (503) 228-9561
Information about and permission to visit Natural Areas—forests, marshes, mountains, preserves—acquired and managed by this nationwide non-profit land conservation organization.

2.2 DEFENDERS OF WILDLIFE

333 S. State Street, Suite 173
Lake Oswego, OR 97034
Telephone (503) 293-1433
May provide 80-page resource, "Wildlife Viewing Guide, which contains regional maps and information about 123 sites (accessible by car, on foot, boat—or a combination of the three) for observing native wildlife and birds in natural settings throughout OREGON.

2.3 NATIONAL WILDLIFE FEDERATION

1412 16th Street, N.W.
Washington, D.C. 20036
Telephone (202) 797-6800
Since 1938 working for the preservation of the nation's natural resources and wildlife.

2.4 NATIONAL AUDUBON SOCIETY

National Headquarters
950 Third Avenue
New York, NY 10022
Telephone (212) 832-3200
Audubon, through its nationwide system of sanctuaries, protects more than a quarter-million acres of essential habitat and unique natural areas for birds, wildlife and rare plant life.

Washington State Office
National Audubon Society
P.O. Box 462
Olympia, WA 98507
Telephone (206) 786-8020
Information may be obtained about regional workshops, treks and
birding areas.

2.5 WASHINGTON NATURAL HERITAGE PROGRAM
Department of Natural Resources
Public Lands Building
Olympia, WA 98504
Preservation of native plants is the program's primary goal.

2.6 AMERICAN BIRDING ASSOCIATION
P.O. Box 4335
Austin, TX 78765
Telephone (512) 474-4804

2.7 NATIONAL PARKS & CONSERVATION ASSOCIATION
1015 - 31st Street N.W., Dept.6
Washington, D.C. 20009

2.8 SIERRA CLUB
530 Bush Street
San Francisco, CA 94108
Telephone (415) 981-8634

2.9 SIERRA CLUB OF CANADA
Suite 308/47 Colborne Street
Toronto, Ontario M5E 1E3
Telephone (416) 366-6692

2.10 CANADIAN WILDLIFE FEDERATION
1673 Carling Avenue
Ottawa, Ontario K2A 1C4
Telephone (613) 725-2191

2.11 BIRDFINDING IN CANADA
P.O. Box 519
Kleinburg, Ontario L0J 1C0

3.0 **TRAVEL PLANNING RESOURCES**
3.1 CALIFORNIA DEPARTMENT OF PARKS & RECREATION
P.O. Box 942896
Sacramento, CA 94296
Telephone (916) 445-6477

3.2 CALIFORNIA NATIONAL PARKS & FORESTS
U.S. Forest Service
630 Sansome Street
San Francisco, CA 94111
Telephone (415) 556-0122

3.3 OREGON STATE PARKS
3554 S.E. 82nd Avenue
Portland, OR 97266
Telephone (503) 238-7488
Oregon State Campsite Information Center
Telephone (503) 238-7488, or toll-free (800) 452-5687

3.4 U.S. FOREST SERVICE (OR, WA)
   Pacific Northwest Regional Headquarters
   319 S.W. Pine Street (P.O. Box 3623)
   Portland, OR 97208
   Telephone (503) 221-2877
   Helpful information about weather, campgrounds and roads within
   northwest National Forests; detailed National Forest maps, trail maps,
   bird and native plant lists.

3.5 WASHINGTON STATE PARKS & RECREATION
   7150 Cleanwater Lane
   Olympia, WA 98504
   Telephone (206) 753-5755

3.6 NATIONAL PARK SERVICE/WASHINGTON
   Pacific Northwest Regional Office (OR,WA,ID)
   83 South King Street
   Seattle, WA 98104
   Telephone (206) 442-4830

3.7 JOINT OUTDOOR RECREATION INFORMATION OFFICE
   U.S. Forest Service/National Park Service
   1018 First Avenue
   Seattle, WA 98104
   Telephone (206) 442-0170
   Inquire about Golden Eagle Passports and Golden Age Passports

3.8 IDAHO DEPARTMENT OF PARKS & RECREATION
   Statehouse Mail
   Boise, ID 83720
   Telephone (208) 334-2154

3.9 IDAHO NATIONAL FORESTS
   Northern Idaho   Southern Idaho
   200 East Broadway Street   Federal Building
   P.O. Box 7669   324 - 25th Street
   Missoula, MT 59807   Ogden, UT 84401
   Telephone (406) 329-3511   Telephone (801) 625-5354

4.0 **HORTICULTURAL & BOTANICAL RESOURCES**
   4.1 National Wildflower Research Center
      2600 FM 973 North
      Austin, TX 78725
      Information about the preservation of native plants and wildflowers
      throughout the U.S.

   4.2 Territorial Seed Company
      P.O. Box 27
      Lorane, OR 97451
      Garden seed for west of the Cascades (the Humid Transition Zone).
      Catalog $1 is a wealth of information on sowing, culture and
      harvesting.

4.3 Nichols Garden Nursery
1190 N. Pacific Highway
Albany, OR 97321
Telephone (503) 928-9280
International and domestic seeds.

4.4 Abundant Life Seed Foundation
P.O. Box 772
Port Townsend, WA 98368
Specializes in seeds for the Pacific Northwest. Catalog/Newsletter $1.

4.5 Tillinghast Seed Co.
P.O. Box 738-A
LaConner, WA 98257
Telephone (206) 466-3329
Founded in 1885, offers seed varieties chosen to thrive in the Northwest's marine climate. Catalog $1.

4.6 McLaughlin's Seeds
Box 550
Mead, WA 99021
Native and naturalized flowers in packets or in bulk. Catalog $1.

4.7 Seeds Blum
Idaho City Stage
Boise, ID 83706
Heirloom seeds from around the world. Catalog $2.

4.8 High-Altitude Gardens
Box 4619
Ketchum, ID 83340
Seeds and custom mixes for short-season gardens. Catalog $2.

5.0 GARDEN CLUBS
Information may be obtained about local chapters.

5.1 Garden Club of America
598 Madison Avenue
New York, NY 10022
Telephone (212) 753-8287

5.2 Men's Garden Clubs of America
P.O. Box 241
Johnston, IA 50131

5.3 Association of Oregon Gardens
c/o 3214 N.E. 69th Avenue
Portland, OR 97213

5.4 The Oregon State Federation of Garden Clubs
c/o 3326 S.W. 13th Avenue
Portland, OR 97201

5.5 Alpine Garden Clubs of British Columbia
303 Mansfield Place
North Vancouver, B.C. V7J 1E4

6.0 HORTICULTURAL & BOTANICAL ASSOCIATIONS

6.1 Botanical Society of America
New York Botanical Garden
Bronx, NY 10458
Telephone (212) 220-8700

6.2 Perennial Plant Association
Ohio State University/Dept. of Horticulture
2001 Fyffe Court
Columbus, OH 43210
Telephone (614) 422-6027

Northwest contact:
c/o Caprice Farms Nursery
15425 S.W. Pleasant Hill
Sherwood, OR 97140

Canadian contact:
c/o William Spaans Greenhouse
Highway 10, R.R. 1
Calendon, Ontario LØN 1CØ

6.3 Hardy Plant Society of Oregon
33530 S.E. Bluff Road
Boring, OR 97009
(Yearly membership $12)

6.4 Oregon Horticultural Society
2015 Yamhill/P.O. Box 1246
McMinnville, OR 97128
Telephone (503) 472-7910

6.5 American Rhododendron Society
14885 S.W. Sunrise Lane
Tigard, OR 97224
Telephone (503) 620-4038

6.6 Northwest Lily Society
c/o 19766 S. Impala Lane
Oregon City, OR 97045

6.7 Friends of the Trees
P.O. Box 1064
Tonasket, WA 98855
A wealth of information on open-pollinated and heirloom flowers, vegetables, trees and shrubs specific to Washington state.

6.8 Washington State Nurseryman's Association
P.O. Box 670
Sumner, WA 98390
Assistance in locating unusual or rare plants, especially ornamentals.

6.9 Washington State Horticultural Association
P.O. Box 136
Wenatchee, WA 98801
Telephone (509) 662-2067

6.10 Washington Native Plant Society
c/o P.O. Box 2653
Olympia, WA 98507

6.11 North West Bulb Growers Association
P.O. Box 303
Mount Vernon, WA 98273
Telephone (206) 424-1375

6.12 Azalea Society of America
P.O. Box 6244
Silver Spring, MO 29096

6.13 American Peony Society
Interlachen Road
Hopkins, MN 55343

6.14 American Rose Society
P.O. Box 30000
Shreveport, LA 71130
Telephone (318) 938-5402

6.15 American Iris Society
6518 Beachy Avenue
Wichita, KS 67206
Telephone (316) 686-8734

6.16 Northwest Iris Society
c/o 608 N.W. 119th Street
Vancouver, WA 98685

6.17 American Fuchsia Society
Hall of Flowers
9th Avenue & Lincoln Way
San Francisco, CA 94122

6.18 American Dahlia Society, Inc.
245 Merritt Avenue
Bergenfield, NJ 07621

6.19 American Daffodil Society, Inc.
89 Chichester Road
New Canaan, CT 06840

6.20 The Herb Society of America
2 Independence Court
Concord, MA 01742
(send $1 for list of publications, including information about the
"Traveler's Guide to Herb Gardens"

6.21 Federation of British Columbia Naturalists
Box 33797 Station D
Vancouver, B.C. V6J 4L6

6.22 Vancouver Natural History Society
Box 3021 M.P.O.
Vancouver, B.C. V6B 3X5

ADDITIONAL RESOURCES:
Your PUBLIC LIBRARY
COUNTY EXTENSION SERVICE
LOCAL BOOKSTORES
MUSEUMS & HISTORICAL SOCIETIES

Index of Gardens
and Natural Areas

KEY

PUB	Public Garden / Nursery
PRI	Private Garden / Nursery
A	Arboretum
W	Wildflowers
BW	Birdlife / Wildlife
NSA	Natural Scenic Area

NORTHERN CALIFORNIA
A coastal sampling
NSA Redwood National Park/1
PUB Mendocino Coast Botanical Gardens, Fort Bragg/1
PUB Trillium Lane Nursery, Fort Bragg/1
PUB Heritage Rose Gardens, Fort Bragg/2
BW Elder Creek Basin, Westport/2
NSA Avenue of the Giants, Redwood Empire/2
W Russ Park, Ferndale/2
PRI Gingerbread Mansion Garden, Ferndale/2
BW Eel River Delta, Ferndale/2
BW National Wildlife Refuge, Eureka/2
PUB Imperiale Square, Eureka/3
PUB Sequoia Park & Zoo, Eureka/3
BW Arcata Marsh and Wildlife Sanctuary, Arcata/3
BW Arcata Bottoms, Arcata/3
PUB Central Plaza, Arcata/3
A Humboldt State University Arboretum, Arcata/3
NSA Arcata Community Forest, Arcata/3
PUB Azalea State Reserve, Arcata/3
NSA Fern Canyon, Redwood National Park, Orick/4
PUB Lily Farms, Smith River/4

OREGON
South Coast
PUB Lily fields, Brookings/5
PUB Azalea State Park, Brookings/5
NSA Loeb State Park, Brookings/5
PUB Shore Acres Botanic Garden, Charleston/5
BW Bandon Marsh, Bandon/7
BW South Slough Estuarine Sanctuary, Charleston/7
NSA Oregon Dunes National Recreation Area, Reedsport/8
NSA Umpqua Dunes Scenic Area, Reedsport/8

Central Coast
NSA Oregon Dunes Overlook, Florence/8
W Darlingtonia Wayside, Florence/8
NSA Heceta Head, Florence/9